DATE DUE

Life and Death at Paloma

Burial 142

Life and Death at Paloma

Society and Mortuary Practices in a Preceramic Peruvian Village

BY JEFFREY QUILTER

With Burial Illustrations by Bernardino Ojeda E.

Foreword by Robert A. Benfer

UNIVERSITY OF IOWA PRESS Ψ IOWA CITY

University of Iowa Press, Iowa City 52242
Copyright © 1989 by the University of Iowa
All rights reserved
Printed in the United States of America
First edition, 1989

Library of Congress Cataloging-in-Publication Data

   Quilter, Jeffrey, 1949–
     Life and death at Paloma: society and mortuary
practices in a preceramic Peruvian village/ by Jeffrey
Quilter; with burial illustrations by Bernardino Ojeda
E.; foreword by Robert A. Benfer.—1st ed.
       p.   cm.
     Bibliography: p.
     Includes index.
     ISBN 0-87745-194-X
     1. Paloma Site (Peru). 2. Indians of South
America—Peru—Mortuary customs. 3. Indians of
South America—Peru—Antiquities. 4. Peru—
Antiquities. I. Title.
    F3429.3.M7Q56   1989   88-31276
    985—dc19   CIP

Typesetting by G & S Typesetters, Austin, Texas
Printing and binding by Braun-Brumfield, Ann Arbor,
  Michigan

FOR MY FAMILY
Thomas and Joan, Sarah, Susanna,
and Betsy

Contents

Foreword, by Robert A. Benfer   ix

Acknowledgments   xi

Preface   xiii

1. Climate, Chronology, and Culture in Early Peru   1

2. The Site of Paloma   10

3. The Archaeological Discoveries at Paloma   26

4. Quantitative Analyses of the Paloma Burials   43

5. Discussion of Paloma Mortuary Practices   53

6. Paloma and Preceramic Cultural History and Processes   68

Appendix 1. Burial Illustrations and Data   87

Appendix 2. Supplementary Tables   163

References Cited   173

Index   183

Foreword

BY ROBERT A. BENFER

The Paloma Archaeological Project was designed to be both a contribution to Andean prehistory and a test case in the study of biological and cultural adaptations of a population isolated from Old World diseases and other influences. Our efforts built upon the work of Frédéric-André Engel and his team of investigators from the Centro de Investigaciones de Zonas Aridas of the National Agrarian University of Peru, who discovered the site in 1964 and excavated there in 1973. From the start, the research was designed to be both multi- and interdisciplinary and to be open to researchers from a variety of institutions, both in the United States and in Peru.

Jeffrey Quilter joined the project while he was a graduate student at the University of California, Santa Barbara, and participated in the 1976 excavations. This book is the product of his research on mortuary customs at the site, including integration of data collected both before and since the 1976 study. The work not only is of value as a summary statement of the Paloma researches but is important in laying the foundation for the study of death rites and society in a seminal period in the development of Andean cultures. For although more than ten years have passed since our work began, relatively little is available concerning funerary practices and what they may tell of the early occupation of western South America. Gradually, however, the corpus of data is increasing (e.g., Stothert 1985; Engel 1987). Given the relatively recent and continuing focus on burials as a rich body of

information on ideological and social systems, this book will help provide a framework for discussion of early Andean mortuary behavior.

The bio-cultural adaptation perspective of the Paloma project in general was followed along several dimensions, including the degree of sedentism, the manipulation of plants and animals, and the role of maritime resources, taking into account both long- and short-term climatic cycles. While we now have a clearer perspective on many of these issues, much regarding them was unknown or debated at the time we first began our work. The high degree of preservation of human remains and other perishables on the coast of Peru made the Paloma site an attractive laboratory in which to test a variety of hypotheses concerning both the specific adaptations of ancient Peruvian populations and ideas concerning nonhorticultural peoples in general. Without such fine preservation, our knowledge of preceramic Peru would be far poorer. Artifacts, including stone projectile points, are both relatively rare and apparently of limited use in studying interconnections of cultural systems in early coastal Peru.

The study of burial customs is therefore interconnected with the other aspects of our researches. The relatively significant changes in mortuary practices which occurred at the site noted in this book, at about the 200 Level, correspond to statistically significant increases in anchovies, demographic changes, and such physical shifts as bony response to musculature and wear gradients on teeth. All of these correlate with our general stratigraphic divisions as demarcated by distinct compositional changes in the Paloma midden deposits.

The Paloma site is significant in its position on the brink of changes in the Andes. As Quilter notes, many of the burial characteristics of mortuary practices at Paloma are widespread in the Americas during the period in question. But hints of change, as more clearly reflected in the later cotton preceramic burials, are also present. It is not surprising that few strong cultural patterns emerged from the Paloma site, given that burial practices in foraging societies today are often marked by considerable idiosyncrasy.

One pattern, first noted in 1976 and confirmed in the 1979 field season, is the abandonment and destruction of houses, as noted in this volume. Careful study of the skeletons showed that in all such cases the central burial was an adult male. This mortuary practice, known today for the Jívaro (Harner 1972), surely indicates a patrilocal society. Such a social system has an advantage for foraging societies in that males can stay close to the resource areas with which they have been familiar since childhood. Marriage is usually outside the local group, often with women from considerable distances away. Modern foragers frequently find their mates 40 or 50 kilometers away (Howell 1979). The need to avoid inbreeding depression may necessitate this for small, dispersed populations. The emphasis on distinctions between the sexes in burial rites at Paloma might thus be due to such insider-outsider divisions on the basis of gender.

The evidence for increased inbreeding (Page 1974; Benfer 1984) suggests that women were not obtained from great distances in the last part of the Preceramic Stage;

instead a much more endogamous situation appears to have existed. With the concentrations of populations in smaller territorial regions, such as valleys, exchange of women in the cotton preceramic may have been more localized than in the times of the Paloma occupation. This is of interest especially in regard to Quilter's observation of decreased status for females near the end of the Paloma occupation, although the relationships between the events are presently obscure and explanations may be quite varied. Nevertheless, a more restricted exchange system for women and other goods may have contributed to the growth of more complexly organized political systems. Running counter to this, however, is the lack of indications of violence one would expect in restricted political territories, as noted in this book, until the very final stages of the Cotton Preceramic Stage.

Certainly, the slight shift in mortuary practices at Paloma—from simple disposal of the dead to an apparent increase in affirming social distinctions—is a significant change in coastal Peruvian society. It foreshadows the more obvious social changes of succeeding societies. Again, such cognitive distinctions were probably part of larger changes such as those distinguishing weed versus crop as noted by Rindos (1984) in the shift to horticulture. Such lines of thought and many more will occur to readers of this book, which directs our thinking to the sociocultural factors that have heretofore been overlooked in many studies on forager societies, including those in Peru. This book is a nucleus of cultural data from which other studies will benefit for many years and provides a source to guide future investigations on the coast of Peru, one of the few regions where the development of complex societies can be studied in such detail.

Acknowledgments

During the long gestation period which led to publication of this book I had the support of many friends and colleagues. I acknowledge their help with deep gratitude.

I must first thank my family, who encouraged me through the day-to-day experience of doing archaeology and thinking and writing about it. My parents, Thomas and Joan Quilter, gave me a love of learning, an appreciation for the past and other cultures, and the courage to pursue a career centered on the heart rather than the purse. My wife Sarah and my children Susanna and Betsy have continued this support, including the pain and difficulty of separation in order to continue research as well as my emotional ups and downs in fieldwork and analysis.

While it is common to separate private and professional lives, such distinctions often become blurred in a field which requires such great commitments. My thanks to teachers and colleagues is thus more than perfunctory.

Dr. Robert A. Benfer, University of Columbia, Missouri, and director of the Paloma Project, was most gracious to accept me as part of the study, even though I was not a graduate student at his institution. Dr. Frédéric-André Engel and Dr. Carlos López Ocaña as heads of the Centro de Investigationes de Zonas Aridas of the National Agrarian University of Peru and the hosts of the North Americans were most hospitable and helpful. I am happy that the relationships established with these colleagues in 1976 continue to grow to this day.

I also wish to thank the entire staff of Peruvian archaeologists and laboratory specialists who worked with the University of Missouri crew, especially Rosa Carbajal, Adrian Fernández, Alejandro Guanilo, Gustavo Guzmán, Lucio Laura, Apolino Lino, Teresa Nicho, Miriam Vallejos, Pilar Valverde, and Gloria Villareal. Special thanks go to Bernardino Ojeda E., who was and continues to be most generous in his willingness to share with me his expert knowledge of Peruvian prehistory and his fine skills as a draftsman.

My colleagues from the University of Missouri included John Greer, Sarah Gehlert, Peggy Wanner Barjenbruch, Barbara Jackson, and John and Jackie Shoplund. Their support in and out of the field is greatly appreciated. Glendon Weir briefly visited the site in 1976 and subsequently conducted extensive research. He continues to be a friend and to aid in discussion of plant remains and other aspects of preceramic sites. Sharon Brock is especially thanked for providing information on the burials excavated in 1979 when she was at the site and I was not.

Many people not directly associated with the Paloma Project were of great assistance to me in the course of fieldwork, data analysis, and the writing phases of research. Thanks to Richard Burger for sound advice and his good sense of humor during the rough times. Junius Bird and Elizabeth Reitz were very helpful in providing some of their knowledge on plant and animal remains, respectively, and I thank them for their help. The Beteta family, in Lima, provided me with the material comforts of home, as did Enrique Mayer and Helaine Silverman. I am forever in their debt. Ernesto Paredes and Mercia Koth de Paredes also proved gracious hosts.

The members of my dissertation committee at Santa Barbara are thanked for their aid: Albert C. Spaulding, Michael A. Glassow, and Elman R. Service. Thomas C. Patterson of Temple University was most kind in consenting to serve on the dissertation committee. He has had great influence on my intellectual development and has given both specific and general help in my archaeological studies. I am indebted to him for many things.

William Stuart of the University of Maryland, College Park, helped during the final stages of writing. John Pousson and Carolyn Smith made helpful comments on style and grammar, and my father was of great help in catching errors in drafts of the dissertation and book.

At Ripon College my colleagues Paul Axelrod and Eric Godfrey have encouraged me to continue research. John Teska of the Mathematics Department helped in statistical analysis. LaVerne A. Toussaint was essential in typing the drafts for this book and is heartily thanked. Many students at Ripon College also helped in many ways, and Elaine P. Sherman is especially thanked for help in final editorial details.

Since the time of my dissertation, an increasingly large number of people have continued to help me in my studies. There are too many to thank, but I must mention Hugo Ludeña, Ramiro Matos, Rolando Paredes, Chela Fattorini de Paredes, Abelardo Sandoval, and Jorge Silva and Nelly Silva, as well as all the staff of the National Institute of Culture and many other friends and colleagues in Peru. In the United States Thomas Lynch, Michael Moseley, and Craig Morris have offered support, for which I am grateful. Robert Feldman reviewed this book and helped make it better by his constructive criticism.

Financial support for the Paloma Project and the fieldwork phase of the resulting dissertation and book was given by the National Science Foundation in grants to Robert A. Benfer (NSF BNS-76-12316, NSF BNS-78-07727a/b, and NSF BNS-81053940).

Preface

One of the hallmarks of Precolumbian Peru is its many well-preserved and elaborate burials. In the postconquest period, the mummies of the Inca attracted the attention of the Spanish because of the reverence and wealth accorded the dead rulers. The cemetery of Ancón excavated by Reiss and Stubel in the 1870s was among the first subjects of Peruvian archaeological study, and much is still being learned from well-preserved burials found in coastal Peru (e.g., Donnan and Mackey 1978). Despite, or perhaps because of, the attention given to later prehistoric burials, few studies of preceramic interments (circa 10,000–1500 B.C.) have been conducted. The only monograph presenting detailed information on large numbers of early Peruvian burials (Engel 1963) deals with relatively late interments dating to 1200 B.C., when pottery was already used in some parts of Peru. Although detailed studies have recently been made on early burials in northern Chile (Allison and Gerszten 1982; Allison 1985; cf. Bird 1943) and Ecuador (Stothert 1985), these regions are outside the core area of the Andes where civilization emerged. Scholarly neglect of preceramic burials has thus impeded an understanding of the development of Peruvian mortuary customs and the societies which practiced them. Burials have held untapped information on the social organization of preceramic people and the changes which coastal cultures experienced during the development of complex Peruvian societies.

Lack of information on social change in preceramic Peru is also partially due to the fact that the concept of a Peruvian Preceramic Stage has only recently developed. It was primarily through the work of Bird (1948) and Engel (1957a, b, 1960) in the 1940s and the 1950s that this long period was defined. Much effort since has been spent in developing a chronology for the period (fig. 1) and in investigating economic and settlement systems. Even today, the great achievements of preceramic peoples are only gradually being realized; some large sites, long thought to date to later periods, have now been identified as the products of preceramic societies (Moseley and Willey 1973; Donnan 1985).

The first occupants of Peru are thought to have relied primarily upon hunting; but by about 7000 B.C., fishing and the gathering of plants and shellfish became important in the subsistence strategies of coastal dwellers, or, at least, became more noticeable in the archaeological record. About 2500 B.C., the last phase of the Preceramic Stage began. By its end, agriculture, monumental architecture, and complex social and political organizations had been developed. The introduction of pottery, circa 1700–1500 B.C., true weaving, and corn agriculture occurred after the establishment of many of the basic patterns of Peruvian civilization.

The Paloma site, a coastal preceramic village dating from about 5000 B.C. to 2500 B.C., was discovered in 1961 by a survey crew of

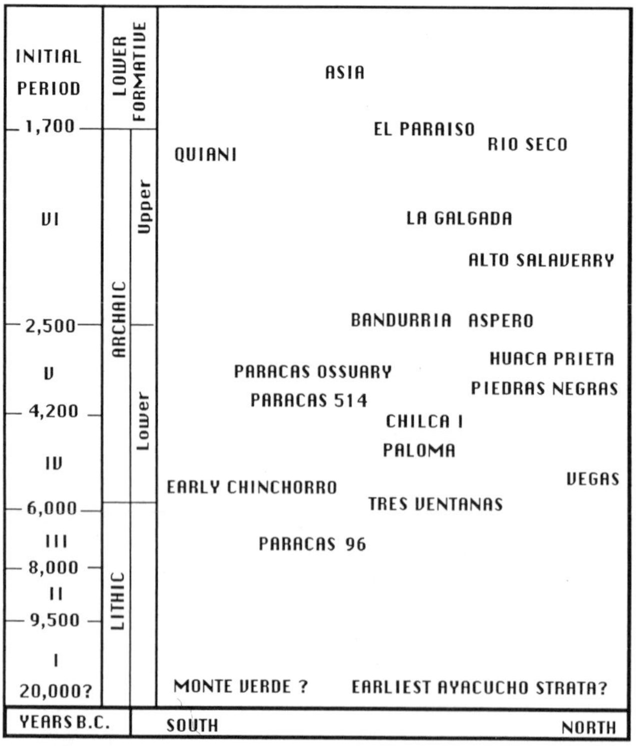
INITIAL
PERIOD
LOWER FORMATIVE
1,700
VI
2,500
V
4,200
IV
6,000
III
8,000
II
9,500
I
20,000?
ARCHAIC
Upper
Lower
LITHIC
ASIA
EL PARAISO
RIO SECO
QUIANI
LA GALGADA
ALTO SALAVERRY
BANDURRIA ASPERO
HUACA PRIETA
PARACAS OSSUARY
PIEDRAS NEGRAS
PARACAS 514
CHILCA I
PALOMA
VEGAS
EARLY CHINCHORRO
TRES VENTANAS
PARACAS 96
MONTE VERDE ?
EARLIEST AYACUCHO STRATA?
YEARS B.C.
SOUTH
NORTH

1. Chronologies of some early Andean sites. Dates not calibrated. Most sites located at date averages. (Roman numerals are preceramic periods after Lanning 1967. Vertically written periods are after Lumbreras 1974, for the central coast of Peru. See chapter 6 for details on many of these sites.)

the Centro de Investigaciones de Zonas Aridas (CIZA) of the National Agrarian University of Peru and given the number 12b-VII-613 in the CIZA catalogue. Limited excavations were carried out until 1973, when the first full-scale work took place under the direction of Fréderic-André Engel. Two large trenches were placed in the center of the largest midden concentration at the site. This excavation uncovered forty-two houses and ninety burials.

In 1976, a team of researchers from the University of Missouri, Columbia, under the direction of Robert Benfer, was invited by CIZA to continue excavations at the site. At this time, I began my participation in the project as burial furniture analyst. The joint project lasted six months. During this fieldwork, two-thirds of the effort was devoted to cleaning the trenches, locating partially excavated burials, studying materials stored in the CIZA laboratory in Lima, and attempting to clarify the relationship of site stratigraphy to features and burials. This work had to be undertaken because the University of Missouri crew discovered that most excavation units in the trenches had not been cleared to sterile soil and because many burials had not been removed from their graves or were only partially excavated.

Some burials, houses, and features could not be located with accuracy because the strata in which they were found had been removed during the 1973 excavations. Even when burials were found in situ, it took time to determine the precise level from which the pit had been excavated.

By the time the excavations ended in December 1976, a total of 178 graves had been recorded, and enough information had been obtained to analyze burial practices.

The University of Missouri crew returned in

1979, but I was not among its members, due to the impending birth of my eldest daughter. During the second and last full field season, more burials and houses were uncovered. Subsequent and briefer work yielded additional data, including information on the ancient environment. The total number of burials listed for the Paloma site is 251.[1] Analysis continues on many topics relating to the aims of the project, although a general picture of ancient life is now fairly clear.

The primary purpose of the research was to study the health and demography of a New World prefarming community, isolated from the effects of European diseases (Benfer 1977, 1981, 1982a, b, 1984, 1986a, b, c). In addition, there were many other general and specific topics of importance relating to human adaptation, nonagricultural communities, and Peruvian prehistory.

My role on the multidisciplinary team was that of mortuary customs analyst. While the subject of how people bury their dead has inherent interest, there were specific reasons why I chose this aspect of the data for investigation. Although I had no interest in developing general mortuary studies theory, the opportunity to apply recent ideas and methods was intriguing, especially because few early nonagricultural communities in the New World had been studied using recent developments in the field and none had ever been systematically analyzed in Peru. Because the occupation of Paloma was at a time during or just before the transition to food production, significant social change might be detected as the society became more dependent on cultivated plants. In addition, in the earlier phase of site occupation, the possible transition of Paloma from a temporary camp to a more permanent settlement may have been correlative with significant cultural changes detectable in mortuary customs.

At the beginning of investigations, of course, the exact nature of Paloma was uncertain, as was the possibility that such research questions could be answered. The reader may judge how well these goals were met in the following pages. It was certain, however, that no full-scale excavation of a coastal site of the middle Preceramic Stage had ever been carried out with subsequent detailed publication of results. Thus, at the very least, a significant contribution could be made by studying a poorly understood era in the culture history of Peru, one of great importance as a crucible for later developments.

Like most publications in archaeology, this book takes the reader from the general to the specific. Chapter 1 discusses the general environmental and cultural background against which the Paloma site and its data can be understood. Chapter 2 then focuses on the Paloma site and its general characteristics. Chapter 3 presents burial goods data. Chapters 4 and 5 analyze and discuss the burials. Chapter 6 compares the Paloma data with other known preceramic burials in western South America and attempts to draw some general conclusions.

An extensive review of the study of mortuary practices in my dissertation has been greatly reduced here since that is not the main purpose of the present volume. A detailed presentation of statistical analyses which ultimately yielded little information of interest has also been reduced. The discussion of Paloma in relation to ethnographic data and other sites presented here, however, is more extensive and detailed than in my dissertation.

Lastly, as a caveat for the more literal-minded who may read this book, "The Lovers of Paloma" should be read as an evocation of the mood of the site and the irony of archaeology, not as factual. An attempt at objectivity follows the poem.

---

1. The number 251 represents the total set of human remains found at Paloma, including isolated bone fragments, crania, and burials excavated before 1976 but subsequently missing. The actual number of remains available for study is much smaller. About 126 burials are complete enough for general comparisons of mortuary practices. Different numbers can be used for specific studies, depending on the nature of the problem to be investigated.

The Lovers of Paloma

The rock was broken long ago, buried in the
sand
with the two of them, forgotten in the shallow
grave.
It was cleanly cut in half, like a cloven skull,
edges polished, curved and shining in the sun.

We stood around the pit, a ring of eyes
looking at the bones embracing in the sand,
thinking
they were lovers, disturbed by our hands.

They were wrapped together in a woven mat
(a tender placement, a symbol, by those who
loved them).
Arranged white bones, interlocking limbs spoke
intimately. One's hand caressed the other's
cheek.

Cleaned by birds, their bones were gathered and
carried
to the grave. And they were given gifts to take
on the journey, an urchin's spiny shell, a crystal
for the light, a gourd for water, feather caps.

They lay together five thousand years, but
tomorrow
we will lift them from their sloping grave, place
them in boxes to be carried by car. Locked
together
for so long, in yellow cardboard boxes, they will
rest uncertain.

Sarah M. Quilter

Life and Death at Paloma

1. Climate, Chronology, and Culture in Early Peru

Climate and Environment

The presence of one of the world's driest deserts on the central coast of western South America (fig. 2) often surprises beginning students used to equating the tropics with rain forests. Rain forests do exist further east in the Amazon Basin; but in between the sand and jungle is one of the world's highest mountain ranges, the Andes. Thus, the geography of Peru and other Andean countries is often simplified as consisting of three vertical strips on the map: coast, sierra, and tropical forest. Although this schema is basically true, there are important complexities primarily caused by three major factors: altitude, winds, and temperature.

The tropic latitude of Peru provides relatively constant temperatures. But the great vertical variability of the landscape results in narrow environmental strips layered like the strata of an ideal archaeological site. While one can travel horizontally for many days in the same environment, vertical movement entails traversing distinct zones—from warm lower altitudes where tropical fruits can be raised, through succeeding levels suitable for maize agriculture and then only root crops, to higher levels where only bunch grass and herding can be practiced, to snow fields, and down again in reverse order. Karl Troll (1931, 1958) and John Murra (1972) have stressed the role of vertically stacked resource zones in Andean culture, in which native peoples have utilized the proximity of different environments to secure a diversity of foods and materials to maintain and enrich their lives.

The geographer Javier Pulgar Vidal (1987) has discussed eight natural regions of Peru primarily defined by their altitude, each having a distinct climate, flora, and fauna. The coast or chala (0–500 meters above sea level) is unique to extreme western Peru and consists of the littoral and its immediate vicinity. Next comes the yunga (500–2,300 meters), the Inca term for warm valley. The lower river valleys were densely populated in prehistory and remain important as the chief areas for irrigation agriculture. On the western side of the Andes the region outside of the productive zones of the littoral and the yunga proper are in a rain shadow and are desertic. The exception to this rule is the lomas, or vegetation nurtured by fogs, of which more will be said below. The quechua (2,300–3,500 meters) is the traditional area for the growing of maize, while the higher suni or jalca (3,500–4,000 meters) is the source of many native Andean foods such as *quinoa* (*Chenopodium quinoa*) and a wide range of root crops, including a great variety of potatoes as well as *oca* (*Oxalis tuberosa*) and *olluca* (*Ullucus tuberosus*). The puna (4,000–4,800 meters) is famed for its camelids and pastoralism, being generally unsuitable for agriculture, while the highest peaks of the janca or cordillera (4,800–6,768 meters) are snowcapped, offering relatively few resources for human exploitation. Descending the east-

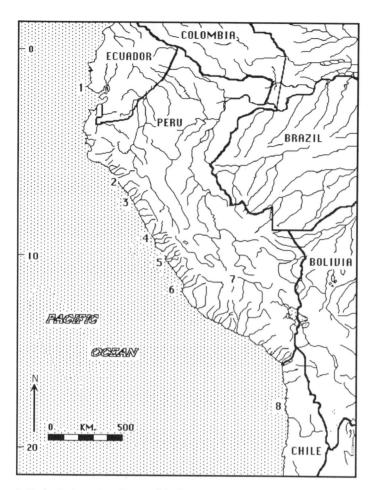

2. Early Andean sites discussed in the text: 1, Vegas; 2, Huaca Prieta, Alto Salaverry; 3, Piedras Negras, Las Haldas; 4, Aspero, Bandurria, Río Seco; 5, Ancón, El Paraíso, Paloma, Chilca 1, Tres Ventanas, Asia; 6, Paracas sites; 7, Ayacucho; 8, early Chilean sites. Due to scale, numbers show general areas of site locations.

ern slopes of the Andes, quechua and yunga zones are again encountered, followed by the rupa rupa or high tropical forest (400–1,000 meters) and the omagua or low tropical forest (80–400 meters) of the Amazon Basin proper. These tropical forests, although relatively distant from the centers of Andean population, were and are sources of exotic plants, animals, and other resources for peoples of the other zones from very early in antiquity.

River valleys vary in altitude as they wend their way to the sea. The continental divide is near the western edge of South America, so that rain falling only a hundred kilometers from Lima flows to the Atlantic. Many rivers formed in the highlands, however, flow directly to the Pacific in roughly parallel routes. The Santa River is an exception, coursing through the central highland valley of the Callejón de Huaylas for almost 300 kilometers only to turn westward and empty into the Pacific. Variations in the course of mountain ranges and rivers exist in different parts of Peru, but these patterns generally hold true for most of the country.

The Peruvian hydrologic system is due not only to topography but also to the pattern of tradewinds which produces the coastal desert and the effect of the cold Peru Current running northward, close to shore. Westerly winds blow across the Pacific picking up moisture, cooling as they pass over the Peru Current. In summer (December to May), the saturated air is immediately warmed as it begins to cross the land surface. The warmed air rises against the western slopes of the Andes and precipitates as rain further east, leaving both the coastal plain and hills dry and barren but feeding the tributaries of the coastal river valleys. In winter the relatively minor temperature difference between the land and the cool offshore water causes the moisture in the winds to be deposited as fog on the coastal hills between 200 and 800 meters above sea level. Within these altitudinal limits the lomas thrive. These are areas of herbaceous plants, grasses, and trees which get their moisture from the condensing fogs. They sometimes stretch for several kilometers along the coastal hills within the limits of the area covered in mist. Thus, the seasons of wet and dry are reversed—the winter coastal fogs occur while the highlands are dry, and heavy rains fall in the sierra when the coast is arid. Highland rains peak in January, and coastal fogs are densest in July and August. Periods of transition equivalent to temperate autumn and spring also exist but, like their northern counterparts, may be irregular.

The unique combination of climate and topography has created an equally fascinating coastal environment. While most of the western flanks of the Andes lie in a barren rain shadow, the coastal hills in the lomas zone support concentrated plant and animal communities. The river valleys also serve as desert oases, thanks to the water they carry. The abundance of resources in lomas and valleys fluctuates with the seasons, however. The lomas are dependent on winter fogs for

moisture and the river plant communities are linked to the cycle of annual floods, with rivers cresting in March. Furthermore, the natural richness of these zones has been altered in recent times.

Both the studies of scholars and the tales of old residents of Lima tell of times when the lomas were rich and abundant, with vast fields present all year in some areas of the central coast (Ramos de Cox 1972:11; Engel 1980:103). At various times in the past, relatively large stands of trees and leafy bushes were to be found in the fog fields. The canopy they provided was sufficient to reduce evaporation and allow year-round growth of the lomas. Grasses (Gramineae), willows (*Salix* spp.), flowers (e.g., *Begonia geraniifolia*), and a wide variety of herbaceous plants relieved the gray monotony of the coastal hills. The plant communities in turn supported deer (*Odocoileus* spp.), wild camelids (*Lama* spp.), foxes (*Desusicyon* sp.), and even an occasional mountain lion (*Puma* sp.) as well as a host of smaller creatures, including flocks of parrots (*Geositta* spp.).

A sense of what the ancient lomas must have been like can be found today in isolated areas, such as the Lomas Lachay (fig. 3) and other reserves set aside by the government of Peru. Studies suggest rapid replacement of different plant communities during the annual cycle of these fields (Torres G. and López Ocaña 1982). There may also have been spatial variation in the fields so that some resources were available in particular regions of the coast and not in others.

The present sparseness of lomas vegetation throughout much of the region is due to overexploitation by humans. Extensive tree felling for firewood first reduced the ability of the fields to hold moisture. The European introduction of close-cropping sheep then further reduced cover, keeping the vegetation down to a sparse green layer of grass during the winter months. It is likely that cycles of destruction and regeneration of the fog fields have occurred many times in the past as the intensity of human use varied.

3. The modern Lomas Lachay gives an impression of what ancient fog fields were like.

The modern river valleys also differ markedly from their natural conditions. Water management was practiced in Peru as early as the late Preceramic Stage (see Grieder and Bueno Mendoza 1981), and irrigation has since played a vital role in coastal agriculture. The upstream diversion of water reduces the amounts available in the lower valleys and also restricts the extent of brackish marsh near river mouths. Before canals were built and cultivated crops replaced natural vegetation, the river valleys were probably extremely rich in plants and game. The intensity of modern exploitation has apparently reduced the biotic richness of river valleys in a relatively short time. The Spanish chronicler Cieza de León (1947, 1959:337), for example, noted that the Mala River, south of the Chilca, was "a very good river flanked by thick woods and groves." María Rostworowski de Diez Canseco (1981:14–15) believes that both coastal valleys and lomas were overexploited in the Colonial Period.

Despite the repeated destruction and regeneration of coastal vegetation zones, their importance can still be seen today. In the past, the river valleys may have served as alternate habitats for some lomas inhabitants. But other plants and creatures were specific to valleys or fog fields, such as crayfish, which remain a treat at small restaurants in valley glades. Freshwater fish are few, however. Marshy areas still play an important role in providing rushes and other materials to manufacture mats to cover floors and even to serve as walls and ceilings in the houses of the poor.

Fresh water is a critical resource for desert dwellers. On the Peruvian coast, outside of the river valleys, an extensive sheet of fresh water rides a hard substratum below the surface soil. The surface topography determines the difficulty of reaching this water. In some areas it rises to the surface as springs. In other areas excavations of a meter or even two reach the aquifer. The use of sunken gardens is a Peruvian tradition—pits are dug deep enough to tap the water (Rowe 1969; Parsons and Psuty 1975; Benfer et al. 1987).

The Peruvian desert is thus an environmental irony, for the two resources necessary for productive agriculture—fertile land and water—are abundant but not in the right places. Most of the land is highly fertile desiccated rock, sand being found only at the beach and in some dune areas. The water is too far below the surface to nurture plant growth unless artificially manipulated by irrigation systems or sunken gardens.

Although the coastal shore is desert, the offshore waters host one of the most productive fisheries in the world. The Peru Current begins far out in the southern Pacific Ocean. As it passes by the Central Andean coastline, it brings up cold waters with rich nutrients from great depths. The upwelling provides nutrients for phytoplankton and an array of sea life, including mollusks, crustaceans, fish, mammals, and birds. The shoreline tends to be either rocky or sandy beach, which host different mollusk communities— primarily mussels (*Choromytilus chorus*, *Mytilus* spp., *Aulacomya ater*) and clams (*Mesodesma* sp., *Donax* sp.), respectively. Away from shore a tremendous variety of sea creatures abound, including sharks, rays, sea lions, dolphins, whales, and fish. Among the fish are dense schools of small varieties including anchovies (*Engraulis ringens*) and others. Peruvian anchovies were harvested for export as cattle feed for many years, and in the nineteenth century the islands were mined for guano fertilizer, the end product of anchovies consumed by the rich diversity of avian fauna in coastal Peru.

In its pristine state, the Peruvian central coast provided a stable and abundant source of food and materials for its ancient inhabitants. Even if the lomas fields decreased in size during the summer months, it is likely that core areas remained productive. The river valleys also waxed and waned due to flood cycles but probably maintained a stock of important resources. The sea provided year-round sources of protein, except when the flow of the cold Peru Current was disrupted. More is said about this in the discussion of ancient subsistence strategies.

Preceramic Lifeways and Cultural Processes

The Peruvian Preceramic Stage begins with the date of human entry into the region. Unfortunately, this date is not known with certainty, although the earliest New World inhabitants are among the most hotly debated topics in archaeology. Prehistoric sites and, especially, radiocarbon dates are the chief data used in such discussions, but linguistic, genetic, and dental studies also have been brought to bear on the problem (Greenberg et al. 1986; West 1987). In a review of the radiocarbon evidence, John Rick (1987:61–64) states that little firm support can be found for human presence in Peru before 10,500 B.P. Seven dates ranging between 10,500 and 13,000 years ago do seem to represent some probability of human occupations, in Rick's view (see also Lynch 1983). The situation is complicated by claims for evidence of very early dates—some more than 18,000 B.P.—in various parts of South America, including Peru (MacNeish et al. 1981; see Bryan 1978; Dillehay 1986).

While other studies (e.g., Richardson 1986) may settle claims for early occupations, the subject does not directly impinge upon understanding of the site and people of Paloma, for it was occupied well after the first settlers arrived on the continent. Indeed, it has been suggested that the coast was occupied for two millennia or more before the first Paloma encampment (Richardson 1981), but that rising sea levels inundated most of these earlier occupations as modern environmental conditions were established.

Ten or twelve thousand years ago, the last great ice age was on the wane. The study of late Pleistocene–early Holocene environments is as trying as other subjects so far mentioned. Such research depends on interpretations of pollen trapped in lake sediments (Heusser 1983), tectonic and shoreline investigations (Sandweiss et al. 1983; Tosdal et al. 1984), weather studies (Pittock 1980), and much speculation. The possibility of rapid changes occurring so long ago and the problems of long-term versus short-term and fluctuating conditions (Cardich 1985) compound both the acquisition of basic knowledge and the assessment of the influence of such events on human lives.

There is no doubt that plants and animals were considerably different during the end of the glacial period. But the effect of low shorelines and more extensive glacial regions in the Andes on the weather patterns and vegetation of the Peruvian coast is uncertain. Pluvial episodes have been suggested (Lanning 1967:44) and disputed (Fung Pineda et al. 1972). Archaeological data have not contributed much to a resolution of such problems. The bones of giant sloths (*Megatherium* and *Mylodon*) and other strange creatures such as *Toxodon* and *Glyptodon* do attest to a world much different than the present one. But modern creatures or their ancestors, such as extinct camelids, were also on the scene. It is generally assumed, although the evidence is tenuous, that early humans in South America hunted these creatures in much the same way that early native North Americans hunted mammoths and mastodons, both of which were present further south. Some of the archaeologists searching for pre-12,000 B.P. human occupations have raised the possibility of a "pre-projectile point" stage or period (Krieger 1964; see Bryan 1978), but no conclusive data have been found in either North or South America for such an occupation. Use of such tools as choppers, scrapers, and other hand-held objects would have made hunting megafauna a very difficult proposition, although perishable weapons such as wooden or bone spears could have been used and smaller and less intractable foods could have been procured without projectiles.

Despite the fascination of searching for very early people in the New World, the first secure evidence of human habitation of South America consists of chipped stone artifacts usually assumed to have been the lethal ends of darts or spears. Among the earliest of these (cf. Mayer-Oakes 1982; Lynch 1986) are Fishtail points first found in the Straits of Magellan by Junius Bird (1969) which share fluting techniques with northern Clovis points. Also found are stemmed varieties such as Magellan I points, from Patagonia, Chobshi stemmed, in southern Ecuador, and Paiján points from northern coastal Peru (Chauchat 1976, 1979). Delicate willow-leaf lanceolate points are also found in Peru (Lynch 1978), but studies of the cultural significance of style differences of points are still in their infancy (e.g., Rick 1980; Malpass 1983).

Gradually, modern environmental conditions were established by about 6000 B.P. Changes in flora and fauna were accompanied by changes in human means of exploiting them, resulting in an Archaic life-style, again similar to processes in North America or Neolithic Europe. In general, smaller animals and a wider variety of plants were taken, reflected by increased use of grinding stones, greater storage facilities, and more nets, bags, and other means for capturing and storing energy sources. Many plants were domesticated or soon would be. As the Archaic or Preceramic Stage continued, developments followed on these trajectories; it is at this time, between 4000 and 2800 B.C., that Paloma was occupied.

The last phase of the preceramic began between 2500 and 2000 B.C. The period is marked by full domestication of many plants and animals, large villages, and monumental architecture. The monumental sites consist of huge constructions of platforms, terraces, plazas, and multiroomed buildings covering many hectares of land. The exact nature of such sites is uncertain (see Donnan 1985). Many appear to have been important ceremonial centers, but it is likely that these building complexes were also major political and economic centers. The ensuing Initial Period began sometime between 1800 and 1500 B.C.; pottery, true weaving, and other major changes occurred, but there seems to have been considerable continuity of traditions established in the late preceramic. Therefore, the period in which Paloma was occupied stands in the same relation to the late preceramic as do the Formative Period villages of Mesoamerica to the Olmec (Flannery 1976) and the Neolithic villages of the Near East to the cities of the Fertile Crescent (e.g., Childe 1952; Fairservis 1975).

Several questions thus become important in studying preceramic Peru. How did people make a living? How did people relate to each other—in what ways did they organize themselves in order to survive and reproduce themselves and their societies? Since societies which are successful in surviving and propagating usually produce surpluses of foods and other goods, how much extra was available and what was done with it? Besides basic problems of chronology, stratigraphy, and data recovery, these are the fundamental questions which archaeology asks. The answers are found through intrepretation of artifacts and other debris, such as food remains, left behind by people as they and the world they live in undergo such changes.

Most of the early studies of preceramic Peru were concentrated on the central coast, in the area between the Mala Valley, to the south of Lima, and the Fortaleza River, northward. Although the first preceramic village of note was excavated by Junius Bird (1948) at Huaca Prieta on the north coast, it was the surveys and excavations conducted by Frédéric-André Engel (1957a, b), Edward Lanning (1963), and Thomas Patterson and Michael Moseley (e.g., 1968), especially in the Ancón-Chillón-Ventanilla area of the central coast, which demonstrated the diversity and density of early archaeological sites available for study. In the highlands research has generally been concentrated in caves and rock shelters (Cardich 1964; Matos 1975; Lynch 1980; Rick 1980). Recently, however, greater attention has been paid to preceramic sites in parts of the coast other than the central area (Richardson 1978; Pozorski and Pozorski 1979), and some early open-air sites have been studied in the highlands (MacNeish et al. 1981).

The greatest number of preceramic stone tools and other artifacts found by Lanning (1963) and his colleagues came from the lomas vegetation in the coastal hills. The logical explanation for this was that preceramic hunters and gatherers camped in the fog oases during the winter months to take advantage of game animals and lomas plants. When the lomas contracted in the summer, one option for people was to go to the highlands. A pattern of transhumance (Lynch 1971) between coastal hills and puna could take advantage of the foggy winters near the Pacific and the food sources nurtured by highland rains beginning in January.

While some groups may have opted for transhumance, Rick (1980) has demonstrated that puna hunters could have lived comfortably year-round in their highland home. Patterson (1971a, b) has shown that coastal dwellers were able to alternate exploitation of local resource zones relatively close at hand. Seafood provided protein throughout the year. When lomas resources shrank, there was always the thorn forest in the river valley, which held water, plants, and animals. Human groups could thus practice a seasonal round of movement among lomas, river valley, and shore. Those locations close to all three major zones could serve as more or less permanent base camps or villages (see Moseley 1972).

Many of the lomas camps seem to have been abandoned about 2500 B.C. Permanent villages began to be located in other zones, including up-valley farming and shoreline fishing communities (Lanning 1963; Patterson 1971a, b; Moseley 1975). The resulting specialization of settlements may have been part of the reason why large architectural complexes developed, serving as centers for regional exchanges of subsistence and other goods. Much study, including development of tight chronological controls on the data, needs to be done before satisfactory explanations for the rise of large centers are established (Quilter n.d.).

As the perspective on the past described above came into focus, a number of questions were raised concerning exactly how hunter-gatherers managed to make a living on the coast. Lanning (1967:59–60) argued that, through time, seafood gradually came to dominate the subsistence economy even as farming became universal on the coast by Preceramic Period VI. Seafood included not only mollusks and fish but also sharks, rays, sea lions, seaweed, and a great number of seabirds. A number of archaeologists rejected the importance of seafood (Parsons 1970; Osborn 1977; Raymond 1981; Wilson 1981), and soon a debate developed as others defended the importance of seafood (Moseley 1968, 1975, 1978; Feldman 1980; Quilter and Stocker 1983). Those arguing that terrestrial foods were the essential ingredients in ancient diets said that deer and camelids provided better and more abundant sources of protein than seafood. Furthermore, some doubted (Wilson 1981:104) that preceramic peoples had watercraft capable of reaching the offshore fisheries—thus they could only exploit the less abundant seafoods close to shore. The proposition that maritime resources served as the foundations for late preceramic complex societies in Peru (Moseley 1975) caused disquiet partly because it was believed that every known civilization in the world was based on intensive agriculture. The possibility that Peru might be an exception to this generalization was disturbing to those who wished to establish a scientific law of the origins of complex societies.

One of the strongest arguments against the maritime hypothesis appeared to be the apparent instability of the oceanic current system as expressed in an event known as El Niño. The richness of the Peruvian fisheries is due to a cold, northward running current which causes the upwelling of nutrients, allowing the growth of abundant phyto-plankton fed on by larger and larger creatures in a complex food chain. The result of this food chain is one of the densest and most varied marine habitats in the world, second only to the Beluga fishery off the coast of South Africa. This same cold current is also essential in producing the coastal desert, as discussed above. Slightly north of the Peru-Ecuador border, the Peru Current turns westward, heading out into the Pacific as it meets a southward-flowing warm current which also turns west. Each of these currents is actually a complicated system of layers of water, and their relationships as well as those of the system as a whole are complex.

Every year, at the beginning of the austral summer, the warmer northern current overrides the Peru Current and pushes southward, but usually not very far. Sometimes the warm waters displace the Peru Current much further south than normal, down to the central coast. This disrupts the food chain. Phytoplankton are not available, so fish and seabirds migrate if they can; others die in droves, as do sea lions and mollusks. Sometimes torrential rains crash onto the central and north coasts, while drought occurs in the southern highlands due to the deprivation of the moisture normally brought to the area by the sea breezes. The term *El Niño* (Christ Child) is derived from the fact that this event occurs close to Christmas time—unlike its sacred counterpart, the epiphany of the natural event is not welcome.

El Niño's arrival on the central coast occurs in a cycle. A detectable, relatively significant event happens once every five to eight years. How often a severe El Niño occurs is uncertain. There have been nineteen lasting six months or more since 1726 (Wilson 1981:100), with the three most recent in 1925, 1972, and 1983 (see Stevenson and Wicks 1975). That ancient El Niños occurred is a certainty. Moseley and Deeds (1982:48) have documented that such an event crippled the fifteenth-century Chimú irrigation system and note legends of similar disasters in earlier times (see Kosok 1965).

Preceramic El Niños are difficult to document, however, although possible evidence for such an event has been detected in the growth rings of mollusk shells found at El Paraíso in the Chillón Valley (Sandweiss and Quilter n.d.), relatively late in the preceramic (circa 1800–1500 B.C.). The problem of when El Niños began after the last glaciation is an important topic yet to be addressed in assessing its role for earlier populations. The focus of recent attention, however, is not so much on whether El Niños occurred, but on what effect they may have had on ancient lives.

Wilson (1981:98–101) has suggested that the resulting "bottleneck" in marine productivity caused by El Niño events would have encouraged early coastal populations to invest their time and energies in agriculture rather than to depend on maritime subsistence economies. But agricultural fields are not immune to the effects of El Niño. Runoff from torrential rains pours down dry canyons and hills, inundates bottomlands, and swamps cultivated fields. Irrigation systems may be severely damaged and nonirrigated fields by the banks of rivers also suffer from such devastation. Furthermore, although the oceanic food chain is broken by El Niño, some fish are driven close to shore—making them easier to catch—and new species quickly take advantage of changed conditions, resulting in a different menu rather than a bare cupboard for coastal fishermen (see Quilter and Stocker 1983:551–553). Early warning signs such as climatic shifts or unusual behavior of animal populations may have forewarned coastal dwellers that El Niño was forthcoming, giving them time to prepare by storing food, temporarily leaving the area, or pursuing other strategies.

Given the millennia of preceramic life on the coast of Peru, it is likely that several severe El Niños occurred, just as it is possible that one or more giant tidal waves or tsunamis pounded the coast (Bird 1985) and huge sections of beach were suddenly stranded by abrupt tectonic events. It is hard to judge, however, how great an effect such calamities

had on the general course of cultural processes. Elsewhere in the Americas volcanism has recently been seen to have caused large-scale abandonment of regions, such as in Mesoamerica (Sheets 1971) and Ecuador (Lippi n.d.), with subsequent effects on sociopolitical systems.

It seems unlikely, however, that major social change was caused by such disasters in preceramic Peru. Neither population densities nor the degrees of infrastructural investment were as great as in Central America. Except for the notable exception of the uplift of Ventanilla Bay, which stranded nine square kilometers, few detectable events were as large or as long-lasting in their impact as the volcanic eruptions to the north. The only comparable events known for historic Peru are massive landslides such as occurred in the Callejón de Huaylas in the central highlands in 1970, blanketing an entire valley with rubble and earth. But this does not directly relate to consideration of coastal subsistence strategies.

Thus, though El Niño events may temporarily have changed the strategies by which preceramic coastal dwellers earned their livelihoods and caused short-term disruptions of normal life, they cannot be cited as evidence to discount the importance of maritime resources in ancient diets. Some of the other questions raised concerning the role of seafood, such as availability and nutritional value, do need to be addressed. The excavations at Paloma have been crucial in helping to clarify these problems, and the solutions to them are presented below in discussion of work at the site. The emerging picture suggests that seafood was indeed important, but was part of a complementary system of terrestrial and maritime resources in a subsistence economy which needed foods from both habitats to be successful. These arguments are based on theory and general observations of the Peruvian Coast. In the next chapter, however, specific evidence from Paloma is presented to demonstrate the economic potential of life by the sea.

2. The Site of Paloma

General Considerations: Strata, Houses, and Features

The site of Paloma is the buried remains of a village of reed huts on the northern edge of the Chilca River Valley, 65 kilometers south of Lima (figs. 4–8; Engel 1980; Benfer 1984, 1986a). Uncalibrated radiocarbon dates place occupations of the site between about 5700 and 2800 B.C. The earliest known occupation has left only faint traces on the sterile desert; the main occupation occurred somewhat later when, apparently, roughly modern environmental conditions existed.

The Chilca Valley drainage system is a combination of east–west trending, irregular parallel valleys, including the Quebrada de Los Perdidos, a dry canyon on its northern edge. Paloma lies between 200 and 250 meters above sea level in hills separating the Quebrada de Los Perdidos from the main valley where the Chilca River flows. The site appears to have been settled so that its inhabitants were within easy walking distance of the Chilca River, 7 to 8 kilometers to the south, and the Pacific shoreline, between 3 and 4 kilometers west.[2] Paloma is situated on the

edge of the lomas, but in years of heavy fog the lomas vegetation spreads over the site.

For desert dwellers, even in the fog-drenched lomas, fresh water was a problem. There were three possible sources of water. Wells may have been excavated to the low water table. There are sunken gardens near the site, but they may be slightly later than its occupation, possibly dating to the time when cotton was in use, probably after 2500 B.C. in the Chilca region. A small spring about a five-minute walk east of the site may have provided water in ancient times. The spring may be intermittent—it was seen in June 1976 but not afterward. Sand-lined pits also could have been used to trap fog moisture. During field-work at the site, one such pit—empty except for beach sand—was found to collect moisture, but it is uncertain whether it and others like it were used for such purposes in the past.

The site is easily detectable by white crushed shell covering the ground surface over 15 hectares. The densest midden deposits lie on the edge of a small canyon on the western side of the site. This appears to have been a garbage dump during at least part of the Paloma occupation, judging from the dense accumulations of food debris and broken artifacts. To the east, these deposits spread out onto a broad fan which gently slopes down into the main canyon of the Quebrada de Los Perdidos. The northern and southern limits of the site are bounded by coastal hills (figs. 5–8).

---

2. These are direct linear distances. Modern Andean people are famous for prodigious feats of walking in which they ignore topography and go directly from point to point. Except when extremely high snow-covered altitudes are involved, the easiest path is not necessarily the route taken. The walking habits of the people of Paloma are, of course, unknown.

Midden deposits vary in thickness across the site. More than a dozen surface shell concentrations appear slightly to overlap the clusters of houses and burials, which are often under relatively light deposits of shell, although subsurface materials are fairly continuous throughout the area. The largest of the shell concentrations is Unit I, occupying approximately 6500 square meters. The thickness of its midden deposits ranges from a few centimeters at its southern limits to over a meter slightly north of its center.

Seven major depositional zones have been observed by CIZA excavators in Unit I:

Level 100   Light gray, relatively sterile, windblown surface dust

Level 120   Medium gray, windblown surface dust with some darker ash, projectile points and other stone tools and flakes, and some shell debris

Level 200   Concentrated crushed mussel shells giving a blue appearance to the level; light gray ashy matrix

Level 300   Usually moderately concentrated shell, especially yellow/white mussels; coprolites; light gray ash; lots of vegetal remains

Level 400   Usually moderately concentrated dark gray ash with plant parts and little shell; sometimes concentrated shell, burnt hearth stones, and plant parts

Level 500   Generally, concentrated dark gray ash with few other contents, usually in contact with sterile pampa (powdered rock)

Level 600   Ashlike layer of yellow pampa dust with some shell, ash, and charcoal; very difficult to recognize when in contact with true pampa.

These strata are general arbitrary units not measured from a specific datum point. Neither are they always found in absolute layer-cake relationships through the site area. Near the east edge of Unit I, for example, Level 500 lies directly below a thin layer of surface dust. But, in general, the stratigraphic sequence holds true. Levels 200, 300, 400, and 500 were the predominant strata found in Unit I.

The other levels are found in varying degrees in other parts of the site. Distinct substrata have been found in some areas. These have been designated in units of tens, such as 210, 220, and 230, signifying successively lower layers within the general 200 level.

There is enough uniformity throughout the areas excavated from 1973 through 1979 to support the view that the same depositional layers exist in the same relationships over much of the site. Radiocarbon samples taken from the strata support the contention that there is relative uniformity and little disturbance of the deposits; a full list of dates may be found elsewhere (Benfer 1984). Weir and Dering (1986:22) note an extreme date of 7735 ± 100 for a "provisional lower level" of Unit I consisting of an organic deposit found beneath a thin layer of sterile soil (pampa) at the deepest point of the midden. Levels 400–500 may then be dated as falling between 7000 and 5500 years B.P., Level 300 at 5500–5200 B.P., and Level 200 at 5200–4600 B.P. These three large groupings have proved to be the most amenable stratigraphic and temporal units for discussion and analysis of Paloma data. They contain the majority of the houses, features, burials, and artifacts and are the most extensive well-defined layers in Unit I.

The range of dates for Paloma corresponds to late Preceramic Period IV and Period V in Lanning's (1967) chronological system. The time of the lomas camps, from about 8000 to 4500 B.P., might also be termed the Middle Preceramic, with the preceding time from first occupation of Peru to 8000 B.P. as Early Preceramic (pending possible future subdivisions) and the period after camps such as Paloma to the introduction of ceramics (circa 4500 B.P.–3500 B.P.) the Late Preceramic.

Engel's 1973 work was concentrated in Unit I, where two large trenches intersected at a 90° angle to form a cross (Engel 1980). The largest trench, 90 meters long, was oriented north to south (fig. 8), while the shorter trench was 72 meters in length and oriented east to west. Each trench was 6 meters wide.

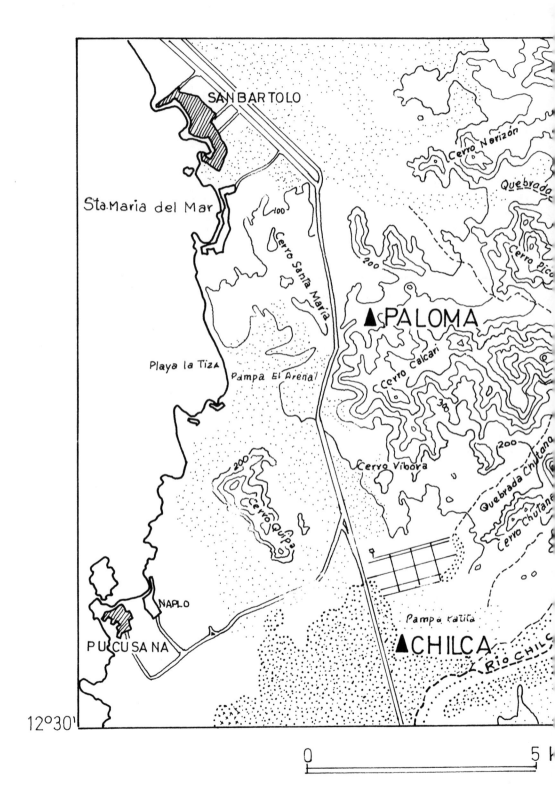

SAN BARTOLO

Sta. Maria del Mar

100

Cerro Santa Maria

200

Cerro Narizón

Quebrada

Cerro Pico

▲PALOMA

Cerro Calcari

Playa la Tiza

Pampa El Arenal

300

Cerro Vibora

200

Quebrada Chutana

200

Cerro Quipa

Cerro Chutana

NAPLO

Pampa Katita

PUCUSANA

▲CHILCA

Rio Chilc

12°30'

0   5 k

4. The Paloma-Chilca region.

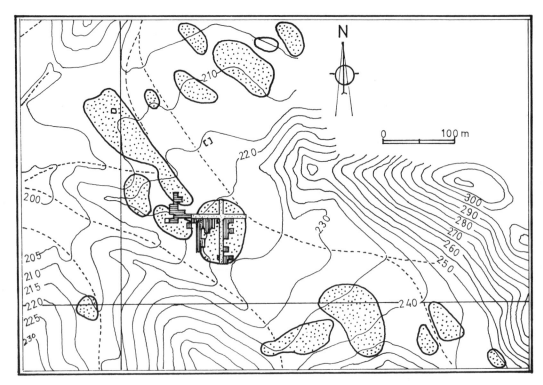

5. Shell concentrations at the Paloma site.

Work began in the center of Unit I and proceeded outward along the length and breadth of the cruciform trench. One meter balks to control for stratigraphy were maintained between adjacent excavation units so that each had dimensions of 6 × 5 meters. Each excavation unit was given a grid provenience based on north to south and east to west datum points. This system was utilized to pinpoint the horizontal locations of burials and other items to within centimeters, although vertical position was sometimes hard to establish (see Key to Data Listings in appendix 1).

In 1976, when the University of Missouri crew began work at Paloma, much time was spent in field checks of the excavated cross-trench as well as examination of skeletal remains and artifacts in the CIZA laboratory in Lima. Over 150 burials were examined during the six-month 1976 field season. An additional 300 square meters were opened in untouched areas of the site, mostly on the

extremity of the western arm of the cross-trench.

The fine powdery deposits made paintbrushes and cane blow-tubes the primary excavation tools. Screens with mesh 1/4" or finer were employed in dense midden and for grave and feature contents. Preservation was good; many layers of deposits were greasy black and some still reeked of organic refuse.

Except for the large refuse pile on the western side of the site, part of Unit II, most burials or other remains were usually associated with a prehistoric house or hut (fig. 9; see Engel 1980 : 106–107). These huts ranged in shape from circular to ovoid to quadrilateral. Floors usually were sloped toward the center and were deliberately excavated to produce a semi-subterranean dwelling 25 to 60 centimeters below the ground surface. The main supports of the structures were willow or cane (*caña brava: Gynerium sagittatum*) poles, sometimes bound together in groups of two to four by reed twine for greater strength. These poles were placed in a compacted, raised ring of earth or midden encircling the floor as a result of the prehistoric excavation of the structure. Poles often had stones wedged at their bases for extra support. Parallel cross poles may have been utilized in house construction to produce a grid system for the walls. Loose bunches of grasses, sedges, or reeds were stuffed between the poles for insulation. It is not entirely certain but seems likely that large reed mats were often placed on top of the pole-grass combination for added insulation against the coastal winter damp and chill. Floors certainly were covered with such mats; they were found in situ.

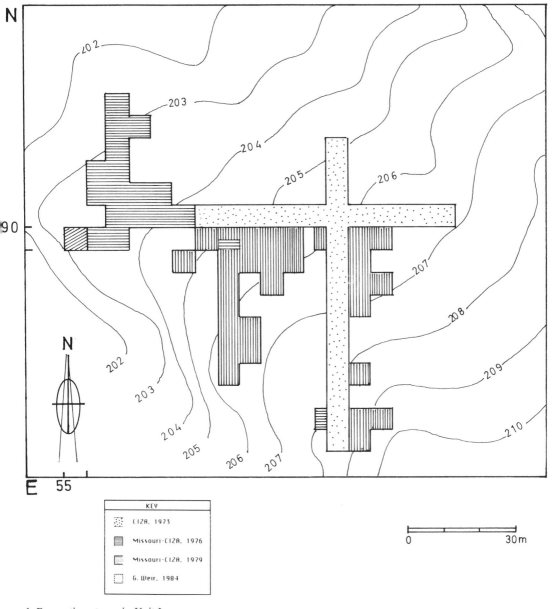

6. Excavation stages in Unit I.

7. The Paloma site: view to the west.

8. View of the trenches in July 1976, looking south.

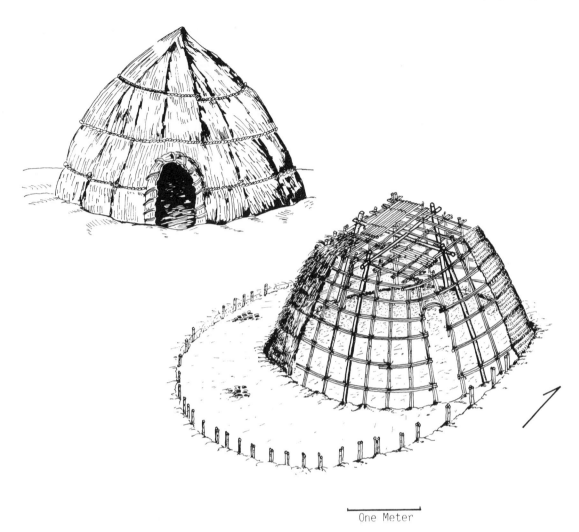

One Meter

9. Two reconstructions of preceramic houses: upper left, Chilca I house after Donnan (1964); lower right, possible squared roof on Paloma house as suggested by Engel.

Another uncertainty is the overall shape of the huts. It first was assumed that the domestic structures were dome-shaped, like the preceramic dwellings at the nearby Chilca I site (Donnan 1964). However, House 101, excavated in 1976 and one of the best-preserved structures at the site, had a collapsed lattice-work cane and reed segment lying on top of its floor. Engel (1980:107) has suggested that this was a flat, square roof over a hut with an oval or circular base. There is no reason to discount the possibility that huts of different

styles were made during the long occupation of the site.

A common feature in Paloma domestic structures was an additional wall, often connected to one point of the circular wall and swinging out in an arc, 20 centimeters or more away from the main domicile. These extra walls may cover as much as two-thirds of the perimeter of the house and are always located on the southwestern sides of huts. The extra space may have served as a storage area. It seems quite likely that an important function of the additional wall was further insulation, as a windbreak. Prevailing winds come from the southwest and probably did so during the prehistoric occupation of Paloma.

Very small poorly constructed houses, often no more than 1.5 meters in diameter, with flat or shallow floors are found in Level 600. These appear to be very temporary structures inhabited by people who may have spent much shorter periods at Paloma than later residents. The more substantial dwellings were occupied longer, as evidenced by more than three floors found in House 101 (see Engel 1980:108).

The Paloma houses averaged 10.9 square meters of covered space. Although this seems relatively small (see Naroll 1962; Howells 1965; Cook 1972), it is probably adequate for a society in which most routine activities were carried on outdoors and close sleeping quarters meant increased warmth. Even today, 10-square-meter huts are common on the coast as basic shelter (Engel 1980:107).

Features found in or near huts included a variety of pits, hearths (fig. 10), and burials.

Most pits were ovoid in cross section, located outside of huts, and ranged in size from small circular holes about 10 centimeters deep and 20 centimeters in diameter to large pits a meter deep and wide. Some of the larger pits were lined with grass stalks, suggesting that the contents were kept away from contact with soil. Perhaps food was stored in such pits, although no direct evidence of this was found. One pit was lined with beach sand and could have trapped fog moisture, as mentioned above, although other uses are certainly possible. Most pits were empty upon discovery, suggesting relatively short-term storage. A fisherman's kit was found in a small pit in House 117 (fig. 10), and small offering pits were found next to burials. Pits seem to have been specially dug and used for particular purposes; only rarely were they re-used for the burial of small infants.

Hearths are of two kinds. Small concentrations of ashes and carbonized twigs were commonly found lying directly on the floor of huts and may have been used to ward off the foggy winter chill. Large, often oval-shaped,

10. Features 340 and 341 in the floor of House 117: a small hearth and a pit containing a fisherman's tool kit.

pavements of burnt cobbles spread up to a meter and sometimes more were encountered outside domestic structures. Burnt bone and shell in these amounts indicate that they were cooking areas.

The midden on the western side of the site consisted of an area of several square meters or more with dense concentrations of burnt rock, animal bones, shells, plant remains, anchovy residues, and coprolites. The area may thus have been not only a garbage dump, but also a place of food preparation and other activities at various times during the occupation of the site. Burials and the remains of part of a house (House 102) in the lower levels suggest that it was not until relatively late in the occupation of the site that this area was used to dispose of trash. The position of the hearth/garbage dump on the edge of the small *quebrada* on the western side of the site is an indication that the Palomans may have systematically cleared their living areas of refuse and maintained a disposal area on the outskirts of their village at least during some portion of the occupation of the site. It has been suggested that use of special garbage dumps is due to relatively high population densities in a given area (Yellen 1977; cf. Binford 1983) and may also indicate relative sedentism, although standards of cleanliness vary worldwide.

The total number of huts at the site and the size of the village at any particular time are uncertain—42 houses were found in Unit I in 1976 and about one-tenth of the midden concentration was excavated, so a total of 420 houses may be extrapolated. This figure seems unduly large, however. John Greer (1977) has suggested that there is a pattern of village growth from the center of Unit I outward, producing a rough horizontal stratigraphy at the site. There is no clear pattern of village organization, however. No empty spaces suggesting a plaza area have been found, for example. In 1979, a house was uncovered with a cache of five large grinding stones in it, one of which appeared to be a blank (Benfer, personal communication). If each stone represents a single domestic unit, then the cache

indicates that at least four or five such units lived at the site simultaneously. It seems improbable that four or five families were associated with a single house; more likely, a number of domestic units agreed to cache their grinding stones in one hut. It is possible that more than one grinding stone was used by each domestic unit, although four or five of similar type seem rather excessive. Subjectively, it seems probable that the village population ranged between one or two families to a maximum of ten or so at any one time during the occupation of Paloma. Engel (1980) and Benfer (personal communication) suggest the population may have been even higher.

Analysis of human physical remains (Benfer 1986) has suggested that a distinct new population inhabited the site during the Level 200 and 300 occupation. Another population shift may be represented by semisubterranean stone structures, northeast of the shell midden. The exact number and nature of these structures have not been determined. But Engel (1980:106) excavated one close to Paloma, only 80 meters northeast of the shell concentration. He found a square stone structure with rounded corners, measuring roughly 9 meters on each side. Two sets of stone steps on opposite sides of the structure led from the ground level to the floor. There may have been more than one floor in the structure, although the lowest one was about a meter deep. Under it a burial was found wrapped in cotton textiles. Radiocarbon analyses of materials associated with the burial produced dates of 2170 ± 200 and 1960 ± 120 B.C. (Engel 1980:106). Thus there appears to have been some continuity of occupation of the Paloma area from early times to the period when cotton was produced and used in the late preceramic.

Another distinct area near the site is a series of thirty-six depressed plots of ground, each about 2 meters square, starting less than 100 meters east of Paloma, south of the semisubterranean rooms and briefly noted previously. These may be sunken garden plots which tapped the relatively high water table. They have not been fully investigated, so their exact nature and period of use are uncertain at present.

Although the shell midden was no longer occupied much later than about 2500 B.C., occasional habitation occurred. In 1979, several ears of maize (*Zea mays*) were found in association with a canine burial in the midden area of Paloma. Radiocarbon dating of the cobs produced an uncorrected age of 1,830 ± 85 years (Benfer 1984). Given the numerous later sites in the vicinity of Paloma, it is not surprising that occasional use was made of the old lomas camp.

Summary of Demography and Paleopathology

Among the most important data at the site are the numerous burials. Most were found wrapped in a reed mat and placed below the level of a hut floor either in or outside of a house. Details on mortuary practices are given below. The physical remains of the ancient inhabitants of the site are also important for what they may reveal concerning ancient health, morbidity, and mortality. Indeed, the primary objective of the project was to study these subjects and the demography of an isolated group of hunter-gatherers in the New World.

Robert Benfer (1981, 1982a, 1984) and other project participants (Gehlert 1979; Jackson 1981) have documented a number of interesting facts concerning physical characteristics of the site inhabitants. Information on survival rates and other matters can be fairly well established due to the good preservation of bones and because all individuals, including fetuses and infants, were apparently buried at the site.

Infants and younger individuals make up the greatest proportion of burials (28%; Benfer 1986b:52). Survivorship curves show that about 42% of the population of the site did not live past childhood. Mortality was most severe between ages 1 and 4 when weaning usually occurs. Once past childhood, however, a person could expect to live to between 20 and 35 years. In 1976, the oldest individual studied was a 50-year-old female

(Burial 11); five other individuals over 50 years of age were found in 1979.

The percentage of fetus and infant burials decreases from 33% in the earliest levels, to 23% in Level 300, to 19% in Level 200 (Benfer 1986b:53). This may indicate that the Palomans improved their adaptation to the coast and became more numerous through time or that population replacement brought better-adapted groups to the site. But Benfer (1986b) notes that the data may be showing that childhood mortality itself decreased rather than indicating a population increase per se. He also cautions that changing site roles, from village to temporary camp, might have biased the data, although no clear evidence for this proposition exists.

While physical data do not necessarily indicate that the Paloma population increased through time, there is evidence for healthier and better-adapted people. Survival rates increase during the site occupation and Harris Lines in bones, indicating periods of growth arrest, decrease through time (Gehlert 1979; Benfer 1986b:54). Studies have determined that these lines are indicative of insufficient nourishment rather than diseases (Benfer 1986b).

The fact that almost twice as many female deaths occurred after the age of 30 at Paloma is different from most simple societies, in which women suffer high mortality rates during childbirth, usually in their 20s. Benfer (1986b) has suggested that this indicates a pattern of delayed birthing, a common means of population control. He further notes a higher number of female infant burials, also increasing in numbers and proportion through time. There are 1.5 times as many male noninfants as female, suggesting female infanticide if a 50:50 birth ratio is assumed. Infanticide is another common means of controlling population size. It may have been carried out due to a perceived, perhaps real, imbalance between birthrate and available resources.

The people of the site suffered from a number of diseases, including tuberculosis and carcinomas (Barjenbruch 1977). A number of ailments also relate to cultural practices, especially in regard to subsistence economies. Broken foot bones were common. Indeed, no evidence for footwear has been found for the Palomans. I discovered the dangers of bare feet in a painful form of unplanned "experimental archaeology" when I broke my toe on a rock hidden by surface dust at the site.

Inflammation in lower back areas, especially osteoarthritis, was in evidence in many of the Paloma skeletons. This affliction was probably the result of the active and rather stressful life of the Palomans. That back problems were found in both sexes and almost all age groups attests to the difficult work done by most members of the communities which lived at the site. Carrying heavy loads of mollusks from the beach and hauling gear in seasonal movements to different exploitation zones could have produced such stresses. Evidence of distinct seasonal differences in food resources appears in studies which show sharp changes in the mineral composition of hair (Benfer 1986a). This may have been brought about by movement of people or by seasonal reorientations of subsistence economies without change of residence.

Eight skeletons were found with inner ear bone growths known as auditory exostoses (Benfer 1977:11). A similar affliction was found in skeletons from the preceramic site (circa 2500 B.C.) of Huaca Prieta on the north coast (Lester 1966; Tattersall 1985). Lester concluded that the growths were due to long periods in cold water, similar to "surfer's knee." At Huaca Prieta and Paloma all skeletons with exostoses were male. Such evidence might be interpreted as demonstrating that fishing was predominantly a male activity since only males exhibit exostoses. Opinion is divided on the question, however. Tattersall (1985:64–65) has argued that women are less susceptible to this ear problem than men, leaving open the possibility that they may also have spent as much time in cold waters as males. Kennedy (1986), however, has used experimental data to show that environmental and geographical variation exists—exostoses are most frequent in the middle lati-tudes (30–45° N and S). In many cases where women dived for shellfish or did other aquatic work they had exostoses, though often less than males. It appears that a very large sample is needed in order to attempt to demonstrate the sexual division of labor (or recreation) in aquatic environments with confidence.

Fauna, Flora, and Subsistence Economy at Paloma

Animal remains from Paloma demonstrate that marine resources were the primary source of animal food at the site (Reitz 1986, 1988). Marine vertebrates, primarily fish, make up 30% of the Minimum Number of Individuals (MNI) and 71% of the biomass; 20% of the biomass (MNI: 68%) came from marine invertebrates. Less than 1% of the animal remains came from birds and mammals, contributing less than 9% as food. Land snails also contributed less than 1%.

The analysis conducted by Elizabeth Reitz shows changes in the relative emphasis of invertebrates and fish at Paloma. Part of the change may be due to larger sample sizes from Level 300, which included the only nonmarine organisms. The increase in invertebrates is due to greater use of mussels, especially *Perumytilus purpuratus* and *Semimytilus algosus*. In Level 300 two clams first appear at the site (*Protothaca thaca* and *Mesodesma donacium*). The mussel *Choromytilus chorus* increases in importance in Level 200, although this may be partly due to a large concentration of the shells found in a single sampling unit. In Level 100 only two members of the mussel family are found, *Aulacomya ater* and *Semimytilus algosus* (Reitz 1986:18–20).

While some of these changes may be due to sampling procedures, the data suggest that the site occupants generally increased their range of exploitation during the Paloma occupation. Rocky shores, where mussels are common, are closest to the site. Clams could only be taken at sandy beaches, which are somewhat farther from the site. Although there are patches of sandy shore directly west of Paloma, the nearest large area for clams begins

6 kilometers directly northwest, at San Bartolo, or southward, near the mouth of the Chilca River. Of course, it is quite possible that clams and other seafoods were eaten in greater amounts but did not all enter the archaeological record as residues at Paloma. At the preceramic site of Avic, on the north coast, dense midden has been found with many sea lion bones, some of which were burnt (Cardenes M. 1978:12).

Clams and other mollusks, like the sea lion meat, could have been eaten at or near the place where they were taken or could have been processed for transport, with the inedible parts left on the beach. Indeed, it seems somewhat strange for the Palomans to have carried heavy loads of shellfish from the water's edge to a lomas camp when the food could have been eaten al fresco at the shoreline. The likely explanation for the huge piles of shell at Paloma and similar sites is that they are the remnants of a process of short-term storage. Wrapped in seaweed or kept in seawater-soaked bags or pits, shellfish can be kept fresh for several days. Such techniques or similar ones seem to be indicated by shell remains found relatively high in the Andes at Tres Ventanas (Engel 1970:56) and other highland sites (e.g., Burger and Burger 1979:149). Thus, the shell remains at the site may underrepresent the total amount of mollusks consumed by the people of Paloma (see Quilter and Stocker 1983).

The great variety and quantity of fish remains at Paloma include large species such as *cabrilla* (*Paralabrax* spp.), *Haemulon* spp., *Paralonchurus peruanus,* and *Sciaena deliciosa.* Small schooling fish, especially anchovies (Engraulidae) and herrings (Clupeidae) were probably very important to the Paloma diet.

The variability of the coastal environment and the resources it provides and the sometimes capricious nature of the archaeological record make interpretation of subsistence economies a difficult task. If it is assumed that the fish listed above were taken under conditions typical of the coast during the present day and without an El Niño present which would have driven deep-water species close

to shore, then these fish remains may indicate fairly sophisticated seafaring abilities for the Palomans. The general elaboration of fishing gear at the site seems to attest to such abilities. No watercraft have been found for the preceramic occupation of Peru, but is likely they were left at or near the beaches and not hauled to lomas sites for the convenience of future archaeologists.

The anchovies and herring may have been especially important resources, providing high-protein, fatty food in bulk. Throughout much of the maritime-terrestrial debate, they were not taken into account because their bones fell through the 1/4" screens used to sift dirt. With greater (Jackson and Stocker 1982) and lesser (Quilter and Stocker 1983) degrees of certainty, the possibility of layers of fish meal at Paloma has been discussed. Reevaluation of the lenses now indicates that the strata in question are composed of coprolites in the garbage dump area of the site (Benfer, personal communication). A diet high in fish foods nevertheless seems to have caused a confusion in the nature of the remains, and it seems likely that the identification of uneaten fish paste is a difficult task, especially since such nutritious portable food would probably not have been allowed to go to waste by either mobile or sedentary peoples.

Fish paste is a common South American food (Lothrop 1946:182; Kirchoff 1948:482; Roosevelt 1980:106–108), especially in the tropical lowlands, and fish oil not only is nutritious but can be prevented from spoiling by heating before use (see Quilter and Stocker 1983). The usefulness of fish paste could have been prolonged by storage in subterranean pits, sealed from the humid air (see Bonavia and Grobman 1979).

Research on the new subsistence data indicates that the available seafood held a greater variety and richness of nutrients than thought by many in the debate on early diets (see Quilter and Stocker 1983). The amount of meat and the quantity and quality of protein of some shellfish are much higher for some species than for the North American riverine clams used in some early calculations (Osborn 1977:171–177). Studies of these aspects of Peruvian oceanic resources are ongoing, but the general picture is that seafood was a rich, varied resource which served as the primary source of protein for preceramic peoples. Relatively small amounts of animal protein from sea lions or the occasional lomas ungulate were probably enough to provide adequate nutrition in a diet with fish, shellfish, and plants as its mainstays. In the Peruvian coastal regime protein was abundant in the form of seafood, but plant foods were relatively scarce in the coastal desert.

Work primarily conducted by Glendon Weir and Phil Dering (1986) has revealed much concerning plants in the Paloma environment and their use. Studies have indicated that between about 4500 and 3000 B.C. it was somewhat cooler on the coast than today (Weir and Dering 1986:23). Although the environment was basically the same, the lomas were much richer in regard to the density and variety of plants compared to the present. Trees were much more common, especially local willow (*Salix* sp.) as well as *chaydo* (*Capparis prisca*) and *Caesalpinia* spp. They and a number of leafy shrubs (e.g., *Piqueria* sp.; *Croton alnifolius; Heliotropium* sp.) helped contain moisture from the winter fogs and reduce evaporation. This in turn fostered the growth of many other plants.

Not only were lomas grasses used in house construction but their seeds served as an important dietary source. In addition, a number of fruits, such as *mito* (*Carica candicans*), *algarrobo* (*Prosopis* spp.), and the fruit from the cactus *Loxanthocereus* sp. were also consumed. A variety of plants still used in folk medicine on the coast (e.g., *Valeriana pinnatifida* [*alberjilla*], and *Schinus molle*) may have found similar uses in ancient times, and *molle* is still used to make a beverage (*chicha*).

Cultivated gourds were common at the site. They are the earliest domesticated plant in South America and their origin is something of a mystery (cf. Lathrap 1977). Some evidence of cultivated squash (*Cucurbita ficifolia*) and beans (*Phaseolus* sp.) is present at Paloma, but these plants apparently did not play major roles in the subsistence economy. Guava (*Psidium quayba*) is also present. It is difficult to determine if this plant was cultivated or harvested as a wild food—little study has been undertaken on morphological differences between wild and domesticated varieties. The same is true for *oca* (*Oxalis* sp.), assumed to be native to the highlands but present in the Paloma midden.

One of the most interesting discoveries concerning flora is the possibility that a lomas plant, a tuberous begonia (*Begonia geraniifolia*), may have been under the process of domestication (Weir and Dering 1986:26). This plant has a large edible tuber with "eyes" similar to potatoes. In certain parts of the site these tubers are the most abundant of the large plant remains. Weir and Dering (1986:26) note that there is no modern, historical, or ethnographic evidence for the use of this plant. They suggest, however, that it may have been encouraged or managed even if it was not completely domesticated.

Through time, there was a decrease in the number of woody plants represented as charcoal and burnt matter in the strata and a reduction in the stem diameters of firewood (Weir and Dering 1986:32). Pollen studies (Weir, Benfer, and Jones 1985) also show that the lomas environment was pauperized through time. Even with a stable population size, the cutting of firewood reduced the lomas overstory, causing increased evaporation rates of ground moisture and a diminution in the quantity and diversity of plants in the fog fields (Vehik 1977; Weir and Dering 1986:33). This may have helped precipitate abandonment of the lomas villages and changes in the settlement system in the coastal region.

A problematic aspect of attempts at reconstructing the ancient environment of Peru is the numerous unidentified pollens found in coprolites and in other contexts (Weir, Benfer, and Jones 1985). The predominant pollen at Paloma and other early sites is morphologically distinct; yet the family to which it belongs is highly uncertain (perhaps *Heliotropium*; J. Jones, personal communication). This suggests that drastic changes have taken place in the fog fields—many species found in them today were introduced after the Spanish conquest. Even though much basic botanical research must still be accomplished, it is possible that a great variety of resources which were once available are now extinct or very rare. All discussions of past subsistence economies must therefore be tempered with caution.

Summary of Subsistence Economy Studies

The analyses of plant and animal remains as well as human skeletal materials from Paloma support the contention that the primary protein source was seafood, with the lomas supplying plants. Whether seafood alone can supply enough calories to support human settlements is still not known (Burger and Burger 1986). But the Paloma data seem to indicate that seafood and lomas plants were sufficient to allow for the maintenance and propagation of peoples in the region.

The evidence also demonstrates that the Palomans could have lived year-round at the site. Enough foods were available, combined with storage techniques, to support a sedentary population, even in El Niño years. Although the nature of maritime resources might change, including the diminution of some foods such as seabirds (not significant in the faunal analyses at Paloma), the lomas zones would blossom in a rare exuberance due to rainfall. While the occupants of the site could have spent the entire year there, there is evidence that some groups may have moved to or been in contact with fairly distant regions.

Three different cacti which today only grow on the western flanks of the Andes were found at the site (Weir and Dering 1986:30, 32). Today one must travel a minimum of 12 to 14 kilometers for two of these cacti and the third may only be found between 25 and 30 kilometers from the coast. Such distances might not require movement of the entire village population. As Binford (1978; Binford and Chasko 1978) has demonstrated, base camps and villages somewhat similar to Pa-

loma are often left for periods of a few days to weeks by groups seeking special foods or other resources. A variety of strategies from portions of the population leaving the site for short or long periods to total abandonment to full sedentism are possible. Given the long period of site occupation, it is likely that at some times Paloma was one station in a seasonal round, while at others it was a relatively permanent village.

Materials from very distant sources were also found at Paloma. These include obsidian, the nearest source of which is 400 kilometers distant, in Huancavelica, in the southern sierra (Burger and Asaro 1977). In a small "grab" sample of midden, a worked proximal femur of a spider monkey (*Ateles* sp.) was discovered (Reitz 1986:25). This primate is an unlikely lomas inhabitant; the nearest source is the *ceja de la selva* on the eastern slopes of the central Peruvian Andes or moister western slopes much farther north near the modern Ecuadorian border. Engel discovered a *Spondylus* sp. shell during earlier work at the site. *Spondylus* habitats are not usually found south of the warm waters of the Gulf of Guayaquil and it is almost certain that this has always been their southern limit. Thus, the bright red-rimmed shell is likely to have reached the site through human agency, as is the case with the obsidian and monkey bone, unless very unusual circumstances such as an extended period of warm waters or a storm could have produced these shells on the central coast. Ecuador is well out of the conceivable range of an annual or even lifetime round of movement of a nomadic foraging group on the central Peruvian coast. It thus seems likely that the shell and probably the bone and volcanic glass reached the site through human exchange systems. While the sources of exotic items may never have been visited by Palomans, exchanges could have been down-the-line (Renfrew 1975).

In summary, the specialist analyses indicate that life was neither easy nor desperate at the time of Paloma's occupation. The people of the site did fairly well for a preindustrial group. Fish and other seafood provided sources of protein but had to be taken by braving the cold offshore waters. The lomas and riverine area yielded industrial materials and plant foods; but the fog fields, especially, were fragile and subject to overexploitation. Even though Paloma is situated in a place where all three of the major resource zones could be efficiently used, their exploitation required considerable effort. The evidence indicates that life was not so good as to encourage permanent residence for all groups that lived at the site. At the very least, small groups took journeys to procure nonlocal materials and foods, and it is likely that the whole village sometimes moved to other areas for part of the year. On the other hand, the data do suggest that sedentary habitation is likely to have occurred during the site's long occupation.

The people of Paloma were also tied to a larger world which included distant lands they did not see. A few exotic items indicate the development of value systems which were elaborated in later epochs. All this is revealed by the data so far presented. The Palomans' social and ideological worlds can be further explored through the discussion of those things directly affected by the intentions of these ancient people—artifacts and burials.

3. The Archaeological Discoveries at Paloma

General Features of Burials

The Paloma soil and midden preserved the bones of the dead in good condition. Small pieces of dried flesh and muscle were occasionally found in areas well protected from disintegration by mat or textile wrappings or at bone joints, but skin was not preserved in any great amount. Head hair, brains, and internal body organs were occasionally found, though body organs usually could be detected only as soil stains. The relative lack of soft body parts is typical of the less than perfect preservation in damp lomas which experience some water seepage below ground.[3] Deeper burials tended to be better preserved because percolation of fog moisture was less. Almost all of the burials appear to have been primary interments. Cases of disturbed burials were noted, but disturbance was relatively minor.

A typical burial was flexed by drawing the knees toward the chest. Hands were often placed in the pelvic or facial region, ropes were sometimes tied around the legs and shoulders, and the corpse was almost always wrapped in a twined straw (junco) mat. The funeral bundle was then buried below the floor level of a hut (fig. 11). Another variation

in mortuary treatment was to place the cadaver on the floor inside a house. This appears to have been carried out late in the occupation of the site (circa Level 200) and was accompanied by house destruction. A similar practice was found at the Chilca I site (Engel 1963; Donnan 1964), contemporaneous with the late occupation of Paloma.

Burial pits were specially dug, except for one or two rare cases in which it appears that infants were placed in abandoned storage pits. Graves were usually oval in shape with flat bottoms and about 30 to 40 centimeters deep. The floors of the pits were often lined with *maicillo,* an unidentified grass. The bundles often had this grass on top of them. Benfer and Edward (1988) suggest that bodies may have been covered with salt before being buried.

Coprolites found in some graves indicate that the dead were probably quickly buried. Broken cervical vertebrae, disjointed long bones, and cuts in hands and feet (Benfer, personal communication) suggest that corpses were sometimes forced into flexion. However, it was common for burials to spill out of their graves, especially the feet. Perhaps these represent burials made just before house or site abandonment. Indeed, the top of the skull of B. 101 (H. 100/101) protruded above the floor level of the house. But the dwelling was abandoned and destroyed shortly after the last interments were made in it.

Burial goods were scarce. Many corpses had no artifacts with them other than a mat wrapping. Some graves contained one or two

---

3. Well-preserved burials with flesh and other soft parts are found in desert sands and, occasionally, cold and dry locales high in the Andes. The fact that preservation in lomas areas is not complete and that some materials deteriorate means that the archaeological record of the fog oases, as is true elsewhere, is less than perfect.

11. Typical subfloor burials (Burial 70 and Burial 143 in House 117).

objects; articles such as ornaments or clothing were most common. Gourd fragments, shell disks and crescents, red pigment, grinding stones, burnt rocks, and a few cases of single valves of mussels filled with hair or other materials were typical goods found in graves. Single animal bones, usually of birds or sea mammals, were commonly found in graves (Brock 1981) and may have represented a bit of meat given to the dead.

After the corpse had been flexed, tied with ropes, wrapped in a mat, and placed in a grave with one or two offerings, a funeral ceremony involving fire appears to have been occasionally performed. Hearth stones, still hot from the fire, were often placed on top of the funeral bundle, as evidenced by singed wrapping. A possible alternate or additional rite was the building of a small fire on the earth covering the burial. A smooth beach pebble was sometimes placed on top of the grave fill. One example (fig. 12) was found wrapped with a piece of fiber string.

12. Stone tied with string on top of grave fill of Burial 35. Length 6.3 cm.

Artifacts and Grave Goods

The following sections discuss burial goods and other objects which, although not found in graves, shed light on Paloma society and culture. Most of the data discussions are drawn from the 1976 excavations, but the numbers of items refer to the totals after the 1979 work. Artifacts found in nonmortuary contexts in 1979 and later years are occasionally noted. Scales in photographs are in millimeters as the smallest unit except where noted. The order of discussion generally proceeds from relatively unmodified materials to more elaborately worked artifacts.

Gourds (Lagenaria *sp.*)

Gourd fragments were found in eight Paloma burials, and numerous fragments were uncovered in the hearth/garbage dump on the western edge of Unit I and elsewhere throughout the site. Gourd fragments were commonly found in the pelvic and cranial areas of Paloma skeletons. Since the qualities of the Paloma soil would have preserved whole vessels or at least most of the pieces of broken gourd vessels, it seems likely that only gourd fragments were generally placed in grave pits, although the sample of gourds is small.

Two nearly complete gourd bowls were found. Both were in shapes resembling variations of olla pottery bowls. In 1973, a fetus or young infant (B. 48) was found buried in a large gourd which has been calculated to have measured more than 20 centimeters across its mouth. In 1976, a well-preserved

14. Gourd fragment with black line drawing. Maximum length 4.8 cm.

bowl, about 7 centimeters across its mouth, was found in the sand fill over B. 159 (fig. 13), and a small gourd bowl was also recovered in 1979.

One of the few pieces of evidence for decorative arts at Paloma was a fragment of gourd with black (charcoal?) lines drawn on it (fig. 14). Other gourd fragments were found with gray-blue encrustations on their outer surfaces. It has not been determined whether this color was deliberately applied, was the result of use, or was the product of chemical processes which occurred after gourds were buried in graves and midden.

Holes near the rims of a few gourd fragments, some with thin cords passing through, may reflect vessel repair—a practice later used by Andean peoples for pottery—or may have been used for hanging bowls by strings. One gourd fragment with numerous holes in it appears to have been part of a sieve or colander.

Unmodified Shells

The use of shell-laden midden as burial fill made the identification of unmodified shell offerings in Paloma a difficult task. Appar-

13. Large fragment of a gourd bowl found in the grave fill of Burial 159. Maximum diameter 7.5 cm.

ently, some shells were used with little or no human modification in everyday life and as grave offerings.

Barnacles (*Peruviensis trapezoidales*) were found in the neck areas of some burials in 1973 (e.g., B. 15), suggesting that they had been strung as necklaces. *Oliva* sp. shells, some with their spires removed or knocked off accidentally, were also found as grave offerings. The shell of lomas snails (*Bulimulus hennahi*) were found in some graves, especially those of infants, and small *Tegula* sp. shells were common in infant and child burials and were often associated with cut shell disks.

As noted above, a *Spondylus* sp. shell was found at Paloma in 1973. Although its exact provenience within the site is unknown, it is one of the earliest examples of this shell species found in central Peru. In later periods of Andean prehistory, *Spondylus* shells were important artifacts in Peruvian religion (see Paulsen 1974).

Single valves of mussels were found in association with fourteen graves (fig. 15 and 16), eight of which were those of infants. These shells were often filled with animal fur or hair and sometimes with red pigment stones. A mussel shell offering was also found in a small straw-filled pit (Feature 224) next to an infant's grave in House 13 and appears to have been a special offering.

Empty mussel valves as well as shells of other species were placed in graves. Some burials appear to have had small unopened mussel shells dropped into them and sprinkled over the burial bundles. But because mussels were the most common shells in the Paloma midden, it was often difficult for excavators to tell whether such shells found in graves were deliberate inclusions or part of the burial fill.

Worked Shells

Small, short, tubular and disk-shaped shell beads of fine workmanship from unknown mollusk species were found at Paloma. Beads were often found in grave fill and could not always be associated with burials with certainty.

The most enigmatic artifacts found at Paloma were small cut shell disks and crescents (figs. 17 and 18), which had been cut from the flat parts of mussel shells. On most specimens the outer cortex had been partially scraped away. The diameters of the shell disks varied, ranging in size from 0.5 to 3 cen-

15. Mussel shell offering containing animal fur or hair. Maximum length 7.8 cm.

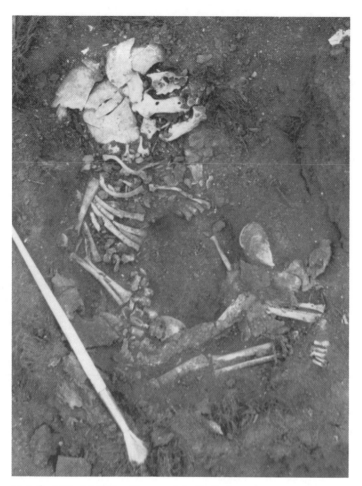

16. Infant (Burial 152) with mussel shell offering above knees.

timeters. The disks were usually about 0.2 centimeter thick.

Shell disks were found in and around Houses 12, 13, and 28. A small disk was found inside the wrappings of B. 112, an infant, and 1973 CIZA notes refer to nine *amuletos* (presumably shell disks or crescents) in B. 51. Small *Tegula* spp. shells were also found in B. 112 and in an adjacent oval grass-lined pit (B. 113), which also contained shell disks. The small *Tegula* shells may have been ritually linked to cut shell disks in mortuary practices.

Few reports of other preceramic site excavations on the central coast of Peru mention cut shell disks and crescents. Moseley (1968:

124) found a shell disk at the Pampa Site and three disks of scallop shell (*Aequipecten plangoctenium purpuratus*) at the Tank Site at Ancón. Lanning (1967:61) mentions the presence of cut gourd disks at late preceramic (Period VI) sites on the central coast; perhaps they served the same or similar functions as shell disks at other sites.

The use of shell disks and crescents other than as grave offerings is unknown. Trianguloid pieces of thick mussel shells with central holes found at Paloma (fig. 19) were probably fishhook blanks, and some of the shell disks may have been by-products of the manufacture of such hooks, although most fishhooks at the site were made of bone. The disks could

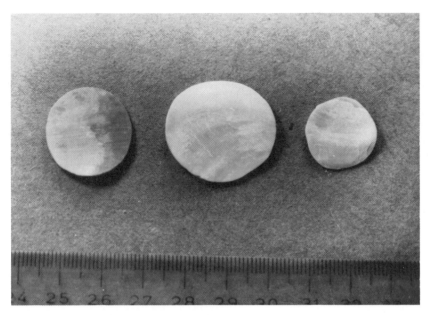

17. Cut shell disks. Maximum diameter of middle shell 2.6 cm.

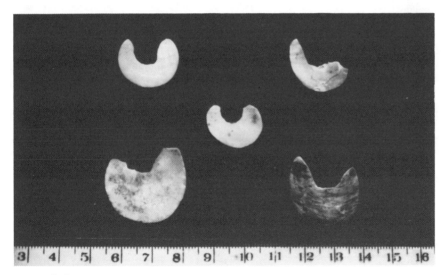

18. Cut shell crescents. Maximum width of middle crescent 1.9 cm.

have been made from the waste material in the area of the concave curve of the hook. They appear to have been too thin for purposes such as fishing, except perhaps as lures. They have no apparent means of attachment to lines and would have been subjected to stress in the water, making a secure link to the line a necessity. The disks and crescents might have served some special function in the ritual or social lives of the Palomans as charms, amulets, or gaming pieces. Jorge Marcos (personal communication) has sug-

19. Blanks for shell disks or fishhooks. Maximum width of left blank 3 cm.

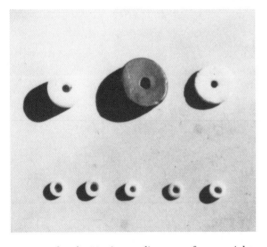

20. Bone beads. Maximum diameter of upper right bead 1.1 cm.

gested that the crescents may have been *narigueras* (nose rings).

Worked Bone

Most of the bone artifacts at Paloma were manufactured by using the long bones of sea mammals, deer, or camelids as raw material. Bone was used to make beads (fig. 20), awls (fig. 21), long pins, fishhooks (fig. 22), and flat, spatula-shaped artifacts (fig. 23).

Among the most interesting items at the site were the spatula-shaped artifacts. They varied in length from 7 to 13 centimeters, in

width from 1 to 1.5 centimeters, and were about 1 centimeter thick. The proximal ends, with drilled holes, were rounded or squared, and the distal ends often showed high polish, presumably from use.

These artifacts were probably used as bodkins for the manufacture of textiles. Similar objects have been found at other preceramic sites on the coast of Peru, such as Huaca Prieta (Bird 1985), Asia (Engel 1963), and El Paraíso (Engel 1966a). CIZA laboratory technicians have used copies of these artifacts to repair cotton textiles found at the Asia site, making it quite probable that the Paloma tools were also used for making twined fiber goods, though not from cotton.

About a dozen of these artifacts have been found in association with burials. It appeared from the 1976 data that the majority of the dead who were buried with bodkins were females. But further research has complicated the picture. For three burials (a male—B. 71, and two females—B. 12 and B. 14) it is not certain that bodkin bone tools were definitely in the graves because the data are available only as 1973 field notes. One burial (B. 21) cannot be given a gender designation with certainty and another (B. 71) was at first considered female but now appears to have been a male. Finally, a burial found in 1979 (B. 231) had a bone tool with a hole for attachment but was shaped with an expanding distal end rather than a point. While it is likely that this tool was used for making fiber objects by the woman with whom it was buried, it is not a bodkin of standard shape.

If all of these difficult cases are set aside, five females and four males were found accompanied by bodkins. It was very common to find these tools in the neck or chest areas of skeletons with string still passed through the holes in the proximal ends of some recovered specimens. The artifacts thus appear to have been worn as pendants when not in use.

The distribution of the tools may be explained in a number of ways. The most likely explanation is that both men and women were involved in fiber craft production. If

21. Bone awls. Length of lower awl 7.3 cm.

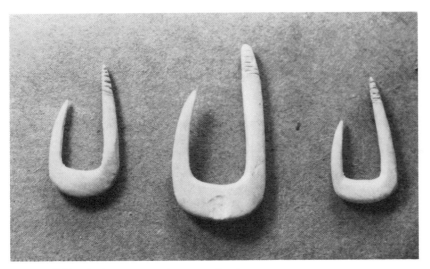

22. Bone fishhooks from Feature 340. Length of middle hook 4.1 cm.

there was a division of labor so that men made and repaired fishing nets and tackle— quite likely, given the subsistence economy— and women made house mats and clothing, it cannot be detected in the data. It is also possible that grave goods were deposited with reference to the sex of the giver rather than of the corpse. In other words, one sex or the other or both may have used bodkins and the items were deposited as tokens of the living to the dead. But this cannot be demonstrated in any event. It does seem more likely that grave goods were associated with the activities of the deceased, as seen in the rather elaborate

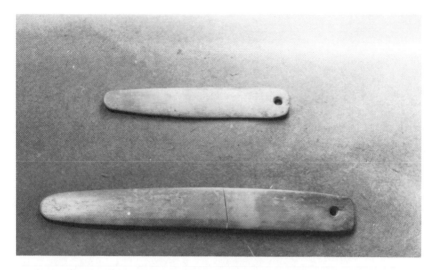

23. Bone textile tools. Length of lower tool 12.6 cm.

interment of a young fisherman (B. 159), discussed below, and general impressions of the site.

Fishhooks and Abraders (Feature 340)

Simple U-shaped bone fishhooks (fig. 22) were found at Paloma. Their size and shape suggest that they were used for catching large deep-water fish. Shell fishhooks were uncommon.

What may have been a fisherman's kit containing three bone fishhooks, pieces of thin cordage, a fragment of a net, small sticks, disintegrated junco, and an abrader was found in a small pit in the floor of House 117 (Feature 340; figs. 10 and 24). Though these tools are referred to here as abraders, their use is uncertain. They appear to have been made from bone (fig. 25) or concretions from colonial worms. Engel (1980:110) believes that the example found with the fisherman's kit was a stopper.

As discussed above, the fisherman's kit was found in the floor of one of the deepest and earliest known houses (Level 400/500) at Paloma. It suggests that fishing techniques were well developed by the time of the first intensive occupation of the site, circa 4500 B.C.

Wood and Cane

Wooden artifacts were rarely found at the site. Thin wooden sticks about the thickness of a pencil, with sharpened ends, were occasionally recovered, and large poles or staves were reportedly found at the site prior to the 1976 excavations.

Caña brava (*Gynerium sagittatum*) and willow (*Salix* sp.) were commonly used for house posts, and a pole of *caña de Guayaquil* (*Guadua angustifolia*) was part of a structure covering B. 159. A meter-long wooden staff found in B. 142 may have been a prized object in a land where wood was becoming increasingly scarce. One piece of wood from Paloma which showed extensive modification was a mushroom-shaped object found in House 117 (fig. 26). This was probably used as a net float or a gourd bottle stopper. A few other miscellaneous wooden objects have been found at Paloma (Engel 1980:108), but they are generally scarce.

Ground Stone Tools

The most commonly found stone tools at Paloma were hand-held manos and large metates. Large stones with convex surfaces that could be rocked over seeds and other foods

24. Feature 340.

25. Worked bone cone. Length 8.2 cm.

26. Carved wood, possibly a net float or bottle stopper. Length 5.4 cm.

(*batanes*) were also recovered from the site. Some grinding stones had slick surfaces from use, as previously noted. Manos were often found in graves, commonly showed signs of burning, and frequently had large flakes removed from their surfaces. A large metate was found on top of the collapsed wall of House 101. Examination of pollen found adhering to the flat surface of this and other grinding stones showed the presence of fossil pollens of Cucurbitaceae, Leguminoseae, *Salix*, Chenopodeae, and Gramineae (Weir and Dering 1986).

Chipped Stone Tools

Most of the formed chipped stone tools found at Paloma were points, except for flaked and battered ovoid tools which Engel has called "Paloma crushers" (Engel 1980:108, fig. 43).

Points were often found a few centimeters below the powdery surface of the site. Only a few were found during 1976 excavations, but a number were recovered before and after

that field season. Most were made of a basalt which was probably available locally. Points were relatively rare in burials.

Six points are shown in figures 27 and 28. Numbers 3, 4, 5, and 6 resemble points Lanning (1967:49) has ascribed to the Corbina and Encanto phases of Preceramic Period VI, which correspond to the time of the occupation of Paloma. Point 1 is similar to a Canario phase point found in an Ancón lomas camp by Lanning (1963). Point 2 was found on the surface of the site. Gloria Villareal, who is studying the chipped stone tools from Paloma, has stated that point 2 is typical of the Early Horizon epochs (circa 1400–400 B.C.[?]; Menzel 1977), suggesting occasional visits to the area after the abandonment of the village.

Small obsidian flakes were found at the site. The one complete obsidian point recovered in the 1976 excavations (fig. 28) was found on the floor of House 117/118, indicating that obsidian was used by the people who

27. Projectile points. Length of center point 6.4 cm. *Left to right:* found south of House 42 backdirt; S. 520–E. 250.5; on surface, east side of small *quebrada;* in fill of Burial 83; 0–5 cm. below surface, N. 90–E. 65.

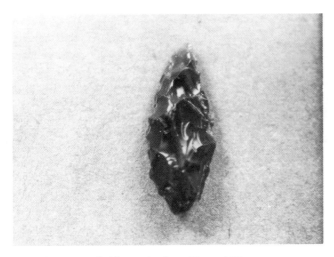

28. Point no. 6: obsidian point from House 117. Length 3.4 cm.

first intensively occupied Paloma. In 1979, over two hundred obsidian flakes were found at the site despite the fact that most of the excavated midden was not sifted through fine screens. This does not necessarily mean that the material was abundant—the working of two or three fist-sized nodules could easily produce such debris. Thus, even several hundred obsidian flakes may only indicate one instance of travel to or contact with obsidian sources. Nevertheless, the presence of volcanic glass flakes at Paloma further demonstrates that people of the site were part of a world which stretched beyond the confines of the lower coastal valleys. The nearest source of obsidian to Paloma is the Quispisisa quarry in Huancavelica Department, in the sierra, 400 kilometers from the central coast (Burger and Asaro 1977). It is likely but not certain that the Paloma obsidian comes from this locale.

Miscellaneous Stone Artifacts

A cylindrical grooved, ground diorite artifact (fig. 29) was probably used as a net weight, though it could also have served as the working end of a bola.

The finest necklace (fig. 30) found at Paloma was around the neck of a young child

29. Grooved cylindrical stone, possibly a net weight. Length 3.5 cm.

(B. 138). It was comprised of three small, flat ground black stones (slate?). The central pendant measured 3 centimeters long, 1 centimeter wide, and 0.2 centimeter thick. Two small crab claws tied together to form a small crescent were also found in the neck area of B. 138 and may have been part of the necklace.

Unmodified smooth beach pebbles were

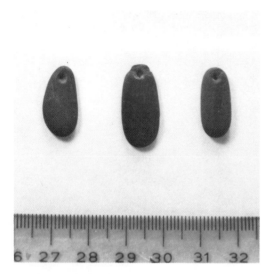

30. Three stone beads from Burial 138. Length of center bead 2.2 cm.

found in some graves; in 1979, it was determined (Benfer, personal communication) that beach pebbles were often placed on top of or in the grave fill, such as one specimen with a string around it from B. 35 (fig. 12). Engel (1963) mentions finding small pebbles in bags in graves at the preceramic Asia site, suggesting that these bags contained magic kits. Perhaps the unmodified stones found at Paloma were also associated with magic or religion. Brock (1981) mentions the presence of "boiling stones" in two graves excavated in 1979.

Red and Yellow Pigments

During the 1976 excavations, red pigment was found in mussel shell offerings and distinctly on the mat wrappings of three burials. Red pigments were detected in three graves in 1979. The body in B. 112 had pieces of red coloring adhering to its funeral wrappings, as did B. 35. Upon removing a piece of matting from the skull of B. 67, a large patch of red paint with a spot of yellow in its center was found on the underside of the mat, which had covered the area of the burial's right temple. Red paint formed an integral part of funeral ceremonies throughout the prehistory of Peru. It was sprinkled over burials and was used

in the painting of grave goods (see Menzel 1977). A positive identification of the chemical composition of the red coloring found at Paloma has not yet been made. The red stones found in mussel shell offerings appear to be hematite (Fe_2O_3).

A shell filled with cinnabar (HgS) was found in an undated Precolumbian burial near Ocucaje (Petersen 1970:6). Though the Ocucaje shell is of a different species (*Concholepus concholepus* B.) than the Paloma shell offerings, it is reminiscent of them in its context. The nearest known source of cinnabar for the Palomans would have been in Huancavelica, 400 kilometers from the site (Petersen 1970: 6), the same region where obsidian was available (Burger and Asaro 1977). Cinnabar was one of the most popular coloring agents used in Andean prehistory (Yacovleff and Muelle 1934:157), and a mano colored with a bright vermilion powder which resembled cinnabar was found in midden at Paloma in 1976.

The yellow coloring found on the matting on B. 62 could have been derived from a number of minerals. Hematite and calcite ($CaCO_3$) are the most likely sources for the Paloman yellow paint (Petersen 1970:6).

Mats and Textiles

Single-warp, twined junco reed mats with two-ply, Z-twisted wefts were the most common artifacts found at Paloma (fig. 31). Almost every burial found at the site had been wrapped in such a mat, and some bodies had been wrapped in two or more. A fragment of a mat from B. 65 showed evidence of irregular split-paired twining, a technique which did not become popular until the Playa Hermosa phase of Preceramic Period VI when cotton textiles were made (Moseley 1975: 29–34). Mats were found as floor coverings in House 100/101, and it is quite possible that the dead were wrapped in mats they had used as sleeping pallets.

Preliminary study of the 1979 materials (Mandeville 1979) suggests that there are two different types of mats at Paloma. Type I mats have warps made of processed fibers, most

31. A typical twined mat of coarse junco; 24 cm. width shown.

commonly treated so that the tough outer tissue was removed, or sometimes the stems were merely flattened. These mats appear to have been used widely—for house construction as well as for wrapping burials. Type II mats are made of complete junco stems with no preparation, and warps are frequently paired. Type II mats were rarely found other than as burial wrappings. While this might suggest the production of special burial mats, it is also possible that Type II mats had a specific (probably personal) use in life—perhaps as sleeping mats—and accompanied their owners to the grave. If further research indicates Type II mats were used only for burial wrappings, then they represent a more elaborate funerary cult than presently considered, but one in which the special mats were items of low energy investment.

Fine twined textiles were also found at Paloma (fig. 32), probably made from the fibers of a small magueylike plant, *Fourcroya andina* sp. (J. Bird, personal communication) and perhaps other species. These fabrics were close to skeletons and probably served as clothing (McAnulty 1977). In fact, Engel's

1973 notes mention the recovery of rush skirts from some Paloma graves, suggesting that a variety of garments may have been worn. B. 100 contained a looped fabric in the pelvic area of a male skeleton; this textile may have been a genital pouch.

Eight specimens of looped material were recovered from Paloma in 1976 (McAnulty 1977:92). Most of these fabrics were found in small pieces and came from the head areas of the skeletons. These fabrics were most likely used as head coverings, and there is also some evidence that animal hair (of camelids or sea mammals) and feathers were used.

The second most common fiber found at Paloma was *maicillo*. These reeds or grasses were used to line burial pits, to cover funeral bundles, and for offerings in small pits next to tombs.

Numerous samples of rope were found at Paloma, most of which were two-ply strands of twisted junco, though three-strand braided ropes and one braided animal hair rope were also found. Most of the rope found at the site had been used to bind corpses. However, two ropes probably used for fishing or hunting

32. Fine twined textile; 23 cm. width shown.

33. Roll of junco tied with string; 40.5 cm. tip to tip.

purposes were found in B. 159. One of these ropes was poorly preserved, though it showed evidence of having an elaborate tassel or knot decoration at one end. The other rope, in excellent condition, was in two fragments (238 and 272 centimeters long). It was in a jumble at the side of the burial, and in its midst lay a sea mammal bone. This piece was so well preserved that it probably could be used today for roping an animal.

Several unusual textiles, or textile-related materials, were found at Paloma, including a

34. Net fragment. Length 8.7 cm.

circular roll of junco wrapped in string (fig. 33), ovals of grass (skeins of unused junco or *maicillo?*), knotted netting (fig. 34), a tightly twined basket (over B. 101), two cord bracelets around the wrists of a child burial (fig. 35), and two textiles which may have been breechclouts or burial wigs. A twined textile found wrapped around an infant (B. 115) may have been a carrying sling or cradle.

A scrap of Z-twined cotton fabric and a fragment of net made from cotton (2^s Z) which may date to the Paloma village have been found at the site (Mandeville 1979: 714). But it does not appear that the people of the site had begun to manufacture cotton textiles on a large scale.

Summary

The material culture of Paloma is relatively elaborate in fiber materials and objects associated with fishing. The most intricate items are nets, cordage, and textiles. Other tools are relatively simple, such as sticks, needles, and the lithic assemblage. All of this suggests that the extraction of food and materials from the environment was a relatively straightforward process which required little technical sophis-

35. Cord bracelets from Burial 152. Maximum diameter of upper bracelet 3.4 cm.

tication, although the strategies involved in surviving may have been quite complex. The exception to this is fishing gear, which received a great amount of energy and care. Nets require much time for manufacture and maintenance, and hooks and other items required relatively great amounts of energy investment.

Given the fact that riverine, maritime, and some lomas materials had to be hauled to the site, the lack of carrying gear is surprising. Baskets are generally rare on the central coast in the preceramic, with only one recovered at Paloma in 1976 (in House 100/101). About 272 fragments of baskets were found at Huaca Prieta on the north coast (Bird 1985: 92–98), some also at Guitarrero Cave, and

they are common on the south coast and in Chile. The usual carrying devices at Paloma probably were nets which could serve numerous functions besides catching fish. Another possibility is that skin bags were used but have not survived in the less than perfect preservational conditions of the Paloma soil.

The people of Paloma had worked out successful ways of living on the central coast. The sophistication of their fishing equipment suggests that maritime resources had been exploited for a considerable period of time. In addition, terrestrial resources were exploited, including those from fairly distant sources. The strongest interregional ties may have been with Huancavelica; even more distant areas supplied goods, though probably indirectly.

4. Quantitative Analyses of the Paloma Burials

Introduction

All archaeological analyses are directed toward the detection of patterns in data which shed light on past human behavior and its contexts. Some data may not have been manipulated by humans, such as the sediments of an ancient riverbed, yet yield information on the environment or other aspects of prehistoric times. Other data rest on a sliding scale of human influence—an unmodified shell or stone recovered at a site far from its source of origin reveals distant contacts. Near one extreme of this scale are those artifacts or clusters highly charged with symbolic content by the people who made them, such as religious objects, artworks, and burials.

Burials have long been recognized as containing important information concerning prehistoric life. In the nineteenth century, J. J. A. Worsaae made the important point that the objects accompanying a burial were usually used simultaneously and commonly placed together in a grave or tomb at the same time (see Rowe 1962). This observation has been useful in cross-dating different classes of objects such as pottery and textiles, as well as helping in the development of relative chronologies.

A second area of burial studies is the interpretation of prehistoric ideology and ritual. The nature of grave goods and treatment of the dead may indicate past beliefs and the acts related to them. The most common examples of this are the elaborate tombs of potentates, which were believed to continue life in the hereafter. Analysis on this level may be complex, because the symbolic aspects of mortuary rites may be couched in specific contexts not easily retrieved by archaeological study.

The ideological and ritual aspects of mortuary data blend with a third category of information which documents the living society that buried the dead. The tombs of pharaohs or Sumerian kings are important partly because they include a wealth of objects which were part of everyday life. Although caution must be used to distinguish the role of specialized grave goods, even they tell of the nature of the society which made them—such as a complex division of labor in which artisans made funerary goods. Furthermore, the preparation of bodies, graves, and grave goods may be carried out at various times and in a variety of social contexts, sometimes with distinct personnel (opposite moiety, low castes, morticians, etc.). Careful excavation with attention to the process of interment or entombment may thus add to the store of knowledge about the past. Indeed, Worsaae's "law" is sometimes violated when a society practices the custom of renewing grave offerings. But this and other variances from normal practice can usually be detected.

Recently, particular emphasis has been placed on studying burials as a means of reconstructing social organization. At one time, it was thought that burial customs, as part of ideology in general, were almost totally divorced from social life and therefore worthless for understanding the societies which practiced them. Alfred Kroeber once argued that mortuary rites have little connection with "those activities which are a frequent or constant portion of living and therefore tend to become interadapted with one another" (1927:314). In other words, burial ceremonies, as part of religion, are epiphenomena which are not articulated with or influenced by economics, politics, and other mundane aspects of daily life. But in the last several years, a number of studies have clearly demonstrated that there is a relationship between a living society and the realm of the dead (Saxe 1970; Binford 1971; Tainter 1975, 1978; Chapman, Kinnes, and Randsborg 1981).

Simply put, it has been suggested that there is a general congruence between the way a society is organized and the way the dead are treated. This is particularly true in terms of recognizing social rank, status, or prestige. Not only are the mighty put in splendid, elaborate tombs while the poor are placed in simple graves, but the kinds of ranks or classes in a society may be revealed through careful analyses. Since burial rites include not only the grave and its contents but also mourning periods, feasts, preparation of the body, and other items, burial activities must be thought of as an often complex series of steps or processes which must be searched for beyond the grave itself.

Some of the general conclusions reached by students of mortuary practices are worth reviewing here. The studies carried out under the influence of the movement known as the New Archaeology used data derived from ethnographic studies and applied them to archaeological data. Lewis Binford (1971) gathered information on the social distinctions recognized by forty different societies grouped into four categories: hunter-gatherers, shifting agriculturalists, settled agriculturalists, and pastoralists. He found that among hunter-gatherers sex and, to a lesser degree, age were the key attributes judged as important in varying mortuary practices (Binford 1971: 12). Among shifting agriculturalists, social position and sex and age differences were

gauged to be roughly equally important in determining funerary rites and goods. Settled agriculturalists considered conditions of death, social position, and social affiliation the most important determinants of burial mode. The number of pastoralists in Binford's sample was too small to reach any conclusions.

This certainly demonstrates that Kroeber's dictum was incorrect. Specifically, Binford's analysis suggests that in relatively simple societies sex and age are the primary reasons for differentiating mortuary practices. In complex societies more criteria, including social position, help determine burial practices.

Other studies enlarged on Binford's findings. Joseph Tainter (1971) found that in almost all of the ninety-three ethnographic cultures he examined there was a high positive correlation between social rank and the amount of energy expended on an individual's mortuary rites. High-ranking individuals almost always have more burial goods, finer funeral offerings, longer mourning periods, and larger funeral feasts than lower-ranked members of society.

A study by Arthur Saxe (1970) showed that three very different cultures all applied the same principles that they followed among the living in distinguishing among the dead in funeral rites. He also demonstrated that as societies develop corporate descent groups, such as lineages, exclusive burial areas for each descent group, such as cemeteries, become more common (Saxe 1970:118).

Recently, sharp criticisms have been voiced concerning the sweeping generalizations and allegedly simplified scientism of the New Archaeology, both in general and in regard to mortuary practices and other specific topics (Hodder 1987). The call has been made for a more historically oriented, particularist study of past societies instead of the search for general laws of human behavior.

Seemingly in response to the conclusions of some of these burial studies, O'Shea (1981) has noted that social differences among the living may be distorted in burial rites and further warped through transformations wrought after interment, such as the disintegration of perishable grave goods which served as status markers. The specific historical development of symbols such as grave goods has also been shown to be understandable only when unique aspects of specific cultures are considered (Hodder 1987).

The relatively coarse typologies used in many recent discussions of social organization have also come under attack. The use of terms such as *bands, tribes,* and *chiefdoms* has been shown to place social systems into pigeonholes which overlook complex phenomena that are of interest and which ignore entities perhaps better discussed on a sliding scale ranging from simple to complex (Feinman and Neitzel 1984).

Most Andeanists have been sensitive and appreciative of the unique aspects of the cultures of western South America; most studies of Peruvian materials, including this one, make use of the rich body of comparative data on prehistory and ongoing traditions of the region. At the same time, however, traditions are not eternal—great cultural variation can be seen even in the same region at the same time. Tools or the opportunity to observe or determine fine distinctions in such things as sociopolitical complexity are not always available; a coarser scale of analysis must sometimes suffice. The current theoretical debates are part of a tradition of a split in anthropology itself between generalized and particularist approaches to subject matter. Both broad-based and specific approaches give insights into the past; the responsible scholar must use all tools appropriate to the task at hand.

Few archaeological studies begin with a total absence of knowledge, or at least reasoned speculation, concerning the ancient culture to be examined—the Paloma work began with a number of suppositions. The site occupants were part of a society more toward the egalitarian, band, or tribal end of the coarse typological scale of measurement. It was thus expected that the primary factors influencing burial activities were the age and sex of the deceased and the social status achieved during a lifetime of interaction with community members rather than a rank ascribed at birth. Since no other site of such antiquity and with so many burials had been excavated in Peru, the study of Paloma mortuary rites also contributed to understanding life at the site in general as well as specific aspects of social organization. On the fine level of study, the fact that burial bundles were an important part of Andean society at the time of Spanish conquest and mortuary ceremonies still drew upon ancient traditions made investigation of Paloma an opportunity to examine an early manifestation of such concerns.

Analytical Techniques

Analysis of Paloma mortuary practices was conducted through the use of both statistical and nonstatistical techniques. Each has advantages and disadvantages. Statistical studies permit the establishment of the degree of confidence or strength of association in observed patterning of data in mathematical terms of considerable precision. They permit the determination of complex patterning, such as the interrelations of several variables, which otherwise might be difficult to detect. But in order to conduct such analyses data must be standardized, often muting subtleties and distinctions.

Nonstatistical studies are often better at noting singular or unique characteristics of data of significance. But such observations are prone to subjective evaluations which may vary depending on the person conducting the study. Presentations made in this analytical mode often can only be judged on the strength of the argument, with no or only poor objective standards independent of both the data under scrutiny and the investigator.

Philosophers of science have explored these topics in great detail in recent years, with special concern for their application to archaeology. The problems are complex. In the present case, both statistics and more subjective analyses were carried out.

Over 200 burials were recovered at Paloma, ranging from complete burials to a few unprovenienced fragments of human bone. Of the more than 100 burials discovered in the 1973 and 1976 field seasons, only 76 were sufficiently complete for statistical analysis of mortuary practices. Preliminary examination of the 52 burials found in 1979 suggests they will not significantly alter the findings based on the earlier data (Benfer 1982b:43). The post-1976 burials do significantly contribute to nonstatistical studies, however.

Statistical Analyses

The first step taken in the statistical analyses was the standardization of burial attributes by development of a coding system. The attributes selected for quantification fell into three general categories: artifacts, skeletal information, and grave location. These attributes were selected because they have been shown to reflect aspects of social organization, although their relative importance may vary among different cultures.

The artifacts which were coded were animal hair, fine textiles, gourds, assumed male-task stone tools (stone points and scrapers), and assumed female-task stone tools (grinding stones). These materials were listed only as present or absent because they were rare or because it was difficult to judge the amount of goods, such as fragments of hair or textiles, placed in the graves. Shell artifacts, beads, mats, and ropes were listed by number; an "other" category was used to lump very rare artifacts.

Skeletal information recorded for quantitative analysis included the age at death and the sex of the burial, skull orientation, the compass direction to which the face was oriented and to which the top of the head pointed, the position of the skeleton (right side, left side, stomach, or back), positions of the hands, and the degree of leg flexion (see appendix 1).

Information on the location of the burial was coded in terms of the stratigraphic level from which the burial pit was excavated and its relationship to the nearest house. The burial was recorded as associated with either the house in which it was found or the house

to which the burial was adjacent. Burials were also coded as either above or below a house floor, the latter usually in postoccupational debris.

One other aspect of mortuary practices was included in the data set: the presence of evidence for the use of fire in mortuary rites. Heavy ash deposits on top of graves, fire-cracked rocks, and singed textiles were the most common signs of the use of fire in Paloma funerals.

Cluster Analysis

Information was recorded on punch cards for a total of 76 burials from 1976. The remaining 102 burials were of limited use in the quantitative analysis. Some burials had been disturbed in previous excavations and therefore provided untrustworthy data. For others, the data were entirely missing. The 76 burials were then subjected to a series of single linkage cluster analyses. The technique was used for the Paloma burials as a sorting device in order to see if any general patterns could be observed to separate large groups of burials.

The cluster procedure (SAS; Barr et al. 1976) combines burials into groups, or clusters, based on the similarity of listed variables. The procedure begins by selecting a burial at random and then searching the data set to find the burial which most closely resembles it. Each burial is linked to the cluster containing a burial which most closely resembles the newly linked burial, rather than using average resemblances as in average link cluster analysis. A "pigeonhole" effect occurs when a burial is included in a cluster even though it might well fit better in another cluster formed later in the procedure.

The joining of single burials or burial clusters into larger groups is accomplished by calculating their similarities on the basis of a Euclidean distance matrix. The distance between any two burials is calculated as the sum of the squares of the total number of differences in the attributes of the burials. A Jaccard coefficient is used so that similarity is only measured on the basis of the presence of data and not by their absence. Otherwise, poorly preserved burials or those with missing data would be grouped as similar because of their paucity of information rather than because they shared similar burial goods or treatment. The clusters can then be diagrammed in the form of a dendrogram (fig. 36).

The first cluster analysis included all of the burials, whereas subsequent analyses were conducted for burials from common stratigraphic levels. Information concerning the age, sex, stratigraphic level, horizontal location, and tomb and laboratory numbers was recorded on the computer cards used in the analyses but was excluded from consideration during the clustering procedure. This was done because the first four variables were those against which patterns in the data were to be measured and because burial laboratory numbers were used only for reference purposes.

Cluster Analysis of Burials from All Levels

The first cluster analysis, including all 76 burials, produced the dendrogram shown in figure 36.[4] No objective test was used to define clusters of burials. Rather, groups were defined on the basis of the way in which clusters of burials were linked with each other during the final stages of the procedure and working backward, going up the branches of the dendrogram. Using this method, three large clusters (1, 2, and 3) were delineated, each with

roughly equal numbers of burials. Further examination of the dendrogram served to define smaller groups of burials (fig. 36: A–F).

After the clusters were defined, the burials in each group were studied to see if they shared common features within clusters which differentiated them from other burials and clusters.

One way to monitor the "pigeonhole" problem is to test if the clusters resulting from analysis are such that they could easily be the result of a random distribution or if it is unlikely that a random pick would produce such groupings. A chi-square test (χ^2) measures the degree to which sets of data are patterned in relation to two or more attributes. This statistical technique states the probability that an observed distribution is due solely to chance. Chi-square analyses were thus performed for the three major clusters on the basis of sex, age, and stratigraphic level (table 1). Both age of burial and level were collapsed into binary categories for two reasons. First, if too many subcategories of the data are made, the strength of analysis is weakened by low numbers in cells. Second, in the case of age groups, the divisions are somewhat arbitrary anyhow: the social designations for infancy, childhood, adolescence, maturity, and the aged may or may not have existed and were not necessarily the same as physical changes. Given the physical evidence for late female pregnancy, it could be argued that a division could exist between women older than, perhaps, 25. But the system would be difficult to apply to males. The twofold division for stratigraphic levels is based on Benfer's (1986b) observation that two major strata may be defined.

The resulting analyses (table 1) suggest that there is no significant clustering in the three groups on the basis of sex ($p = .5–.3$). There is considerable patterning on the basis of age at death ($p < .01$), most sharply discerned in Cluster 2. This group has more old burials and fewer younger burials than might be expected in a random assortment. The distribution of burials in clusters on the basis of

---

4. The original analysis of 1976 is presented here, rather than a new one including all recent burials, because subsequent contingency table analyses demonstrate that the general conclusions implied by the cluster analyses are sound. The cluster analysis is primarily a heuristic device. Burials as arranged on the dendrogram are listed in order, from left to right: CLUSTER 1—A: 008, 010, 138, 019, 139, 137, 064, 112, 009, 065, 031, 039; B: 015, 072, 017, 109, 025A, 037, 089, 050, 083, 085; C: 044, 076, 153B, 063, 060, 081; CLUSTER 2—D: 011, 119, 025B, 110, 069; E: 012, 018, 014, 102, 021, 086, 073, 070, 032, 087, 059, 100, 101, 117, 053, 020, 071, 143, 159; CLUSTER 3—F: 013, 103A, 075, 026, 066, 104, 035, 041, 128, 047, 079, 057, 061, 152, 058, 118, 115, 042, 051, 052, 084, 067.

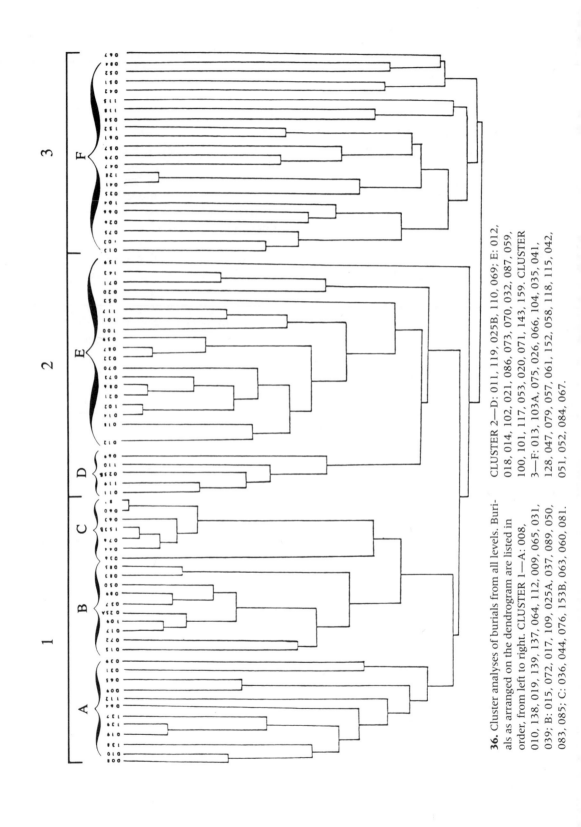

36. Cluster analyses of burials from all levels. Burials as arranged on the dendrogram are listed in order, from left to right. CLUSTER 1—A: 008, 010, 138, 019, 139, 137, 064, 112, 009, 065, 031, 039; B: 015, 072, 017, 109, 025A, 037, 089, 050, 083, 085; C: 036, 044, 076, 153B, 063, 060, 081. CLUSTER 2—D: 011, 119, 025B, 110, 069; E: 012, 018, 014, 102, 021, 086, 073, 070, 032, 087, 059, 100, 101, 117, 053, 020, 071, 143, 159. CLUSTER 3—F: 013, 103A, 075, 026, 066, 104, 035, 041, 128, 047, 079, 057, 061, 152, 058, 118, 115, 042, 051, 052, 084, 067.

TABLE 1. Chi-square Analyses of Major Clusters and All Burials

| CLUSTER | SEX | | AGE | | LEVEL | |
	Male	Female	Young (≤16)	Old (≥17)	Upper (100–300)	Lower (400–600)
1	(11.8) 14	(12.2) 10	(10.5) 14	(17.5) 14	(13.2) 11	(19.8) 22
2	(10.3) 08	(10.7) 13	(8.25) 02	(13.75) 20	(7.2) 12	(10.8) 06
3	(8.9) 09	(9.1) 09	(8.25) 11	(13.75) 11	(7.6) 05	(11.4) 14

$$N = 63$$
$$\chi^2 = 1.84$$
$$(2\ \text{d.f.})$$
$$p = .5-.3$$

$$N = 72$$
$$\chi^2 = 10.91$$
$$(2\ \text{d.f.})$$
$$p < .01$$

$$N = 70$$
$$\chi^2 = 7.43$$
$$(2\ \text{d.f.})$$
$$p = .05-.02$$

Expected numbers shown in parentheses.

level also appears to be such that chance alone would rarely produce it ($p = .05-.02$). Cluster 2 again varies from expectation, with more burials from upper levels and fewer from lower ones than expected with random distributions. This does not preclude the possibility that the observed clusters are due to chance. But it does suggest that there is patterning in the data which is probably the result of human intentions—specifically, that mortuary practices varied according to the age of the deceased and that practices vary by level, suggesting change through time.

It is questionable whether the smaller clusters, designated by letters, exhibit meaningful patterning. They each contain too few burials to use a chi-square test with confidence. On examination, they do appear to be grouped on the basis of age and stratigraphic level but show little grouping by sex, conforming to the study of the entire group. In an earlier study (Quilter 1980) further cluster analyses were conducted on burials by strata (400/500, 300, 100/200). But chi-square tests of the resulting clusters failed to provide powerful evidence that distinctions of hand placement, leg flexion, side of burial placement, or age of death could be demonstrated for the resulting groups.

Contingency Table Analyses

Despite the apparent lack of patterning except for age and level, further study was warranted for the burial data. A number of contingency tables were thus made and analyzed. Few of them produced interesting results, but discussion of the problems in these analyses as well as those which did produce results of interest is worthwhile.

The side on which a burial was placed might have been of importance to the ancient inhabitants of the site. Given the known patterning of the cluster analysis, age and stratigraphic level appeared to be the two variables which are worth examining in relation to the side on which a corpse was laid. Furthermore, the sex of the burial should be considered in case the cluster analysis masked its significance.

Many burials were clearly placed on either their right or left side. In some cases, however, the side on which the burials rested was difficult to determine. For purposes of this analysis, only those burials in which there was a fairly clear indication of an orientation were listed as being on their right or left sides. Tabulation of all burials excavated in 1973, 1976, and 1979 produced 79 cases distributed as shown in table 2.

TABLE 2. Distribution of Burials on Right or Left Side

| | | Level 400/500 | | Level 300 | | Level 200 | | |
		Males	Females	Males	Females	Males	Females	Total
Right	Young	0	4	0	3	0	0	7
Side	Old	3	4	4	6	5	5	27
Left	Young	1	2	7	3	0	0	13
Side	Old	5	6	8	4	4	5	32
Total		9	16	19	16	9	10	79

Despite the relatively great number of cases and the narrow limit of two possibilities for burial position, as well as the lumping of age into either young or old, the data are too dispersed in the table, with frequent empty cells or low numbers in them, for statistical manipulations to proceed with confidence. Further collapsing of the variables produced tables 3, 4, and 5.

Surprisingly, the only table which suggests that nonrandom patterning may be in evidence is table 4 ($p = .1-.05$), in which females are more frequently found on their right sides and males on their left than might be expected in a random distribution. Nevertheless, the patterning and probability are not so strong as to produce a high degree of confidence that the people of Paloma deliberately buried males on their left sides and females on their right sides.

Returning to table 2, it is noteworthy that the number of younger-aged burials buried on *any* side is relatively low. Indeed, for many infants and fetuses the most common position of burial was supine. It seems likely that there are two possible reasons for this, one natural, one cultural. The natural reason is that it is hard to position a small child, given the lack of fixed joints and the inherent flexed fetal position which is maintained for at least a year after birth. The different lengths of torso and limbs of early childhood perhaps are not conducive to positioning. The cultural explanation, related to the physical properties of infants, may be that the marginal social status of the young was recognized by burying them differently than adults in a "natural" rather than cultural form.

Another aspect of body position examined through the use of contingency tables was the position of the hands. The workmen at Paloma, with long experience in excavating burials, joked that women were buried with their hands at their faces "because they died of fright"; men had their hands between their legs "because they died of the cold"! This subject was clearly worth pursuing.

Several manipulations of the data were required. First, patterns in the stratigraphic levels were ignored, given their poor results and the similar thinness of the data spread over so many cells. Second, the hand positions were treated as upper body—above the pelvis—or lower body—below the pelvis—since many burials did not have hands directly on the face or crotch area. In addition, only those burials which had hands in the same sector of the body were used; examples of mixed hand positions were ignored. As before, age was divided between young (fetuses, infants, children, and juveniles) and old (adults and old adults). A total of 126 burials were suitable for the analysis.

The results were of interest. Table 6 ($p = .05-.02$) suggests that some nonrandom patterning is present with the young, especially males, more commonly exhibiting hands in the upper body area and the old, fairly evenly between the sexes, with hands in the lower body region. Subsequent analyses (tables 7 and 8) suggest that age more than sex is at work in the data. The young, in general, more commonly have hands at the upper body and the old more frequently have hands placed at or below the pelvis. Again, the natural position at rest of infants and

TABLE 3. Chi-square of Burial Side by Level

| | Level | | | |
	400/500	300	200	Total
Right Side	(10.8) 11	(15.1) 13	(8.2) 10	34
Left Side	(14.2) 14	(19.9) 22	(10.8) 9	45
Total	25	35	19	79

$$2 \text{ d.f.} \quad \chi^2 = 1.22$$
$$p = .7 - .5$$

Expected numbers are shown in parentheses.

TABLE 4. Chi-square of Burial Side by Sex

	Male	Female	Total
Right	(15.9) 12	(18.1) 22	34
Left	(21.1) 25	(23.9) 20	45
Total	37	42	79

$$1 \text{ d.f.} \quad \chi^2 = 3.19$$
$$p = .1 - .05$$

TABLE 5. Chi-square of Burial Side by Age

	Young	Old	Total
Right	(8.6) 7	(25.4) 27	34
Left	(11.4) 13	(33.6) 32	45
Total	20	59	79

$$1 \text{ d.f.} \quad \chi^2 = .71$$
$$p = .5 - .3$$

young children might have some influence on this patterning. The fact that a fairly low probability is exhibited for hand positions based on sex, however, suggests that deliberate positions occurred in mortuary rites. More subjectively, it seems that the ideal positions were hands either in the neck-face area or at the pelvis but that this preference was not a rigid rule to be followed in rites of death.

Many other aspects of burial data were worthy of study but could not be statistically examined due to a number of problems. Some mortuary behavior occurred too infrequently, including the use of red pigment in graves, the presence of stone grave markers, gourd fragments, animal fibers or hides, traces of fire, and other relatively rare objects or practices. A summary discussion of these data is presented below.

Another subject of interest is the use of plant fiber materials in graves, including straw linings of pits, the number and types of mats, and the use of fine textiles. A full report on the most abundant materials at the site and objects made from them is available elsewhere (McAnulty 1977). Findings suggest that animal hides and their products decrease in time at Paloma, while textiles increase. Other than this observation, the fiber materials present a difficult category for study because of the deterioration they have suffered in graves. In some cases, mats could not be distinguished from straw due to their poor state of preservation. It is not entirely certain if some of the apparently processed material, such as retted or crushed junco, is merely junco which deteriorated during burial. As noted in chapter 3, it is likely that retting was done but its frequency is uncertain.

Stone tools constitute one category of artifacts both distinctive and frequent enough for quantitative study. Lithic artifacts in graves at the site included active and passive grinding stones, projectile points, flakes, and rare and infrequent miscellaneous tools such as wedges and "preforms." Hearth stones, grave markers, and most unmodified rocks found in graves were not included in the analysis. The unmodified stones present problems for analysis since it is likely that some were used as

TABLE 6. Hand Positions of Paloma Burials

| | Upper Body | | Lower Body | | |
	Male	Female	Male	Female	Total
Young	(27.0) 33	(21.9) 23	(12.9) 9	(19.3) 16	81
Old	(15) 9	(12.1) 11	(7.1) 11	(10.7) 14	45
Total	42	34	20	30	126

3 d.f. $\chi^2 = 8.71$
$p = .05 - .02$

TABLE 7. Hand Positions of Paloma Burials by Age

	Upper Body	Lower Body	Total
Young	(48.9) 56	(32.1) 25	81
Old	(27.1) 20	(17.9) 25	45
Total	76	50	126

1 d.f. $\chi^2 = 7.37$
$p = < .01$

TABLE 8. Hand Positions of Paloma Burials by Sex

	Upper Body	Lower Body	Total
Male	(37.4) 42	(24.6) 20	62
Female	(38.6) 34	(25.4) 30	64
Total	76	50	126

1 d.f. $\chi^2 = 2.81$
$p = < .1$

TABLE 9. Stone Tools at Paloma

	Males	Females	Total
"Male Task" Tools	(7.1) 9	(2.9) 1	10
"Female Task" Tools	(4.9) 3	(2.1) 4	7
	12	5	17

$\chi^2 = 4.41$ 1 d.f.
$p = .05 - .02$

tools. Burial 142A held a rock in its right hand, which might have attracted little attention if found in a different context.

Only 17 stone artifacts were found in the burials excavated by the end of the 1979 field season. The gender of two burials could not be determined, and two artifacts were found in grave fill rather than in direct association with the burial. Given the small number of instances, the 2 questionable grave-fill occurrences were included in a contingency table (table 9) testing for sex only. Only 2 of the 17 cases represented nonadult burials. The other axis of the table was divided between those tools stereotypically considered as related to male tasks such as hunting—including projectile points, flakes, and miscellaneous tools—and those often considered related to female work in preparing foods close to home—primarily grinding stones. The results suggested a weak nonrandom patterning of males with hunting and small processing tools and females with grinding stones. As in other cases in this study, however, the low frequency of counts in the cells necessitates caution in making too much of the results.

In summary, the quantitative analyses suggest that patterning resulting from human intentions is present and observable in the Paloma burials and that it varies on the basis of age, stratigraphic level, and gender. Few attributes of the burial data show very strong patterning, however, and many of the specific burial practices, such as use of red pigment and others mentioned above, occur too infrequently to be statistically studied. These topics can nevertheless be further explored.

5. Discussion of Paloma Mortuary Practices

General Character of Mortuary Practices

It is remarkable that burial practices at the site were basically the same through the great span of time during which Paloma was occupied. Even if variations have been missed due to lack of evidence for ephemeral rituals of mourning or vanished due to the less than perfect preservation of artifacts, the general impression in viewing the data is of a conservative mortuary tradition. The standard practices of flexing limbs, tying the cadaver with ropes, wrapping it with a mat, and burying it with a few goods below a house floor continued through the occupation of the site. This is especially interesting given Benfer's (1984) suggestion of population replacement at the site. Even if a different genetic group was at Paloma during the Level 200 and 300 period, it maintained mortuary rites similar to those of previous occupants.

However, the cluster analyses (table 1) did suggest different frequencies of mortuary traits in the upper versus the lower levels at the site, providing some support for cultural as well as biological change. It is quite likely that many somewhat differing cultural groups occupied Paloma during the millennia of its existence and that some of the different mortuary rituals they carried out are masked by the coarse temporal units represented by the stratigraphy. Indeed, there was a tendency in the cluster analyses for burials from the same house to fall in the same cluster. Perhaps this reflects micro-styles of burial practices associated with family groups or very brief periods of site occupation. A false sense of normative mortuary behavior is thus produced—what appear to be variations of a "typical" burial may in fact be somewhat different traditions. Since this study represents an initial attempt at examining preceramic burial customs, the coarse focus is demanded; but future studies may help to see sharp distinctions where only blurred gradations can presently be discerned. For now, all the burials must be discussed in terms of a general Paloma mortuary tradition.

A number of changes may be observed in the burial data. Of the fifteen burials with beads or shells, commonly strung as beads, two-thirds were found in the 400/500 Level. This seems significant considering that more 200 Level burials have been recovered through careful excavations than burials of any other level. A decrease in articles of personal adornment is surprising, given the assumed increase in complex social interactions in coastal Peru occurring during the late Paloma occupation (cf. Bender 1985). Perhaps status items changed to include objects which were curated or do not appear in burials for other reasons during the Level 200 period. Increased importance of textiles may be one change related to these events. Thus, the observed decrease in animal fur and hides may not be linked solely to depletion of animals due to lomas degradation but also to changing social values.

Another change evident in the burial data

is the use of fire in burial rituals. Of the twelve graves with evidence of fire, seven are in the (general) 200 Level, four were found in Level 300, and only one in Level 500. In addition, the practice of destroying a house and setting fire to it was unique to the late occupation of the site, as discussed below. Most of the burials found with evidence of fire were those little disturbed by pre-1976 excavations; it is likely that many of the earlier excavated graves had such evidence which was destroyed but not noted. Nevertheless, the change seems to be genuine and not the result of variations in excavation techniques.

The household was the primary focus of attention in burial rites. Although some human remains were found without clear association with a house, the majority of burials were interred in association with a domestic structure. Those burials without association may represent victims of unusual circumstances, such as death away from home or some other misfortune. In some cases the house remains have left little trace over the millennia. Burial in or near houses rather than cemeteries suggests that loyalty to the household group outweighed any considerations of larger social units.

An attempt to examine the body orientations of burials at the site (Quilter 1980) yielded no clear patterning except for a slight tendency for heads to point toward the west. Orientation to significant landscape features is not in evidence. Rather, as many burials as possible were included inside a house. Findings in 1979 (Benfer, personal communication) suggest that burials were usually first placed in the west side of a house. Additional interments were then made around the interior perimeter of the hut until all wall areas were used. Finally, an adult male was placed in the center of the floor. This may have signaled the end of the burial program for a house and the conclusion of its occupation.

The temporal association of burials found immediately outside a house is uncertain. It is possible that two or more huts formed a domestic unit, although there is no conclusive evidence for this supposition. It seems likely

that exterior burials were related to the inside group. Perhaps these burials were of people who died within the memory of inhabitants who associated them with the house, or they may have been individuals who were peripheral members of the social group buried inside the house, such as cousins, who for some reason were not buried in their own domicile.

The patterned placement of individuals in a house, with the center reserved for a male adult, possibly a head of household, is a clear indication that burial in a hut was a deliberate act—part of a symbolic system. The placement of the dead may have replicated and, in a sense, continued the social unit after death. In conjunction with this system, the primary locus of production also appears to have been the household. The artifact inventory indicates that surplus labor and goods were not expended in the production of fine items such as elaborate cotton textiles, fancy stone beads, pyrite mirrors, and ceramic figurines that exist in the archaeological record shortly after the time of Paloma's abandonment.

The excavation of the best-preserved house at Paloma, House 100/101 (figs. 37–39) has brought many of these aspects of mortuary ritual into focus. Several burials were found in the structure with B. 109, an adult male, in its center. A number of floor layers were found inside the hut, indicating that occupation lasted for some time. As noted previously, the top of the skull of B. 101 was above the level of the last floor, suggesting that house abandonment may have occurred shortly after this interment rather than the central burial, unless there were multiple deaths. An additional possibility is that the protrusion of a deceased relative's head above the house floor was culturally acceptable, but this seems unlikely—or at least is uncomfortable for modern sensitivities—and no other such cases are known for the site.

Evidence for the deliberate destruction of the house was found in the form of charred house poles showing heaviest signs of burning near their bases, collapsed walls, and a large grinding stone placed on top of the fallen walls. Although a fire could have been

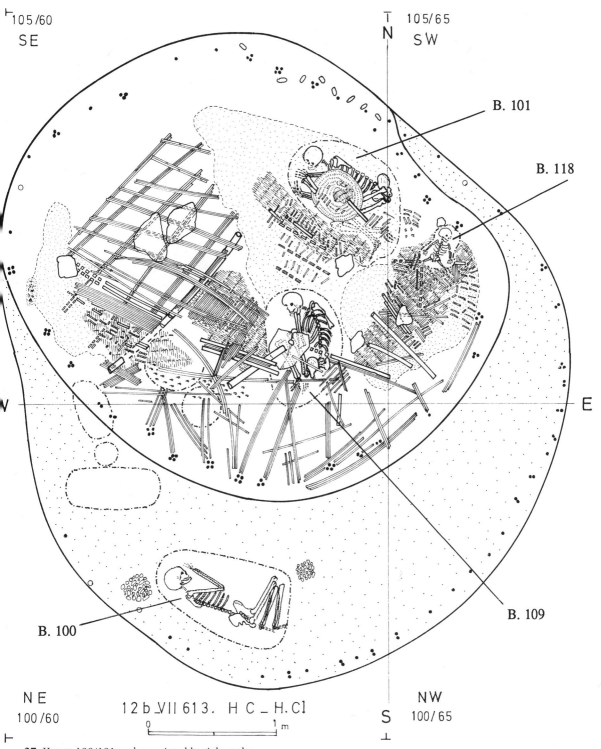

37. House 100/101 and associated burials at the
close of the 1976 excavation (after Engel 1980:
fig. 25).

38. Excavation of House 100/101.

started by accident in the house, the charred bases of the poles suggest that someone began the fire by lighting the bases of the poles in the vicinity of B. 101, where the heaviest burning is found, thus supporting the notion that this burial was the last in the house. The southern edge of the structure shows little evidence of burning, indicating that the fire was not allowed to consume the structure totally. All of the poles show inward breaks along their bases, so that the walls appear to have been deliberately collapsed, and the large grinding stone on top of the house rubble was a final gesture in the destruction of the dwelling.

Another destroyed house (H. 102) was found a few feet south of House 100/101. It contained the remains of a male (B. 103) with a young child. The adult was in a semi-extended position in a manner suggesting little or no formal arrangement of the body. The skeletal remains were covered with and

tangled in house post fragments and burnt matting. The evidence suggests lack of care or haste in this burial, lying above ground rather than in a pit. The roughly contemporary and nearby site of Chilca I also contained burials on floor surfaces, although they were more carefully treated (Donnan 1964).

The shallowness of B. 101, careless treatment of B. 102, and, probably, the position of B. 101 denote a concern with quick burial. The breaking of joints, mentioned previously, may indicate burial while rigor mortis was present, also suggesting relatively speedy interment. Ethnographic accounts (Metraux 1947) of funerary rites in the Amazon note that house destruction commonly occurs when the head of household dies, when the hut floors are filled with burials, or when extraordinary circumstances, such as disease, result in multiple deaths. It is likely that one or more of these causes was in operation during the late occupation of Paloma, to which

39. Cleaning the wall/roof of House 100/101.

the houses with clear evidence of destruction date. The practice is less clear for lower levels.

House destruction necessitated relocation of any surviving kin of the deceased. How far they moved—whether a few yards or to another site—is unknown. The extensive spread of houses at Paloma certainly shows that the site was reoccupied many times in the presence of older burials and abandoned houses.

From ethnographic accounts (Metraux 1947) it seems that house destruction usually calls for removal of the resident population from the general site area to a considerable distance away. If this was true for the practice of house abandonment and destruction at Paloma, it may indicate that the later site inhabitants were relatively mobile, although not necessarily more or less so than the previous residents based on burial avoidance alone. But the very early pre–Level 500 occupation and the late Level 200 occupation may bracket the most permanent settlement of the site.

While the earliest groups may have used Paloma as a temporary camp in a nomadic life, the later mobility occurred during the time of the abandonment of the lomas. Fog field degradation, shifts to valley farming and onshore fishing communities, and increased sociopolitical complexity may have played roles in these changes.

Whether reoccupation was by different ethnic or biological groups or not, subsequent inhabitants respected the graves of earlier site occupants. Burials could be detected by observing the outline of graves and the edge of grass pit linings, as was done during the modern excavations. Very few graves were substantially disturbed by subsequent occupants of the site, and the avoidance of burials must have been deliberate. Since houses continued to be occupied as burials were placed under floors, avoidance solely because of the presence of death seems unlikely. More complex reasons may have been involved. Perhaps, if indeed families are represented in houses, it was acceptable to be near dead relatives but not burials of unknown or nonkin. Although such speculation may be futile, it is striking that Paloma occupants should be so apparently comfortable with burials in their houses while at the same time avoiding them elsewhere. The relative lack of grave disturbance at Paloma implies that the tradition of burial avoidance continued throughout the occupation of the site.

Distinctive Burials

As a whole, the mortuary data suggest that all the occupants of Paloma were members of relatively egalitarian societies. No burials were differentiated to the degree that would indicate status achieved except by personal lifetime effort. But some graves are distinctive in the number of grave goods, different grave locations and burial positions, and special interment facilities. These distinctive burials give insights into the complexity of Paloma social organizations beyond the simple heuristic term *egalitarian.*

The burials (51, 52, 112, and 113) in House 15/16 (Level 400 or late 500) were more elaborately interred than their contemporaries in other parts of the village. B. 51 consisted of a male adult (25 years) in a loosely flexed, almost extended, position. The head pointed west, the hands were at the face, and the body was wrapped in a fur robe and covered with a large amount of grass. An oval biface, nine cut shell amulets, and a bone pin fragment had been placed in the burial pit. The lower left leg of this burial protruded out of the grave, possibly indicating house abandonment after interment. B. 52, a female adult (24 years), was found next to B. 51, with the same kinds of wrappings as well as twenty-five bone beads. B. 52's body position was the same as that of its male companion. The quality of treatment suggests that women may have shared status with their husbands or other family members of Paloman households. Such apparent equality between the sexes is not in evidence in later mortuary rites at the site. Fewer grave goods in female buri-

als in later periods suggest a diminution of female status in the Paloma village during the late occupations. There is little information available on the other interments in the house. B. 112 was an infant placed either in an extension of the grave of B. 52 or in a pit which cut into the edge of the adjacent grave. It contained the bones of an infant, possibly female, about 2 months old. A cut shell disk, fragmentary animal skin or fur, and a fine fabric with traces of red pigment were found in direct association with the skeleton. Less than 10 centimeters north of B. 112 a small straw-lined oval pit (B. 113) was found to contain three cut shell disks and a small *Tegula* shell lying on an ash layer on top of the lining. A few poorly preserved teeth belonging to a 2-year-old child were also found in the pit. While other examples of relatively elaborate infant burials were found at Paloma, B. 112 is unique in the goods found in the grave, and the nearby pit is also unusual.

40. Burial 159: straw border and cane structure.

The equal treatment for males and females in House 15/16 contrasts with the single adult males in the center of later houses such as House 100/101. Evidence of special attention to male burials during the late occupation of the site is represented by B. 159 (late Level 300?). This 17-year-old male was the most elaborately interred individual found during excavations at Paloma. The grave (fig. 40) consisted of a long oval pit (170 × 100 × 90 centimeters) covered with a cane grid over which at least three mats had been placed to form a cover. When excavated, the grid structure was found collapsed into the burial pit, but bent and broken crosspieces of the cane poles forming the grid were found placed in the ground, suggesting that the grid originally formed a long vaulted roof over the grave. Funeral goods were numerous: a shell offering, a mano, a tabular shaped rock, gourd fragments, and several ropes were found in the burial chamber. One rope fragment was badly decayed at the time of its recovery, but the remains of an elaborate series of knots and a tassel could be detected at one end lying near the head of the burial. Another rope fragment was found twisted around a sea mammal bone.

The individual in B. 159 (fig. 41) appeared to have been in generally excellent health prior to his death (Benfer, personal communication). However, the entire left leg of the skeleton, from toes to pelvis, was missing from the grave, and cut marks were detected on the left ilium and right humerus of the skeleton. Examination of the characteristics of the cut marks indicates the likelihood that the leg was removed by a shark (Benfer, personal communication). It seems inescapable that the reason for the elaborate treatment of B. 159 was his accidental and violent death. The fact that this death occurred in the water and was subsequently honored by such an elaborate grave may denote the importance given to fishing as a social role by the people of the site. Other accidental or unusual deaths may have been similarly celebrated, but the evidence for B. 159 allows easy identification of the cause of death.

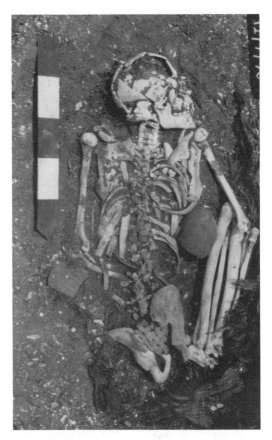

41. Skeleton of Burial 159, a 17-year-old male, missing left leg.

In 1979, the remains of two adult females (B. 215 and B. 222) and an adult male and a juvenile male (B. 213 and B. 214) were found in a square pit lined with mats and associated with Level 220 (fig. 42). The square shape is unusual, and the bodies appear to have been thrown over each other rather than formally buried. Burial goods were few among these individuals so there is no clear evidence that interment in this square grave was an honor. It seems that the group represents a common and perhaps contemporary demise which deserved special treatment but not necessarily honor—nor clear disgrace save, perhaps, for the rough handling of the bodies. Perhaps all died at nearly the same time due to disease or another cause, such as drowning. These burials may further demonstrate the way in which participants in the

42. Burials in a special grave facility found in 1979.

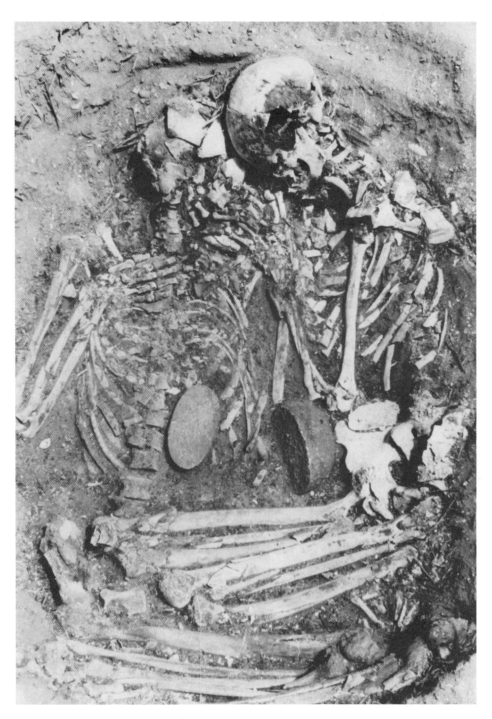

43. Burial 142: A on left, B on right.

Paloma mortuary tradition made exceptions in the standard mortuary rites for unusual deaths or circumstances associated with them.

Another burial pit which contained evidence of special attention for some individuals at Paloma was found on the eastern edge of Unit I (fig. 43). As in the case of B. 159, no clear house association could be established for this pit. Two male adults (B. 142a and 142b) were found with their skeletons partially interlocked in a large circular burial pit (Level 300). They were covered with one or two large mats; a large wooden stick, a calcite crystal, cactus fruits, animal hair, and gourd fragments were found in the burial pit. On the southeastern edge of the grave a small pit was found filled with a bunch of grass coiled in a ring.

Burial 142a was judged to be a 21-year-old male; Burial 142b was another male, about 47 years of age. These two individuals appear to have been special members of the Paloma community. Although some double infant burials were found at Paloma, this grave is the only evidence of a double adult burial. Furthermore, the nature and number of burial offerings and the time and trouble expended in placing the bodies in an embrace suggest that these individuals were of special concern to the Paloma community. Crystals are associated with shamanism throughout the Americas, and staves are both symbols of authority and religious symbols in the Andes (Sharon 1978). Although the evidence is slim, these items in the double burial may indicate a religious or authoritative role for one or both of the individuals.

Another example of special mortuary treatment at Paloma is the special care given to infant burials, which received some of the finest grave goods found at the site, such as the three stone pendants discussed in chapter 3. Similar care for younger members of society is indicated in House 28 (Level 400), a special structure with a floor plan tending to a quadrangular rather than circular shape (fig. 44).

Although some residences at Paloma had floor plans closer to the square than the circle,

House 28 was clearly a special structure. It was small by site standards, with a floor area of only 8 square meters. On the eastern side of the floor, twelve small burial pits for fetuses or neonatal infants were found. Although most of these had been cleaned out before the 1976 work, some remains as well as the small size of the pits indicated that these were the graves of very young individuals. A complete skeleton of a child was indeed recovered in 1979 when the remaining portion of the structure examined in 1976 was excavated. The western side of the floor, however, was devoid of graves—nor were any other features or artifacts discovered.

South of House 28, another structure, House 13, with the usual circular floor plan, contained the burials of many juveniles from the Level 400 or early 300 period. Unfortunately, many of these burials had been removed in the 1973 excavations and the larger grave sizes could not be used as a criterion. Some of the pits are large, suggesting adult burials. Review of the available field notes seems to support the assignment of the dead to a young age category; some of the younger or older burials appear to have been interred before or after the period in which adolescents were the exclusive age group buried in the structure.

To have so many infants in a single house or to have such a concentration of infant deaths over time represented in one house is quite unusual. Even taking into consideration the uncertain information available for House 13, House 28 appears to have been a special mortuary facility for infants and, perhaps, fetuses. The evidence at least suggests that at one time the people of Paloma may have recognized social roles that went beyond the nuclear family; children who died in infancy were given special treatment in death rites.

It is also interesting to note that the infant burials are concentrated on the eastern side of the floor of House 28, while the standard burial program has been suggested to have begun on the western side of a house. A charnel house found at the Real Alto site (circa 3400–1500 B.C.) in Ecuador also displayed

44. House 28; excavator is near corner of house.

this bilateral configuration (Lathrap, Marcos, and Zeidler 1977). Although much larger in size than House 28, this structure contained burials only in its northern half. Perhaps the plan of a burial area opposed by an empty space is a common pattern. In the Real Alto house, cultural remains on the floor space with no burials suggest it was an area for ritual. No objects were found in the cleared area of House 28, but similar activities could have taken place there. When the special treatment of infants in general at the site is taken into consideration, House 28 at least reinforces the inference that the very young were given special treatment by the people of the site.

Discussion

The analyses of the burials suggested distinctions in mortuary practices on the basis of the individual's age and the stratigraphic level. Special treatment was given to the very young. Distinctions on the basis of sex have been also established. Unique burials have revealed differences between house groups (House 16)—presumably domestic units or families—on the basis of relative wealth of the burial goods and special interment facilities. Further distinctions have been noted in regard to manner of death (B. 159) and perhaps distinctive social roles such as shamanism, although the magical items in B. 142 could be due to the unusual occurrence of simultaneous deaths.

This practice and such goods were not found elsewhere, however. The data only hint that age-grouping organizations may have united separate households, as in House 28; but in the main, the primary emphasis in death and life was on the household or family. Little temporal change has been noted except for the use of fire, an increase in fine textiles with a decrease in animal products and beads, and, possibly, the late introduction of the practice of home destruction. It also seems that special graves, such as group burials of adults and special graves for certain individuals (B. 142 and B. 159), are more common later in the occupation of Paloma. If group burials for younger individuals are in evidence, the practice occurred early.

Males appear to have had higher status than females. Their central burial in house floors probably mimics their central roles in the social structure. There may have been a sexual division of labor in which men were the chief hunters and fishermen and women the collectors and preparers of plants.

Benfer (1984) notes a significant diminishing of sexual dimorphism in musculature of burials from early to late levels at the site. The implication of this is that men and women may have begun to perform similar kinds of work so that the sexual division of labor was less pronounced later in the occupation of the site. This trend seems to be separate from any population replacement of site occupants. The trend in deceased dimorphism runs parallel with other trends, including a diminution of some lomas resources such as fur-bearing animals, and perhaps a decrease in the extent, richness, or variety of lomas resources in general. Another trend is the decrease in grave goods for adult female burials, which may indicate decreased status of women in the communities that lived in Paloma.

Maintaining the coarse analysis of previous pages, it may be worthwhile to note that the final abandonment of Paloma as a precotton lomas village was part of a general shift to new locales where horticulture assumed a greater importance in subsistence economies or where people specialized in fishing. The

decrease in the social standing of women and increased role of horticulture were possibly interrelated. But work may have been harder for all in a degraded lomas environment— Benfer (1986a, b, c) found signs of greater stress in some aspects of Paloma skeletons over time despite an overall improvement in health and life expectancy. While the argument is at best a hypothesis based on current data, it may be worth pursuing.

In one of the few ethnographic studies which documents social change in the shift from mobile foraging to sedentary horticulture, Patricia Draper (1975) has noted a decrease in women's autonomy and influence in society. In her case study of the !Kung of Botswana, women have an essential role in contributing gathered plants to the subsistence economy and are as mobile as males in their foraging activities; domestic chores and child socialization practices are similar for both males and females. All of this occurs with small group sizes, concomitant sanctions against physical aggression, and relatively little privacy with a strong sense of group identity. In sedentary life, however, there is a more defined and narrowed sex-typing of adult work and more permanent attachment to particular places and people. Men have more control over important resources such as domestic animals and are more mobile than women, having more contact with the world outside the settlement. With more material goods and a greater investment in a particular settlement, women tend to spend more time at home, and child-rearing practices differ—boys and girls are trained for more specialized adult work.

These observations might be applicable to the Paloma data except for some very important differences. One is that the people of Paloma had not yet completely made the shift to sedentary horticultural life, as far as can be ascertained, during the occupation of the site. The second difference is that the evidence of musculature suggests that men and women were doing more similar work near the end of the occupation of the site, rather than different activities as was the case among the

!Kung. The degradation of the lomas may have pushed the activities of men and women closer together rather than further apart. Yet the burial data suggest a decreased status for females.

While there may be factors which elude detection in studying these changes, perhaps the key to understanding differing results of similar processes is to note that social equality is an ideology and thus different from a quantitative judgment of the amount or nature of work. There are many societies in the world in which women do equal or more work than men in providing basic necessities of life yet are dominated by males, and women generally contribute more work in horticultural societies with low dependence on crops (Martin and Voorhies 1975:215) as was probably the case at Paloma for some time after its occupation. Patrilineal kinship also predominates in horticultural communities (Martin and Voorhies 1975:219), and Patterson (1983) has argued that such a social system existed for early farmers in coastal Peru.

Although intercommunal violence is not in evidence until relatively late in the preceramic and not universally found throughout the coast, the constriction of resources which contributed to raiding and warfare began during the occupation of Paloma. The degradation of the lomas decreased necessary food and materials. The shift to valley farming for some communities would have accentuated concerns with resource limitations. Indeed, Martin and Voorhies (1975:233) note that the localization of males is an adaptation in times and places where resources are scarce.

The solutions to perceived or actual problems of scarcity were not solved, for the most part, by recourse to raiding and warfare. Instead, at least for a while, the elaboration of material goods and the exchange of these and surplus foodstuffs temporarily solved the problems of imbalances between communities. Within communities, however, the loss of women's status may have been the result of ideological factors interacting with changes in economic systems.

During most of the occupation of Paloma, success was probably measured in terms of providing food for one's family and propagating the social unit in the next generation. There are few artifacts which appear to have had inherent value. While stone or worked bone beads may have been valued more than strung barnacles, items of high labor investment are rare. Obsidian and *Spondylus* shells may have been valued due to their rarity on the coast, and the superior cutting abilities of volcanic glass were probably appreciated. *Spondylus* was a prestige good in later prehistory and may have begun to assume such a role at the time of Paloma's occupation, although it is so rarely found at such an early date that its role is hard to assess.

Within a few centuries after the abandonment of Paloma, the number and quality of mats and cloths in a burial appear to denote relatively distinct differences in access to wealth (Moseley 1978). Paloma adult burials with many grave offerings tend to have many textile objects as well, and there are clear distinctions in the quality of mats and the fineness of twined textiles. It thus appears that the importance of fabric goods in Peruvian society, which continues to the present, was established by or during the time of the occupation of Paloma and increased in importance through the preceramic. Study of these materials has revealed little of the elaborate treatment and skilled workmanship in textiles exhibited in the fabrics from the slightly later site of Huaca Prieta (Bird 1985). The Paloma textiles are competently and skillfully done, but there is little decoration. The emphasis is utilitarian, with soft pliable materials next to the skin and coarser, tougher outer goods for additional warmth.

Paloma was not an arcadia. The physical studies, especially, show hunger, disease, and sudden death. A high mortality rate inflicted pain and suffering on young and old, male and female. Congenital afflictions, accidental traumas, and degenerative conditions all brought their special miseries. If a fairly good system of extracting food and other necessities from the land and sea was developed, there were, nevertheless, times of shortages and unpredictability as well as abundance and certainty.

Even if the men of B. 142 were not shamans, it is certain that some knew techniques to attempt to control or influence fate. It may be that the grave goods accompanying the dead were not part of religious ritual as we know it. But the care with which the dead were laid to rest imparts a sense of loss, a retention in memory, a spiritual feeling, across the millennia. The embrace of the double burial, the 17-year-old shark victim so elaborately interred in his special burial vault, and the infant burials evoke a sense of pathos. Subjective analysis infers that this was not the first time such sentiments were felt at Paloma.

Easily identifiable symbolic icons are rare at the site. Red (and yellow) pigment found in graves and almost universally associated with funerary rites may just as easily been body decoration in life. The filled mussel valves are the only objects which suggest the possibility of a concept of an afterlife. The cut shell disks and crescents are enigmatic. No clear use among the living can be determined for them. Their shapes suggest the sun and crescent moon, but this is speculation.

The burning of at least some houses at the end of their burial programs is surely more than a utilitarian or hygienic act. Even if insect infestation was an incentive, why burn a house if it was to be abandoned in any case? Signs of burning also have been found in burials; hearths on top of graves appear to be deliberate, not accidental events, especially considering that grave sites may have been known.

The use of fire in mortuary rituals is probably linked to concepts of regeneration or renewal. This symbolic role of fire is widespread in ancient America as well as in other regions of the world. Whether the fire meant a renewed life for the dead in another existence or the affirmation of continued existence of the social group or both cannot be determined.

More than religious ideology, the identity of the dead was expressed in mortuary practices in terms of *who* a person was rather than *what* rank or status the dead held in life. Even

if the possibility of special burial facilities is considered strong, the identities expressed in age groups are of corporate members of a social group defined in terms of life cycle. Moreover, the emphasis on house burial and personal goods in grave offerings, including the tools of production, stresses the importance of a personalized social status.

Above all, children, especially infants, received particular attention in burial ceremonies. They have the greatest number of special grave goods. Perhaps this is because, being young, babies had not acquired clothing, grinding stones, bodkins, and other paraphernalia of active adults. The more exotic materials may have been allotted to the young in part because every burial was required to contain at least some artifacts. But there seems to be more to this than simple adjustment of burial rites for the very young.

It is remarkable that so many infant burials, even fetus burials, are to be found at Paloma. In many societies with high infant mortality, true social identity is not given; a person is not considered a real "human being" until a time well after the period when early death is most likely. This delay in incorporation into the social unit can also serve to justify infanticide—since the victims are not truly human, the act is officially a neutral one, not murder. Disposal of the young dead is often informal, resulting in low numbers of infant burials in later archaeological investigations, and the fragility of small bones often prevents their preservation.

This is not the case at Paloma. Nevertheless, the demographic studies of the skeletal remains indicate that female infanticide was practiced. Further evidence of population stress has been detected in late procreation patterns. Despite this, infants and even fetuses were buried in houses (or special structures) as if they were part of society. It is unfortunate that the skeletons of the young children in House 28 are not available for study. The case for infanticide rests on the fact that only seven male but eighteen female infants less than one year old were excavated. As noted by Benfer, this distribution is unlikely due to chance (chi-square = 5.8, $p <$ .02, 1 d.f.; 1986c:351). Only two infant or fetal remains could be sexed in Level 200, leaving the problem of continued infanticide open. But the burial of infants in houses rather than a special mortuary facility suggests a possible renewed emphasis on the household.

Irene Silverblatt (1987:34–35, 67) cites a number of ethnohistoric sources for the Inca in which special shrines for fertility contained offerings of aborted fetuses and children who died shortly after birth. Although a great length of time separates Paloma from the Inca, it seems possible that such concepts of fertility were expressed in House 28.

There are many ethnographic examples of societies in which infanticide is practiced. In some, it is almost a casual affair; in others, a painful, bitter, and regretted event. Among some groups, the fact that infants are being selectively killed, often by not feeding them, may even be denied by the parents. It is likely that infanticide was carried out at Paloma either regretfully or "unintentionally," given the apparent importance of households and families in the burial data. The people of Paloma were caught in a conflict between the desire to have children and the need to control population size. Furthermore, the evidence shows that Paloma society was increasingly successful in providing relatively healthy and longer lives at the same time that lomas resources were decreasing. These two facts may have been important in ending the life-style represented by the site as well as actual abandonment of the site itself, circa 2500 B.C. With the assertion of a more male-oriented social system, decrease in women's status, yet an equalization in the sexual division of labor and the general breakup of old lifeways, children may have been more desirable than ever as families calculated their strategies for survival in a changing world. If descent reckoning became more important in a world of limited resources, a shift away from common burial of infants to burial within the family house may have been stressed.

New problems came with the apparent solutions, however. Concepts of property became more important as land and water resources played critical roles in the new economy. Economic specialization made communities less independent than in the lomas. These processes partly led to the development of complex societies in the forms of the great states and civilizations of later Peruvian prehistory.

6. Paloma and Preceramic Cultural History and Processes

Comparative Mortuary Practices: Chile and Ecuador

The Paloma burials are not the oldest known for the continent or region. Interments have been found at a number of Andean sites which date many centuries earlier. Many of these sites were occupied by hunters at the end of the Pleistocene epoch. They resemble the Paloma burials in that they are frequently simple, flexed interments with a few everyday items as grave furniture. Usually, only a few burials are found at any one site, so mortuary patterns are hard to determine. What is striking, however, is that these early remains more resemble the Paloma burials than those of subsequent periods. If burials reflect society and culture, they suggest that Paloma lifeways are more closely related to the old foraging and hunting tradition than to the following emphasis on farming and fishing on the coast of Peru and that Paloma society truly was on the brink of major sociocultural changes. Yet it is also striking that the preceramic mortuary tradition is quite conservative, with practices continuing through many centuries. Even though large architectural complexes were built relatively soon after the abandonment of Paloma, there is a continuity in burial practices and little evidence for sharp distinctions in social rank despite the impressiveness of the buildings at such sites.

The most complete records of mortuary practices predating those of Paloma come from areas far distant from the central coast of Peru. Both on the north coast of Chile (Al-lison 1985) and the southern coast of Ecuador (Stothert 1985), burial complexes have been found which antedate the Peruvian central coast materials.

In 1919, Max Uhle was the first archaeologist to note an early fishing culture in the Atacama Desert of northern Chile. Mummies were also recovered from this Chinchorro culture, named for the prehistoric people's use of gill nets. But, as noted previously, the antiquity of this culture was uncertain and little more research was done until the work of Junius Bird (1943). Continued research (Allison 1985) has recovered over 1,500 burials and clarified the prehistoric lifeways dated to as early as 7800 B.P.

The Chinchorro (7800–3800 B.P.) and Quiani (3400–3200 B.P.) archaeological cultures represent human groups who adapted to some of the harshest desert conditions in the world. Few lomas zones relieve the barren landscape of the Atacama Desert, springs are rare, rivers thin and seasonal, but the sea is rich in resources. Groups probably moved between coastal fishing areas and interior hunting grounds. Even if conditions were somewhat more amenable to human life in the past, the central coast of Peru was a veritable eden of resources compared to northern Chile.

Yet despite the harshness of the desert regime, humans survived and even prospered. The inventory of their material culture is small but includes some very sophisticated equipment. As in Peru, the sea was a crucial resource; composite sinker hooks, squid hook barbs, fish harpoons, and other special gear were all found during shell midden excavations by Bird (1943:240–244). As at Paloma, there were few frills in the material life of these people. Simple garments, stone and shell beads, and other ornaments were the only luxuries found.

But despite this simple life, mortuary practices were extremely elaborate. The Chinchorro practiced forms of mummification ranging from simple air drying of a body to practices involving many stages in manipulation of the cadaver. In the most complex forms, all the internal organs were removed, including the brain, hooked out through the foramen magnum. Skin and hair were also cut away, and major muscles were removed. Hot coals and ashes were placed in the body cavities to dry the body thoroughly, and the limbs and torso were made rigid by grinding knee and elbow joints, inserting sticks along the major axes of the body, and binding the corpse with ropes. Once dry, the remains were wrapped in reed matting and cavities were stuffed with wool, feathers, earth, grass, and shells. Clay was modeled over limbs; skin was sewn up over major joints. A face mask of clay included orifices and a modeled nose. The corpse's hair was added to the mask and the mummy was painted black or red, depending on the period.

Study of the burials is ongoing (Allison 1985), and a sequence of mortuary styles remains to be established. Analysis has revealed, however, that the mummies were propped up in groups (Allison 1985:78). As at Paloma, the dead were important to the living, but they were treated in a very different way. The great variation in body treatment may eventually be sorted into a chronological sequence, but perhaps there was a certain sense of craft, art, or showmanship in such preparations. In a barren environment with low population density and relatively constant climate and resource availability, mortuary rituals may have been foci of social interactions. The display of the elaborately prepared dead may have occasioned the con-

gregation of many small groups into a larger unit or macroband to honor the dead and surviving kin. Like the *fandangos* of the Great Basin Shoshoni (Steward 1936), such meetings, founded on ritual premises, could have served as social gatherings where information on hunting, marriage arrangements, and other communications and interactions vital for survival and a sense of community occurred.

Analogies may also be drawn between the Chilean mummies and ethnographic practices of the South Pacific, especially Melanesia (Krieger 1943:59). In the New Hebrides, Solomon Islands, New Ireland, and the Sepik River area of New Guinea, the features of the dead are modeled over the skull in clay or other materials. In some cases, long bones are also incorporated in a display. Such activities are sometimes associated with fertility and are carried out by the clan, more as entertainment than as a strict religious ritual (Bateson 1967:233); in other cases, the emphasis is on the achievements of the deceased individual. These activities can serve both to reinforce group identity of members of the dead or sponsor's group and to engender competition between social divisions.

Two thousand kilometers north of the Atacama, the Vegas culture was a contemporary of the Chinchorro. Karen Stothert (1985) has excavated 192 individuals who lived and died in the Late Vegas Period between 8250 and 6600 B.P. on the Santa Elena Peninsula of southern Ecuador. This region was more humid than central Peru or northern Chile and preservation is not as good, but much has been revealed about mortuary practices through the careful analyses of Stothert and her colleagues.

The Vegans practiced a broad-based subsistence strategy including hunting, harvesting mangrove mollusks (*concha prieta: Anadara tuberculosa*), and collecting wild plants. Significantly, no bifaces, including projectile points, are found at Vegas sites. The bottle gourd appears to have been domesticated; Stothert (1985:621) cites evidence for maize. The evidence consists of opal phytoliths, nonperishable silica crystals found in plant parts. Phytolith studies are new, however, and their characteristics, including travel through the atmosphere and soil, are only now being determined. Some doubt, therefore, remains as to whether maize was being grown in Santa Elena between 7,000 and 8,000 years ago, as Stothert claims. Regardless of this problem, the people of Vegas appear to have been broad-based hunter-gatherers not too different from the people of Paloma, except that fishing was more important to the latter.

The burials (fig. 45) were found in deep midden and were usually flexed and resting on their sides. The positions of the interments suggest they had been wrapped. Burial on the right side was slightly (1.5 times) more popular than on the left, although subadults were more frequently found on their left sides. Males tended to be buried with heads oriented west, women in all directions, and subadults also in all directions, perhaps with an avoidance of a western orientation. As at Paloma, small sample sizes make it difficult to establish clear patterns.

Two primary double burials were found. One consisted of two adults of undetermined gender, in flexed positions and opposite orientations. The second was of a man and woman who both died in their early twenties and were oriented to the east.

Grave goods were rare. They consisted of such things as shell spoons, perforated conch shells, flat pebbles, groups of shells, lithic flakes, and red pigment. A polished stone axe head may have been imported from northern Peru (Stothert 1985:632). Stones were found on top of an infant burial and on the male and female double burial.

Few features were found in association with the Vegas burials. Root penetration in sandy soil made identification of houses difficult, but some traces of structures remained. It is likely that the site was a residence, given the evidence for structures and the midden. An adult female was found buried in the threshold of an east-facing circular structure; this may have ceremonial significance, as has been suggested for a much later but perhaps related practice found at the Valdivia site of Real Alto (Lathrap et al. 1977).

Secondary burial was a popular practice: 157 of the 192 individuals were secondary burials. It was more common for males (Stothert 1985:625). Burials were stripped of flesh, disjointed, and either arranged in packets or placed in irregular piles. In addition, four massive secondary burial groups were found, with at least one group contained in what may have been a structure. One ossuary is described as containing the partial remains of at least 17 adults and 21 subadults. Bones are distinctly grouped, suggesting they were in perishable containers. In one group all skulls faced east. Two children (8 and 9 years old) were found within the bone pile, as well as a partially articulated adult male. Another articulated subadult was found immediately beneath the ossuary.

Although the secondary burials of individuals contained no burial goods, the larger groups were accompanied by some rather fancy items, including small pebbles rubbed with red pigment, a shell charm, a peccary canine, a group of fox teeth, and other shell and stone artifacts.

Stothert sees the Vegas burial patterns as related to others in the Intermediate Area, especially Cerro Mangote (McGimsey 1958), an early site (6800 B.P.) in Panama.

In comparing Paloma, Chinchorro, and Vegas burial practices, common features may be identified in all three, such as group burials and special attention to subadults. Distinctions are clear, including the elaborate treatment of the Chilean remains and the secondary burials of Vegas. But before a full discussion of these similarities and contrasts can be fruitfully presented, it is worthwhile to review some slightly later preceramic Peruvian burials.

Comparative Mortuary Practices: Preceramic Peru

The earliest burials found in Peru come from the same Chilca Valley as Paloma, but from a site much further up-valley, at an altitude of 3,925 meters above sea level, in the caves of Tres Ventanas (Engel 1987). Two of the tree caves yielded burials. Cave 2 contained two adults wrapped in camelid skins, one of which had blue lines painted on it. A radiocarbon date associated with one of these burials (Vallejos A. 1982:21) placed it at 8030 ± B.P. (1-3108). Tight flexing of the limbs and placement on the side characterized the burials. In Cave 1 a small house was found (Engel 1987:23) in the lowest level. The structure was made of high-altitude *ichu* grass placed over poles. The same level contained the burial of a young child laid on a cushion of fiber. It had a fine fiber textile, a shell amulet, a bone needle, and a mantle of leather with it and was wrapped in a fiber mat. No detailed presentation of the stratigraphic context of the burial has been presented, but Engel (1987: 23) claims that this burial belongs to the earliest occupation of the cave, which has produced a radiocarbon date of 10,030 ± 170 years (Vallejos A. 1982:21). Another young child burial found in the cave is claimed to date later in the preceramic. Planned future work at Tres Ventanas (Benfer, personal communication) will be important in determining if it contains Peru's earliest human burials.

Engel (1966b, 1976, 1981) has excavated sites near Paracas Bay on the south coast which yielded evidence of preceramic mortuary practices. One area consists of two components, given separate site numbers and names (Engel 1981:32–33). Encampment 96 (14a-VI-96) is the lower and older of the two, said to date to between 8000 and 9000 B.P., while Village 514, Santo Domingo de Paracas (14a-VI-514) overlies the earlier occupation and contains cotton as well as *jícama* (*Pachyrrhizus* sp.; Engel 1981:38).

Two burials were found in association with Encampment 96. They consisted of the remains of an adult lying on the back with hands over the face, wrapped in a junco mat. Two very fine coverings as well as a third slightly coarser textile were found around the body. A bone textile tool lay on the chest. The

second grave contained the remains of an individual of undetermined age or sex. The body was tightly flexed and wrapped in penguin hides. Grave goods consisted of a ball of fiber twine, miscellaneous strings and reeds, and a junco mat covering the body.

Eleven burials have been reported for Village 514. Two graves may be associated with the earlier Encampment 96, according to Engel (1981:36): 1b, an adult wearing a bead necklace, may have been disturbed when a later house was built. Burial 2 consisted of an adult and a child. Both are reported to have been wrapped in vicuña garments and covered together in a twined reed mat. The rest of the burials belonging to Village 514 proper include both sexes and ages ranging from adult to juveniles to infant (1–2 years old). Burial practices resemble those of Paloma, with objects of everyday life used as grave offerings and outer wrappings of junco mats. Red pigments were occasionally found on fabrics, and looped net textiles were encountered on some skulls. While only one basket has been identified at Paloma, seven were discovered at this site. Two were flat and rectangular, and some had been decorated with alternating blue and red bands of pigment (Engel 1981:37).

Another site excavated by Engel (1966b, 1981:31–32) is the ossuary of Paracas, sometimes referred to as Cabezas Largas, a later site nearby. Fifty-six skulls are shown in the published illustration of the ossuary (Engel 1966b:106), giving a tentative minimum number of individuals. There is a mass of skeletons, many of which are partly to fully disarticulated; many skulls are shown separate from other skeletal parts. Engel reports that some skeletons were wrapped in unique mantles of fine fibers with distinctive knotted fringes on their lower edges. The only other recurring artifacts are slender stakes or poles, some measuring two meters in length. All of

45. *Overleaf:* Excavations by Karen Stothert at Site 80 on the Santa Elena Peninsula, Ecuador.

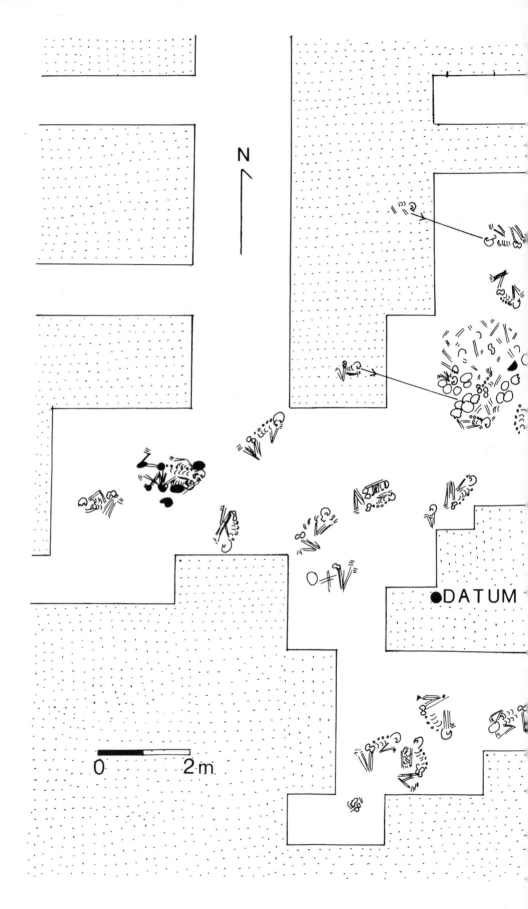

N

0   2 m.

●DATUM

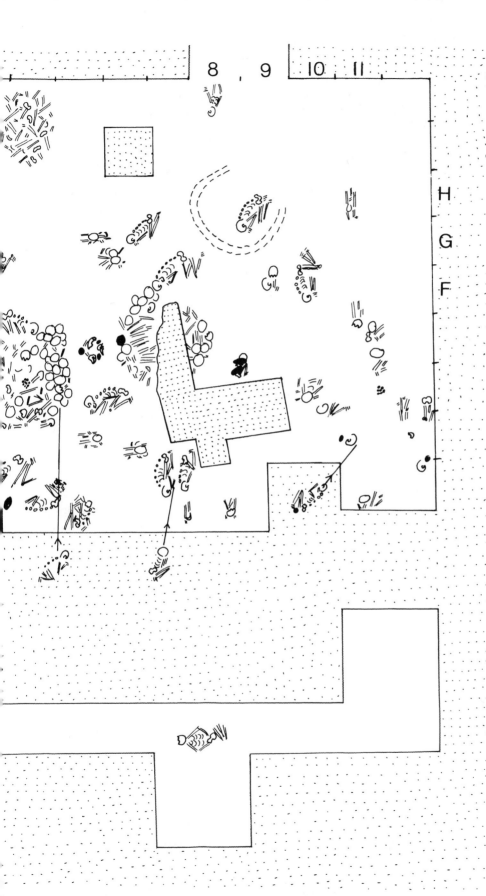

8 , 9   10 , 11

H

G

F

the human remains were of adults; sex determinations are not available. Reported carbon dates are 5020 ± 120 and 5175 ± 200 B.P. (Engel 1981:31); cotton wefts are present in some of the finer textiles.

The ossuary is not directly associated with a preceramic settlement, although there are sites nearby which are likely candidates. This remarkable interment deserves additional study, such as pathological analyses of the human remains which might determine cause of death and shed light on the possible reasons for this special grave. Whatever the circumstances surrounding the deaths of these individuals, the ossuary appears to highlight the practice of group interment as a method to denote either distinct social roles or unusual death in the preceramic.

Ancón Bay is about 100 kilometers north of Chilca; a single burial from the site of Colinas, although dated late (circa 1900 B.C.), resembles the Paloma customs (Muelle and Ravines 1973). An adult, possibly male, corpse was semiflexed with the head pointing east. A mat wrapped the body, as did a thin rope and a net fabric which covered the lower waist. The hair had been formed into small braids. Grave goods included four sea snail shells (*Thais chocolata* Dc.), an *achira* leaf, an unidentified fruit, an anchovy, a thin human hair rope, and an oval shell fragment worked on its side.

One of the few sites which has received attention comparable to the Paloma excavations is Chilca Monument I, relatively nearby, on the northern bank of the Chilca River, only 8 kilometers from Paloma. The site is divided into a village (126VII-1) of about 50 huts over an area of 100 × 300 meters and an adjacent cemetery (126VII-680), both dating to the preceramic, circa 5700–3600 B.P. (Engel 1984:31, 36), with a second, later, pottery-bearing component present. Engel (1976:97) believes that the site was much larger but has been subjected to erosion by the Chilca River. Donnan (1964) has reported on the study of a single house with a more extensive report recently published by Engel (1987, 1988), who directed the excavations. House 12, re-

ported by Donnan, was a circular, semisubterranean conical structure, 2.5 meters in diameter, made of junco, cane and whalebone. Except for the use of whalebone, and a hypothetical domed shape, the Chilca house generally resembles those of Paloma.

Seven burials were found inside House 12. All were oriented with heads pointed north or northwest. They were extended, supine, with hands at the sides. One burial (No. 6) was placed in a shallow pit dug into the house floor, but both ends of the mat wrapping protruded above the floor, reminiscent of the protruding skull of B.105 at Paloma. Three fine-grained igneous rocks were on the chest of the burial bundle. The only other nontextile objects found with burials was a limpet shell bracelet with the youngest male (No. 5, 20 years). Five of the burials were adult males (20–40 years) and two were young females (18 and 20 years).

Other burials found at Chilca I include the remains of women, each with five wooden pegs driven through them. The practice of giving great care to the burials of infants and fetuses as seen at Paloma was apparently continued at Chilca I (Engel 1976:96–97).

An ossuarylike structure (House 6) was also discovered, consisting of eight flexed burials with hands at their faces. Most of the bodies had been placed side by side in a row with heads oriented north or south. The bodies had been partially burned and other human remains and mammal bones were mixed with the eight individuals (Lumbreras 1974:39; Engel 1976:94). A large whale vertebra rested on top of the remains.

Forty burials of individuals of varying ages were outside around House 6. Some of the burials may have been oriented with their heads pointing to the ossuary, although the general pattern appears random. All burials had flexed legs and hands at faces, similar to the interior burials. Most of these exterior graves were on the southern and southwestern sides of the structure and were irregularly scattered around House 6.

Chilca I is especially interesting in its proximity to and overlapping dates with Paloma.

The general mortuary patterns are similar. The ossuary at Chilca I seems somewhat more formalized than that found at Paloma. Nevertheless, similarities are present. Not only do both contain groups of burials, but the remains at Paloma show signs of burning as at Chilca. It seems quite possible that the Paloma crypt represents a burial facility which was not filled. The disturbance of the burials, such as missing or mixed bones, suggests that the tomb was opened a number of times to admit new burials but was not filled, whereas the Chilca ossuary was perhaps finished. Engel (1984:36) notes the presence of "kidney beans" in House 1 at the site; its riverine location strengthens the suggestion that farming may have played a more important role in the subsistence economy, although the mortuary practices are fairly similar.

Preceramic sites later than Paloma have also yielded burials. They were occupied by people who practiced horticulture more intensively than the people of Paloma and who made rather elaborate twined cotton textiles.

An example of an isolated preceramic burial was found on the northern edge of the central coast at the site of Las Haldas. The site itself is filled with monumental architecture dating to the Initial Period. However, excavations by Pozorski and Pozorski (1987:20) uncovered an infant burial in what appeared to be late preceramic refuse, when cotton was in use. The burial was of a child of less than 6 months of age, flexed and on its back. One or more twined cotton textiles had been wrapped around the body and the whole was encased in a layer of junco. Several large boulders appear to have been deliberately placed on the grave. Though this is only a single example from fairly extensive deposits, it is interesting to note the careful treatment of infants as found at Paloma in earlier times and the use of stones to cover the grave.

An important site has been discovered, studied, and recently reported (Deza 1988) on the southern north coast, fronting the preceramic monumental complex of Salinas de Chao (Alva 1986) and closer to the sea. This site, Piedras Negras, has not been directly associated with the large-scale architecture, but it contains burials of interest, with an occupation from about 6500 B.P. through the cotton preceramic (4150 ± 90 B.P.; Deza 1988) with extremely late, nonpreceramic dates also registered (1350 ± B.P.; Deza 1988), perhaps the result of mixture from later visitors to the area—no later occupation has been reported.

Four burials have been excavated which appear to date to the early use of cotton, judging by the use of cotton wefts in mats with junco warps. These burials were found in graves cushioned with fibers, lined with mats, covered with fine sand and small stones, and sealed with large rocks. The burials also appear to have been flexed and tied with large ropes. All of these mortuary practices resemble those of Paloma. However, the burials were well burnt, so that the skeletal remains are mostly fragmentary.

Also within the site boundaries are semi-subterranean rectangular buildings measuring 3 × 4 meters with steps which resemble the cotton preceramic structures near Paloma. One such structure is located slightly inland from the area of earlier preceramic burials and is surrounded by burials containing cotton fabrics. The building has been badly looted, but on its surface cotton was present, as were many skulls of young children, the approximate ages of which were indicated by lack of molar eruption (Deza, personal communication). It is unfortunate that the site has been looted and that further work may not be done, for the evidence suggests that this structure may have been a special mortuary facility for the young.

Huaca Prieta, at the mouth of the Chicama Valley, was first occupied around 3000 B.C. and continued for several hundred years more. Thirty-three burials dating to the preceramic were found at the site by Bird (1985) during his 1946 excavations on the large mound which had been built up through successive occupations.

Three of the Huaca Prieta burials (896, 897, 901) had been covered with a mixture of water, ash, and dirt poured on the body after death, perhaps as part of a ritual (Bird 1985:

68). Examples of similar treatment were found at Paloma. Burial 110, found in the refuse on the west side of the site, had a consolidated mixture of ash and caliche rising from its head in a wide funnel shape to the ancient ground surface, suggesting that liquid had deliberately been poured into the grave once most of the body was underground. Burials 117 and 119 exhibited similar treatment. If this practice was a part of a ritual, perhaps it was associated with the use of fire in mortuary ceremonies, the water serving to extinguish the flames. No evidence of fire was noted at Huaca Prieta, however, but burials in midden are difficult to evaluate—burnt rock in the grave fill may be assumed to be from later activities not associated with burial rites.

The general impression gained from studying the report on the Huaca Prieta excavations is that preservation was not quite as good there as at Paloma. Nevertheless, it appears that grave goods other than textiles were rare at the Huaca Prieta site; only two burials contained such articles.

One of the burials with grave goods was the remains of a child in a clay-lined storage pit. The skeleton was wrapped in a junco mat on the bottom of the pit associated with a worn basalt flake, five unworked basalt flakes, two unfinished cobble sinkers, and a worn chunk of whalebone (Bird 1985:74). The excavator was uncertain if these materials were deliberate grave inclusions or not. Stone flakes, *lucuma* seeds, gourd fragments, and mussel shells were also found in the upper grave fill; again, their status is uncertain. At least five different kinds of textiles were in the grave, suggesting that care was taken in the burial of this young individual.

The other elaborate grave (fig. 46) was of an old (over 45) woman in a shallow unlined pit (B. 903). The hands were in the facial area and the legs were tightly flexed. Excrement and undigested plant remains and possibly fish bones were found in the pelvic cavity. A wad of slightly chewed plant remains was found in the mouth. Part of the mass included a small *turi* flower. This plant is still used as

medicine for afflictions of the kidneys and toothaches.

The body was wrapped with a junco mat with cotton wefts. Above the mat a worn junco cord pouch rested on a small piece of matting. Inside the pouch was a gourd bottle containing a gourd vine stem, two gourd seeds, willowlike leaves, small *turi* flowers, and two pieces of junco tuber. Under the mats were the remains of at least six fabrics.

Some of the most famous Peruvian preceramic artifacts were found inside a cotton pouch in this grave. These were two pyroengraved gourds elaborately decorated with highly stylized renditions of humanoid faces—and on one (fig. 46) also torsos—all very similar to the Valdivia (Phase IV or V) style of Ecuador (see Lathrap 1975).

The Asia site (Engel 1963, 1976) is somewhat later than Huaca Prieta, abandoned circa 1400 B.C. It consisted of a low mound, 15 meters in diameter, near the mouth of the Omas River, south of Chilca. This mound, Unit I, contained a rectangular walled compound made of adobe, loose rocks, and stone slabs. Forty-nine burials were found in and around the compound. Clam (*Mesodesma* sp.) shells, cotton fabrics, seeds, fruits, and other refuse were recovered from midden scattered around Unit I.

Burials were flexed, wrapped in mats, and placed in oval pits. Body positions were highly standardized, with all but two burials oriented with the heads pointing west. Nine burials were found with hands between the knees, while the rest of them had hands at the chin or face. Although problems exist in identifying the ages and sexes of the remains (cf. Hartweg 1958; Engel 1963) it seems likely that body positions crosscut age and gender categories.

Red pigment was common in graves and stones usually weighted burial bundles. Some of the dead were wrapped in extra mats so that the final shape of the bundle was unusual, resembling tubular sections joined together. Moseley (1975:76−77) has shown that the number of mats corresponds to the

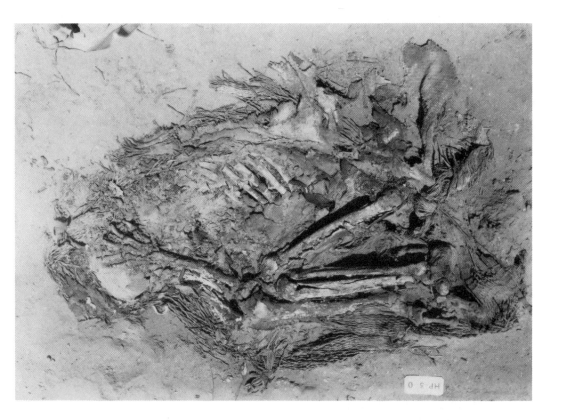

46. *Top,* Burial 903 at Huaca Prieta; *bottom,* two decorated gourds found with it by Junius Bird. Courtesy American Museum of Natural History.

general wealth—quantity and quality of grave goods—of a burial. Graves were marked by driving wooden stakes into the ground above the burial pit.

Artifacts were abundant as offerings. A variety of beads, pins, bone tubes, fancy textiles, and elaborate objects such as baked clay tablets, pyrite mirrors, engraved spindle whorls, incised bone pendants, and carved wooden trays were also found at the site. Snuff tubes and trays indicate that substances, possibly drugs, were inhaled by the people of Asia. Slings, spears, and a wooden baton embedded with shark teeth suggest that armed conflict occurred during the site's occupation.

Violence is also in evidence in the form of headless burials and heads without bodies. Headless burials generally conform to the treatment of complete individuals, although they seem to have fewer grave offerings, mostly textiles. One (No. 23) was found with a sling tied around its abdomen (Engel 1963: 100). Heads without bodies, however, were elaborately treated, often wrapped in many textiles. Another (No. 10) had an incision across its forehead (Engel 1963:94—95), parallel to the brow ridges, with the lower facial skin removed. Another skull had a hole in it which would have permitted a rope attachment for a trophy (Lumbreras 1974:47). This suggests not only that raiding occurred but that the taking of trophy heads probably began in the preceramic.

Bandurria is located south of Huacho on the central coast. Two preceramic occupations are present, according to Fung Pineda (1988:77). One radiocarbon date (4420 ± 140; 1-7448) placing occupation circa 2470 B.C. has been reported (Lynch 1974:385) for the lower level, while the date of the second occupation has not been determined. A pyramid mound is present at the site, as are many burials. Burial practices seem to conform to preceramic patterns. Infants were sometimes accorded burials with adults. Bundles which resembled burials but contained matting, sticks, and plant materials were also found. Artifacts include unbaked clay figurines and

beads made of reddish stone, rectanguloid in shape, lentoid in cross section, and drilled with two holes (Feldman 1980:148).

Aspero is close to Bandurria and dates to roughly the same time period. Robert Feldman (1980:114, 122) conducted excavations at the site, including work on top of two large pyramids. Seven burials were encountered.

An adult and a neonate were found on a floor atop the Huaca de los Sacrificios. The infant was slightly flexed, on the right side, with the head to the north and facing west. A large number of clay or mudstone beads, some of which had green pigment on them, covered the head of the infant in a form suggesting a cap. The body had been wrapped in a cotton textile and placed in a basket also wrapped in a textile. A cane mat covered all this. A gourd bowl was associated with the burial, as well as two large pieces of twined cotton cloth. The burial bundle had been placed under an inverted four-legged, shallow stone bowl which probably had served as a grinding stone. The adult was about 3.5 meters away from the infant and rested on the same floor. The remains were in poor condition but appeared to have been slightly flexed, perhaps even partly disarticulated, placed on the left side, head to the east, facing south. Traces of textiles indicated the burial had once been wrapped, but no other grave goods were noted.

On the north end of Aspero an infant and an adult (perhaps two adults) were found buried together in low unfaced terraces. Several stones were found north of the infant's body along with a large gourd container. Like the infant on top of the *huaca*, this infant was less than 2 months old at the time of death. On top of the gourd two ropes coiled around each other, extending 70 centimeters below the infant to the adult bundle burial. The adult was tightly flexed, on the right side, head to the west, facing south. The hands were on the chest and face. Fragments of a fine cotton textile were found near the head. A gourd container, a twined grass basket, and netting were also in the grave. The body and grave goods had been wrapped in two grass mats and tied with ropes. Stones surrounded the adult and were also piled over the head area. A third body was revealed by a looter after excavation when Feldman was away from the site. The remains appeared to be of a male young adult (17–22 years). Remnants of textiles and matting were found in association with this burial, to the side and slightly above the infant.

The other two burials were of an adult male below a plaza wall north of the Huaca de los Idolos and an infant on the west side of the Huaca Alta. The adult was tightly flexed, supine, right hand on the abdomen, left hand near the left shoulder. The head pointed north, and the burial was wrapped in a grass mat and covered with rocks. The skeletal remains revealed evidence of arthritis and dental problems, which may have contributed to the individual's death. The infant was possibly a female who died at about 1 month of age. The body was extended between two thin pieces of wood or bark with three shell artifacts. Cotton textiles appear to have wrapped the burial and bark.

Miscellaneous bone fragments were found elsewhere at Aspero, suggesting that more burials are present and that many have been disturbed through subsequent excavations.

Some of the other artifacts retrieved from Aspero deserve mention. They include about 135 short carved sticks and part of a carved wooden bowl found together in a cache located on the center line of the Huaca de los Sacrificios. More than half of the small (1.5– 8.5 centimeters) sticks were undecorated, while the rest were carved with lines, grooves, bumps, chevrons, or corrugations. The bowl fragment had two frogs carved on it and would have had two more if the complete vessel was symmetrically designed.

Another cache of artifacts was made up of at least thirteen unbaked clay figurines (fig. 47) placed with twined baskets, matting, plant material, and fur, and occupying the entire space below the uppermost floor in Room

2 of the Huaca de los Idolos. All but one of the figures whose posture can be determined are seated. Eleven of the thirteen are females, four of which might be rendered as pregnant. Headdresses and clothing styles are shown, and several figurines are wearing necklaces of the beads described for Bandurria. An isolated figurine hand shows a bead band around the wrist. Two actual red square beads were also found at Aspero.

The site of Río Seco, south of Aspero, is somewhat smaller and later than its northerly neighbor, dating to circa 1790 B.C. (Wendt 1964:253). Wendt (1964) discusses two of the six or more platform mounds at the site, 10 to 15 meters across and 3 meters in height—at least one has rooms on its summit. Occupation of the area is in evidence in the form of houses which are also present at Bandurria; the two sites, along with Aspero and the later occupation of Huaca Prieta, are probably contemporaneous. Forty-two burials (thirteen adults, ten children, nineteen infants) were

47. Figurine found by Robert Feldman at Aspero. Height 16 cm.

found, mostly in small pits on the site margins. The usual pattern of flexed bodies with no clear head orientation was present at Río Seco, and mats and ropes commonly bound bodies. A double infant burial was discovered. Two skulls were found with infant bones covered with cloth and stones.

Cotton textiles, baskets, gourds, and bone and red square stone beads were found in graves, as were two wooden needles. Except for four burials, the interments had at least one stone on top of the burial bundle with between three and six stones for most burials and as many as twenty for others.

Alto Salaverry (Pozorski and Pozorski 1979) is dated roughly to 2500–1800 B.C. It is on the southern edge of the Moche Valley but resembles Asia in its quadrangular room complexes. The rooms are semisubterranean, made of cobbles and boulders set in mud mortar as well as some adobes. A circular subterranean structure is also present at the site and was presumably used for nondomestic purposes, and an uninvestigated cemetery is found near the settlement. Beans, squash, avocados, and cotton were raised; fish and shellfish were the primary protein sources.

Two burials were discovered in the settlement. One was found in the fill of a platform and consisted of the remains of an old man tightly flexed and buried on his back, leaning to the left. The legs were crossed and drawn, and both arms were crossed with hands near the chin. The body was oriented with the head to the south and pelvis to the north. Cotton textiles including a possible cap were found on the body. A mat covered the remains and was tied with a cotton cord.

The other burial found by the Pozorskis was in domestic refuse near a structure in a burial pit which had been dug through refuse to sterile sand, but later accumulations of midden had covered the grave. Two small boulders had been placed on the central area of the burial bundle—a practice seen at a number of sites already discussed. The outer junco mat covered inner layers of twined cotton textiles, including a headpiece as sus-

pected in the other burial. The body was tightly flexed, on the right side, with the head to the south and feet to the north. The legs were parallel, while the arms were crossed and under the chin. The remains were of a young child approximately 10 or 11 years old.

El Paraíso (fig. 48), also sometimes called Chuquitanta, is one of the largest late preceramic sites in coastal Peru. At least seven large stone buildings cover an area of over 50 hectares. Excavations at the site have been limited in extent, however (Engel 1966a; Quilter 1985). Only the relatively small but centrally located building, Unit I, and sections of Units II and IV have been studied in some detail. No elaborate burials like those at Aspero were encountered, but graves were found in the floors and immediately outside of Unit I.

Four of the five burials found at the site were of young infants and adults. The fifth individual was an adult male found next to the north (front) wall of Unit I. All of the burials were flexed and wrapped in cotton textiles in the general mode described for many sites. A carved mammal bone was found with the adult male.

La Galgada (Grieder and Bueno Mendoza 1981), in contrast to coastal sites, is located further up the western slopes of the Andes. This monumental site yielded spectacular burials and therefore deserves mention here. The site was refurbished many times, and burials were placed in former ritual chambers as the site was rebuilt. Between three to five bodies were placed in flexed or extended supine positions in these rooms. They were accompanied with fancy twined textiles, including purselike bags decorated with bird, snake, or geometrical designs somewhat resembling the twined textile decorations at Huaca Prieta. Shell pendants and bone hairpins were common burial goods. Thin, square, centrally pierced beads of turquoiselike stone were found, sometimes serving as inlays for the hairpins. The shape of these beads re-

48. El Paraíso, one of the large late preceramic monumental complexes.

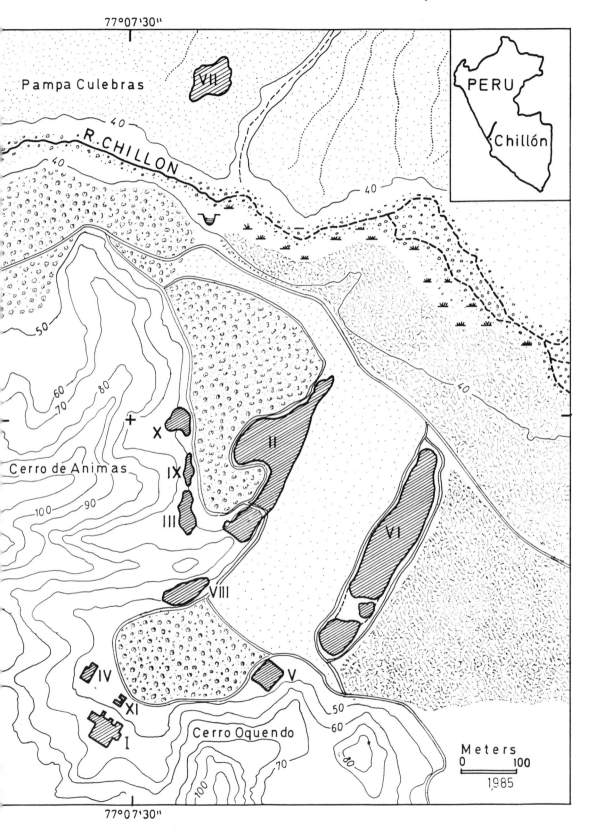

sembles that of those found by Feldman on the infant burial from Huaca de los Sacrificios.

Discussion

The sites discussed above cover a great span of time and a wide area. They are the major Andean preceramic sites with reported burials; while a few may have escaped discussion here, a general pattern can be seen. This common pattern involves burying the dead in a flexed position, wrapped in textiles, and accompanied by a few artifacts—in short, the general mortuary system seen at Paloma. Other common, though not universally detected, practices include the use of red pigment, traces of fire rituals, such as ashes in the grave, and rocks on top of burials.

An important and widespread phenomenon is the special treatment of burials of young infants with emphasis on, presumably, mother-and-infant burials. Double burials occur, as do multiple burials, and special burial facilities for groups of interments are fairly widespread, generally for earlier sites. The apparent emphasis on women and infants is sometimes matched by special treatment of at least some adult males at those sites where the gender of burials has been carefully determined or reported. At Vegas and Paloma certain males are given special mortuary rites.

The orientation of burials generally appears to be unimportant in the preceramic Andes. Of course, it may be that some patterns exist but have not been detected, such as orientation to landmarks or celestial phenomena, but this seems unlikely. When burials are oriented to a cardinal direction, it is generally west, as is the case at Asia, Vegas, and to some degree at Paloma.

Many of these basic patterns of mortuary rites, such as the use of red pigment, may have entered the New World with the first Asian immigrants. Several of the practices—house burning, elaborate postmortem treatment of the corpse, and others—resemble recent practices by Amazonian peoples. At Paloma the down feathers in the head areas of some burials match decorations of eth-

nographically known tropical forest peoples, such as the Sirionó, who glue down on their hair (Holmberg 1969:40–41).

There are two theories which may explain the similarities of early preceramic cultures and tropical forest cultures. Donald Lathrap (1977), elaborating on Spinden (1917), has argued that a "Mother Culture" developed in the northwestern Amazon which then diffused, spreading northward into Central America and Mesoamerica, and west and south into the Andes. An alternate explanation has been voiced by Anthony Ranere (1980), who argues that a Tropical Forest Archaic adaptation was already in existence when northern South America was settled by people who had become accustomed to the similar environment of the Isthmian region. Ranere's discussion focuses primarily on the similarities within the Intermediate Area—southern Ecuador through lower Central America—but the proposal can be extended to include a larger area. Peruvian preceramic societies can then be seen as continuing a tropical forest tradition with local adaptations to specific environments such as the coast where fishing and lomas resources called for new ways of life.

These proposals cannot be adequately assessed at present, given the poor state of knowledge of the earliest inhabitants of Central and South America, including the possibility of several epochs of migration and countermovements. It can be said, however, that a tropical "flavor" is present in the Paloma data which is strong enough to assert itself through the more specific regional adaptations of coastal fishing and lomas exploitation. On the other hand, the distinctive elaborations of burial customs in evidence at the earliest sites of Vegas and northern Chile demonstrate that specific local cultural developments were already in place very early in prehistory. Any common tradition must lie deep in the past or underwent rapid modifications in a relatively short time after societies began to diverge from it. If the lomas were much richer in the past, however, it does not seem unwarranted to suggest that Paloma society and others like it in Peru were part of a continuum of tropical forest–like cultures which were part of a widespread system in western South America.

Perhaps a better way of conceiving this phenomenon is to consider the similarities of these early Peruvian sites in the same way the Archaic Period is viewed in the prehistory of the eastern United States. There is, in both North America and the Andes, a broad similarity of cultures with regional and local differences. The similarities are the result of a combination of a common cultural heritage from earlier societies and broad-based subsistence economies.

The symbolic meanings of many of the mortuary practices are difficult to determine but burial customs do offer insights into the earliest expressions of South American religious life and ideology. Mortuary rites serve to mark the transition from life to death as a rite of passage for the deceased individual. They mark a change in the composition of the social group through the loss of a member and usually emphasize a sense of social solidarity, community, and shared identity. Both of these functions are usually enacted with symbols which express concepts of change and continuity and are frequently voiced in the form of a religious ideology. Such religious concepts employ specific symbols within a general system of beliefs which address fundamental concerns of life, death, and ultimate meaning and reality. Considerable research over many years enables the interpretation of mortuary rites and symbols with appropriate caveats. Burial goods and mortuary rites do not automatically imply a belief in an afterlife, but they do serve to infer ideological concerns.

Several practices found at Paloma and elsewhere suggest an emphasis on fertility and possibly regeneration or even life after death. Red pigment, one of the most ancient and ubiquitous funerary items, has been widely and generally considered to represent blood and therefore to be related to vitality and the life force. Fire, too, also commonly found in Andean preceramic burials, has often been seen as cleanser, purifier, and therefore renewer of life.

Emphasis on infant burials is another common denominator in many of the Andean burials discussed. As noted previously, such attention to the young must contain a symbolic element beyond the circumstances of high infant mortality or infanticide. This symbolism seems fairly clear in the straightforward role of the very young as encapsulating the life force. In many societies the soul or life force of those who die in infancy is believed to be recycled in new babies; as noted above, fetuses were important elements in Inca worship and beliefs concerning fertility and the propagation of society.

Conceptions of the continuity of an individual's spirit or life force do seem to be present in the burial data in two forms. The first consists of grave goods, sometimes in the form of food such as sea mammal bones, and, of course, the use of red pigment. While the inclusion of tools, clothing, and decorative items may be interpreted as a means of disposing of the personal belongings of the deceased, these other items speak of something more than an immediate concern with the burial of a corpse. The shell disks and crescents may also represent a special class of burial goods associated with ideas on events after death, although, as previously stated, they are rather enigmatic items.

The second set of evidence for concepts associated with postmortem activities by the dead is the common placing of stones on graves as seen at Vegas, Chilca I, Piedras Negras, Río Seco, and, to some degree, Paloma. The rocks are often in the grave, directly on top of the burial bundle and covered with fill so they could not have easily served as grave markers. The other function of weights on burials may have been to prevent them from rising as the "living dead" and threatening the living. Concern with the dead coming back to life is an expression of fear of the disruption of the social order, resulting in chaos.

Female burials at Chilca I are interesting in regard to these concepts. The stakes may be a variation of the use of stones. It cannot be determined if they were driven into the bodies after death. The fact that stakes or pegs were found in only five female burials may be an indication that this treatment was reserved for particular individuals and is related to the gender of the burial—that is, that particular female social roles were marked in graves by the use of stakes. Although equal burial treatment is generally seen for males and females at Paloma, women have fewer goods during the late occupation of the site. Perhaps these burials at Chilca also reflect a diminution in the status of women as lomas resources declined and their social role changed. Indeed, the stakes suggest a form of punishment.

Finally, the elaborate postmortem treatment of the dead at Vegas, in northern Chile, and elsewhere indicates that the deceased continued to play a role among the living whether or not they were seen as maintaining a separate, continuing existence. The dead were respected, and their remains were processed as a means of justifying the actions of the living.

So, too, it is likely that group burials represent a concern with social groups. Even if the simultaneous death of a number of individuals occurred, placement in a single grave might indicate an expression of their social links in life. At Vegas and Paloma such social links may have been those of kinship. At Chilca I and Cabezas Largas the ossuaries have not been studied in enough detail, but the latter might contain a special social group since all are adults equipped with the unique items of staves and special textiles. The elaborate mummies of northern Chile suggest that some social ties may have existed beyond the nuclear family, while the possibility of special interment areas for young children at Paloma and Piedras Negras may show social concerns again stretching beyond an emphasis solely on immediate kin. The Asia site, as the latest preceramic site without monumental architecture represented here, has an almost cemeterylike organization; other evidence such as the possible trophy heads suggests

that changes were taking place in the Andes at the time of the site's occupation.

While study of changing social organization in preceramic Peru is still in its infancy, a number of trends are at least suggested, given present information. In general, the earliest sites show emphasis on family units crosscut by larger social structures. Burials tend to be associated with dwellings. Evidence for special social roles and achievements includes B. 159, the fisherman at Paloma, and infant burials which might represent the fertility and renewal of the social group as a whole. These trends continue through the later phase of the preceramic such as at Chilca I, where another ossurary exists, through the later cotton preceramic, such as at Piedras Negras.

Social and mortuary changes appear to have occurred during the time when cotton was in use. The emphasis on fertility continued; infant burials were still commonly placed in elaborate graves. But a transformation took place in which older beliefs and practices were put to use in new social contexts. Instead of representing the continued existence of the social group, child burials were placed on tops of pyramids, such as at Aspero. The development of monumental architecture and social distinctions was thus accompanied by a reinterpretation of mortuary practices. Unfortunately, not enough is known about the nature of the political systems of monumental complexes to suggest the specific social changes which took place, but some social changes toward less egalitarian systems were probably occurring.

Although no elaborate burials matching the richness of kings or potentates have been found for preceramic Peru, some of the later graves do suggest that social differentiation was becoming more pronounced when monumental architecture was erected. The La Galgada tombs hold the remains of people who took a fair amount of wealth with them to the grave, although these may have been personal possessions.

Although only one possible stone axe was found in one grave at Vegas, other relatively fancy items were fairly evenly distributed except that they were more frequent in mass graves. As at Paloma, this suggests that special grave goods and treatment were probably based on personal achievements or circumstances of death. If social inequalities existed, they were probably not supported by laws or customs which restricted social mobility. At Huaca Prieta, although the sample is small, only one individual was buried with imports from Ecuador. But at Río Seco (Wendt 1964) one burial contained all of the stone beads found in graves at the site—nine or ten of the rectangular red stone variety and two cylindrical beads—the rest of the beads in graves were of bone. Society was thus beginning to be organized in terms of new criteria, although it had not yet been transformed into a new order (see Patterson 1983). The rectangular red stone beads are the most easily recognized prestige goods for the time in which these changes took place. Nevertheless, the degree of social ranking is uncertain, and all of the examples cited above could easily represent individuals who achieved their status through personal effort in relatively egalitarian social systems.

The causes of social change are uncertain but of great interest. In searching for the origins of social complexity, scholars are divided as to whether centralized governments developed due to strife or for mutual advantage such as in agriculture or exchange systems. The burial information cannot answer this question completely but does contribute some interesting data. In general, evidence for violence is relatively low. J. Topic (1987) has raised the possibility of early violence at the Ostra Camp Site on the north coast, where piles of sling stones were found surrounding a ridge. But weapons are found relatively early only at Paracas 514 and then much more definitively at the late preceramic site of Asia. It would be well worth the trouble for physical anthropologists to reexamine skeletal evidence for death by trauma to explore this topic. At Paloma there is one case (B. 204) of a cranium buried by itself and apparently baked in ashes. This is slim evidence for trophy heads, and other signs of possible violent death are rare. At present it appears that intercommunal violence was relatively low in the preceramic.

Exchange systems may have been important factors in the development of complexity. The red beads mentioned above are evidence of exchanges in specially made prestige items, probably of relatively rare raw materials. But to what degree the fancy items were traded among high-ranking individuals and whether subsistence goods were the main items exchanged within and between regions remains to be determined (see Quilter and Stocker 1983).

Sharp social distinctions did eventually come to the Andes, although when is somewhat uncertain. The early preceramic burials set the basic format for later practices. The wrapping of the dead in a mat or cloth and the inclusion of grave goods associated with life reached their culmination in the elaborate mummies of the Inca emperors. The dead rulers were treated as living entities in charge of vast estates and servants. For the rulers, at least, the boundary between life and death was abolished. The beginnings of this elaborate system are in evidence in the preceramic as found at Paloma.

Appendix 1. Burial Illustrations and Data

The illustrations of burials presented here have been reworked by Bernardino Ojeda E. from drawings made by members of the field crews during the various excavation seasons at Paloma. The information presented with the drawings is the primary data base for the burials. Therefore, information is listed in cases where no burial drawings are available. Burials for which only age, sex, or level is available are not listed here but may be found in the additional tables in appendix 2.

The gaps in the sequence of numbered burials are due to the discounting of pits numbered in the field which later proved not to contain human remains. Some "burials" are not illustrated because they consisted of fragmentary human remains, sometimes found in contexts other than graves, such as backdirt.

All scales in the drawings represent 10 centimeters. All arrows point north. All grave or pit profiles are oriented along the axis on which they are drawn unless otherwise noted. Absence of scales and north arrows in some drawings is due to unavailability.

KEY TO DATA LISTINGS
Sample Burial List

(1) 1976   (2) B. 118   (3) N 105—E 60
(4) 1 month, (5) male?   (6) V. 4869
(7) H. 101, in, under (Floor 3)   (8) L. 200

(1) **Date of Excavation.** "Pre-1976" indicates that the exact date of excavation is unknown. Many burials so designated were probably excavated during the 1973 CIZA field season.

Dates indicate time of first excavation. Many burials were reexcavated in 1976 or later and are so noted in Comments.

(2) **Burial Number.** The number given to excavated skeletal remains in the field and the main reference for burials in this book. Some of the burials with numbers greater than 100 are individuals excavated in 1973 but not removed from graves. Original field numbers are sometimes suggested.

(3) **Grid Provenience.** A designation in the horizontal control system used at Paloma based on the location of the skull of the burial. The number in the example signifies that the burial was located in grid N(orth) 105—E(ast) 60 based on datum points on the southern and western edges of the site. Decimal numbers refer to locations within each excavation unit (e.g., 105.400 = 400 centimeters from the southeast corner of unit N 105—E 60) and pinpoint the skull of the burial.

(4) **Age of Burial at Death.** The ages of burials were based on a number of different observations of the skeletons. Accuracy is within two years for adults.

(5) **Sex of Burial.** The Palomans generally exhibited strong sexual dimorphism in their skeletons. It is likely that there is a high degree of accuracy in the sex designations of the burials. If field or preliminary studies determined a sex for a burial but it was later decided that gender was indeterminate, I have chosen to retain the sex as first assigned. Such questions of doubt, or general uncertainty,

are indicated by a question mark after the designation.

(6) V. Number. Laboratory numbers of burials, provided for future reference to collections. A "V.—" indicates that the materials were not found in the CIZA laboratories and no check on age, sex, or other information was made on them by University of Missouri personnel.

(7) House Relationship. The house in which a burial was buried or the house closest to a burial is indicated by an "H." and its number. The following shorthand is also used:

in:	inside a house
out:	outside a house
under:	under the level of a floor in a house
on:	on the floor of a house or at the same level as a floor if outside
over:	above the floor level of the house with which it was associated; commonly, in postoccupational fill.

Parenthetical statements such as the one in the example above comment on the general information. For example, Floor 3 is the floor under which B. 118 was found.

(8) Level Designation. The level with which the burial was associated.

The Artifacts and Comments sections supply details concerning the burials and goods. They are sometimes combined when only a few artifacts were present. Details on burials excavated in 1979 were kindly provided by Sharon Brock and Robert Benfer. Some observations seem to differ between 1976 and 1979. The generic term *straw* was used for grave linings in the earlier field season while the more precise term *junco* was used in 1979. Presumably, the later field crews were better able to differentiate the materials. Laboratory ("V.") numbers were not available for these burials and some uncertainty exists as to the relationships of burials to houses. In most cases where a house association is listed, the burial was probably in the house and under the floor.

Pre-1976   B. 3A   ?   28, female   V. 2675
H. 10?   L. 500

Artifacts: Textile tool next to back of the skeleton. Shell bead in thoracic region. A fine textile of junco was in the center of the skeleton.

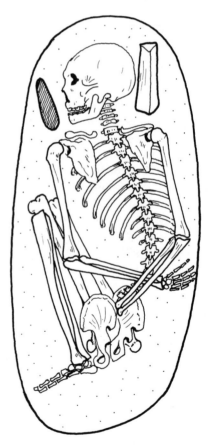

Pre-1976   B. 8   N 95.400–E 115.365
24, male   V. 3244   H. 11, out, above
L. 500

Artifacts: A mano in front of the face. A stone behind the head. Three junco mats, two beads, and a rope also reported by CIZA.

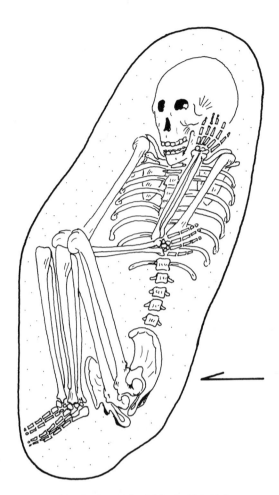

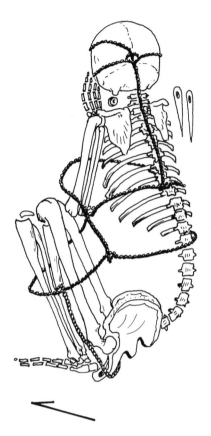

Pre-1976   B. 9   N 95.300—E 115.350
31, female   V. 3246   H. 11, out, above
L. 500

Artifacts (not shown in illustration): Looped cap on skull, hank of strings, braided rope, roll of junco tied with string, two mats, skeleton tied with rope, outer straw wrapping.
Comments: Three ropes were tied around the inner mat covering the skeleton.

Pre-1976   B. 10   N 95.325—E 115.260
34, female   V. 3243   H. 11, in, above
L. 500

Artifacts: Two textile tools next to the right shoulder. A bead in the neck area. A (camelid?) fur skin, wrapping of straw, and a junco mat were all tied over the body with a decorative rope tied to form a square.
Comments: CIZA notes report a necklace of shells of *P. trapezoidales* (barnacles) and another necklace of unspecified shell beads with one stone bead. Red coloring was noted in the soil near the skull.

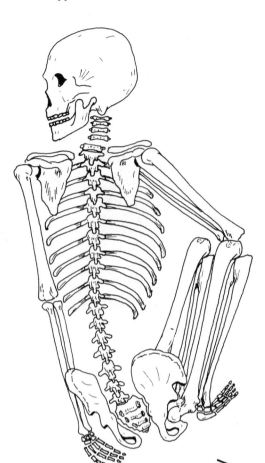

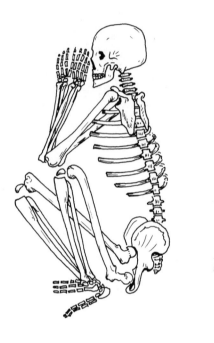

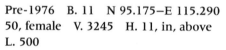

Pre-1976   B. 11   N 95.175−E 115.290
50, female   V. 3245   H. 11, in, above
L. 500

Artifacts: CIZA notes report same general
wrappings as B. 10.

Comments: CIZA notes report that B. 10 and
B. 11 were found in the same grave.

Pre-1976   B. 12   N 95.000−E 115.280
40, female   V. 3284   H. 29, out, above
L. 300?

Artifacts: CIZA notes report a needle or point,
four monovalve mollusk shells (*Babosa* sp.?),
P. trapezoidales shells, a perforated bivalve, an
outer mat of crushed junco stems bound by
a braided rope, a second mat, and (camelid?) fur.

Comments: CIZA notes report remains of di-
gested food in the stomach area.

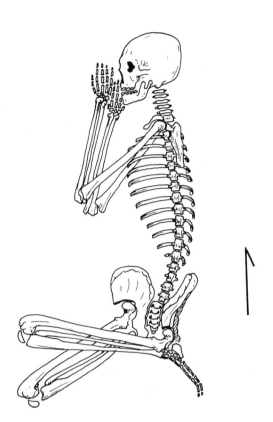

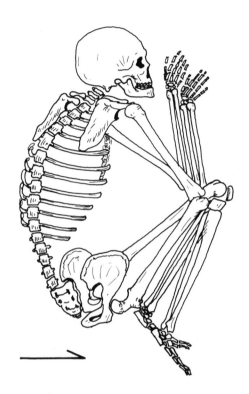

Pre-1976   B. 13   N 95.000–E 115.530
42, male   V. 3256   H. 29, out, above
L. 300?

Artifacts: CIZA notes report two beads and a
mat of crushed junco stems.

Pre-1976   B. 14   N 100.220–E 115.110
27, female   V. 3255   H. 29, in, above
L. 400

Artifacts: CIZA notes report a needle or point,
15 *P. trapezoidales* shells, and a stone tool
(grinding stone?). Notes also state that there
was a wrapping of straw and that the body
was in a looped and knotted fabric and sea
lion fur.

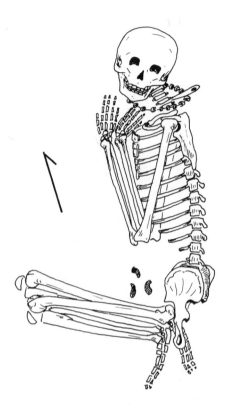

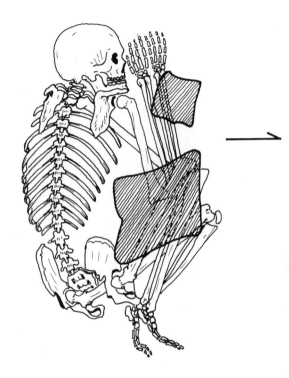

Pre-1976   B. 15   N 105.360–E 115.440
31, male   V. 3289   Data not available
L. 300/400/500?

Artifacts: A textile tool and a necklace of 15
P. trapezoidales shells were in the neck area.
Two mats of crushed junco stems.
Comments: Food remains reported in the
stomach area.

Pre-1976   B. 17   N 100.090–E 115.050
42, female   V. 3286   H. 15, ?, ?
L. 500

Artifacts: A whale vertebra covered part of
the right forearm and a grinding stone covered the right leg and lower right forearm.
Junco mat covered the entire skeleton.

1973   B. 18   N 110.190–E 115.050
42, female   V. 3288   H. 24, in, ?
L. 400?

Comments: 1973 CIZA notes state that the
body was flexed, lying on the left side, the
head pointing west. A small (4 mm. diameter)
stick was reported to have been placed parallel
to a radius, but its exact position is unknown.
A complete *Mytilus* shell was found under the
proximal end of the remaining arm. Fragments of straw and shell were also found in
the pit in 1976 work.

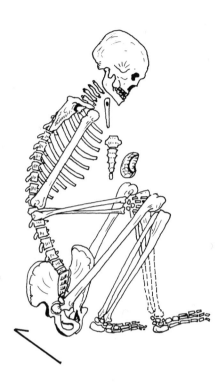

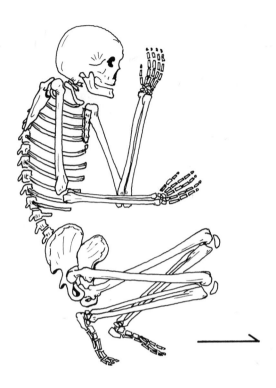

Pre-1976   B. 19   N 110.210—E 115.290
25, male   V. 3348   Data not available
L. 500

Artifacts: A bone textile tool near the neck and
an unidentified shell in front of the chest.
There was a wrapping of straw.

Pre-1976   B. 20   N 110.190—E 115.000
32, female   V. 3283   H. 24, ?, ?
L. 500

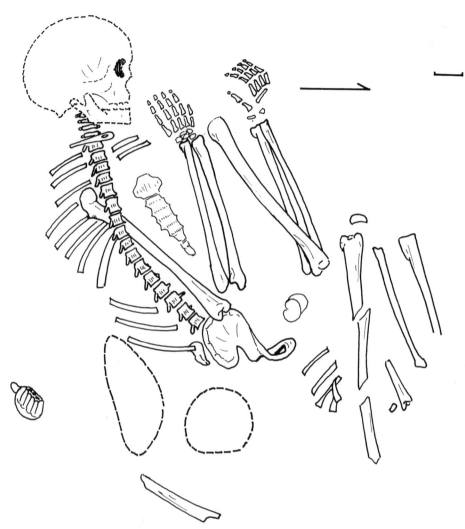

1976 (Reexcavated)   B. 21
N 110.440–E 115.050   Old adult, female?
V. 4881   H. 25, ?, ?   L. 200?

Artifacts: One of two whelk shells previously
reported by CIZA to be in the grave was near
the back of the skeleton. A bone textile tool
was found in the neck area.

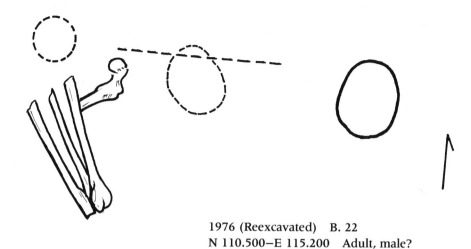

1976 (Reexcavated)   B. 22
N 110.500−E 115.200   Adult, male?
V. 4880   H. 25, ?, ?   L. 200?

Artifacts: Traces of straw pit lining and junco.
Comments: Remains in poor state of preservation. No pit could be defined. The dashed
line in the illustration shows general vertebral
column bone fragments and the enclosed
dashes indicate bone concentrations.

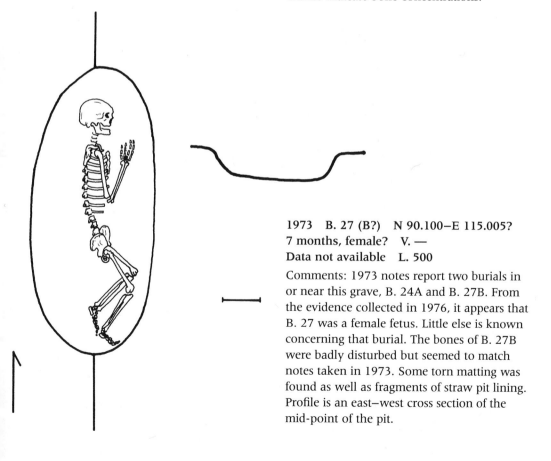

1973   B. 27 (B?)   N 90.100−E 115.005?
7 months, female?   V. —
Data not available   L. 500

Comments: 1973 notes report two burials in
or near this grave, B. 24A and B. 27B. From
the evidence collected in 1976, it appears that
B. 27 was a female fetus. Little else is known
concerning that burial. The bones of B. 27B
were badly disturbed but seemed to match
notes taken in 1973. Some torn matting was
found as well as fragments of straw pit lining.
Profile is an east−west cross section of the
mid-point of the pit.

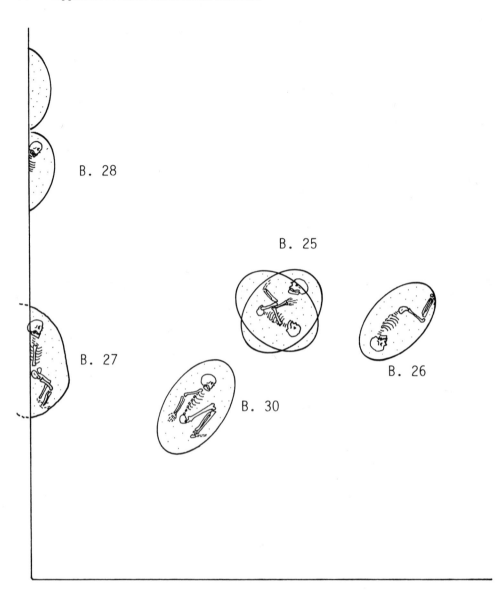

Burials in Unit N 90 - E 115

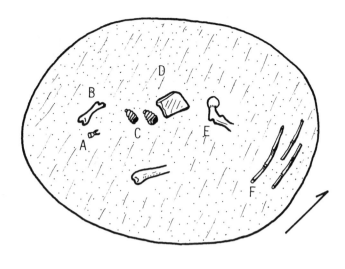

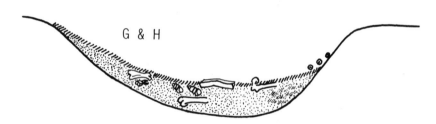

1976 (Reexcavated)   B. 31
N 85.225–E 115.355   43, male
V. 3330   H. 12, out, ?   L. 300

Artifacts: A, human tooth; B, mammal bone; C, lomas snail shells; D, quartzite flake; E, human bone; F, cane fragments; G, straw lining; H, fine gray ash.
Comments: CIZA notes state that the burial was semiflexed, facing west, on the left side with the hands at the face and with a junco mat.

1973–1976   B. 32   N 85.270–E 120.030
40, male   V. 3397   Data not available
L. 300

Comments: This burial was the first uncovered by CIZA crew members in 1973. From re-excavation of the burial in 1976, it was determined that the humeri, pelvis, legs, and feet probably were still in situ. It appears that the body had been buried tightly flexed on the right side with the head pointing west and the hand at the face. The right foot was found under the left foot and both appeared to have been crammed into the grave. A red stain was found on the skull and on some of the bones. A rib and other bones showed signs of burning and a mixture of burnt rocks and midden was found among the skeletal remains. Though much of the burial was destroyed, what remained measured 100 cm. by 50 cm. in its maximum dimensions and was 45 cm. below the ground surface. A straw lining was found in the grave, close to the skeleton. Below the straw were braided ropes which had probably encircled the body, and below the ropes was a junco mat.

1973   B. 33   N 85.110–E 115.500
Child?   V. —   ?, ?, ?   L. 400/500

Comments: No bones were found in this burial in 1976 and none could be located in the CIZA laboratories. The burial pit was difficult to define but appeared to be about 23 cm. deep, 70 cm. long, and about 35 cm. wide. The long axis of the grave was oriented northeast to southwest.

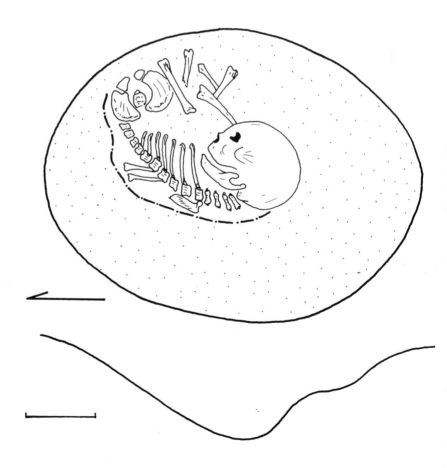

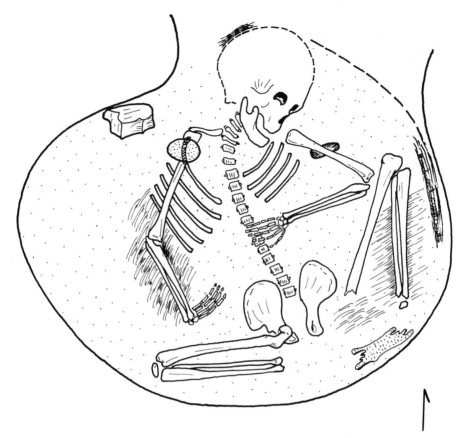

1976   B. 35   N 080.580−E 115.290
7, male?   V. 4891   H. 13, in, under
L. 300?

Artifacts: Red pigment found on *maicillo* on
the skull. Unworked rock on the pit edge near
the right shoulder. A beach pebble with string
in grave fill above the skeleton above the right
shoulder. Red-brown organic matter around
the left humerus; straw pit lining; matted animal fur (?) near the proximal left femur.
Comments: This is a good example of a well-
preserved child burial.

◀

1976 (Reexcavated)   B. 34
N 85.130−E 115.445   5 months, female?
V. 4988   H. 13, out, under   L. 300

Artifacts: A *maicillo* pad was found under the
skeleton with brown soil surrounding bones,
perhaps the remains of disintegrated fabric.
Comments: Bones disturbed by previous work.

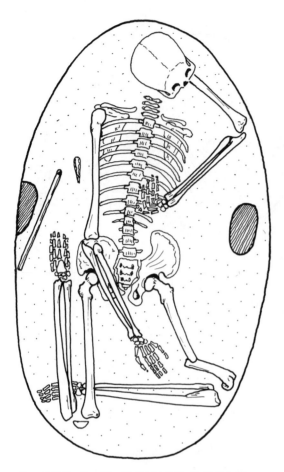

Pre-1976   B. 47   N 75.395 0–E 115.060
23, male   V. 3343   H. 14, in, under
L. 500

Artifacts: Manos to left and right of the skeleton's midsection. Point alongside the right humerus. Wooden pole next to the western mano. Straw pit lining and junco mat also found in the grave.
Comments: CIZA notes state that the burial bundle was rectangular.

1973   B. 48   No data available
Fetus or infant   V. —

All that is known concerning this burial is that it was an infant or fetus buried in a large gourd bowl. B. 48 may be one of the burials now listed as 121A, B, or C.

1973   B. 50   N 70.420–E 115.200
Adult, female?   V. —   H. 15/16, in, ?
L. 300

Artifacts: CIZA notes report a wrapping of straw, a mat of crushed reeds, braided rope in the burial bundle, a fine mat around the body, and a skirt made of reeds in the pelvis area.
Comments: CIZA notes also report that the burial was flexed on the left side, the skull pointed north, and the hands were at the face. Reexcavation in 1976 recovered only bone fragments, two teeth, and traces of straw pit lining.

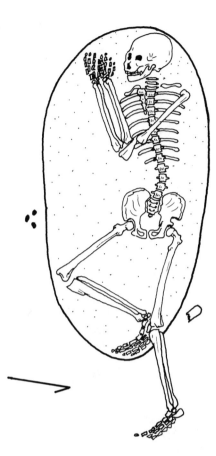

1973   B. 51   N 70.200–E 115.245
25, male   V. 3342   H. 15/16, in, under
L. 500

Artifacts: CIZA notes report an oval preform,
nine *amuletos,* a wrapping of straw, and camelid skin around the body with the fur side
out; a proximal end fragment of a bone pin;
and an unidentified stone artifact on the north
edge of the grave; three house posts on the
south side of the grave.

1973   B. 52   N 70.230–E 115.245
24, female   V. 3344
H. 15/16, in, on or under   L. 500

Artifacts: CIZA notes for 1973 report twenty-
five beads, same wrappings as B. 51, straw,
and the skin of a camelid with the fur side out.
Comments: CIZA notes for 1973 report a half-
flexed burial, the head to the east, the hands at
the face. Reexcavation in 1976 uncovered
many coprolites on the bottom of the pit or
house floor, a straw ring around the edge of
part of the grave, below the straw, a folded
junco mat or two mats, more straw below the
mat(s), and a piece of nonhuman bone, possibly that of a sea mammal, on the edge of the
grave. A portion of the side selvage of the
mat(s) found in the grave was similar to that
on a mat found by Donnan (1964) in House
12 at Chilca I. Wefts were 3 mm. thick with
3.5 wefts per 2.5 cm. Warps were spaced 6 cm.
apart, and the side selvage consisted of an
8 mm. braid of junco.

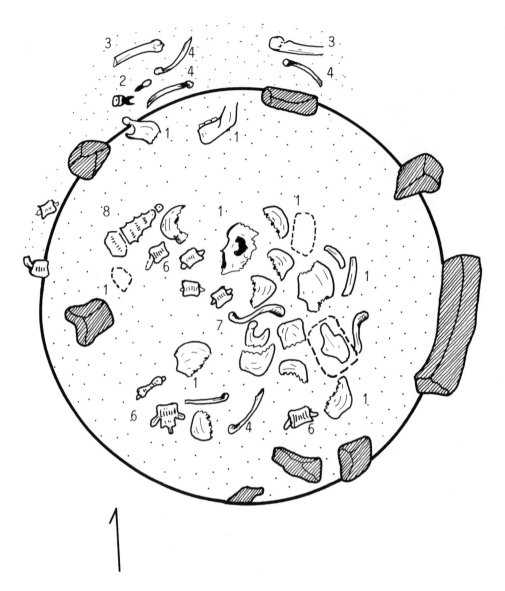

1973   B. 53   N 95.130—E 105.010
1, female?   V. 3897   Data not available
L. 500

Comments: 1, skull; 2, teeth; 3, long bones; 4, ribs; 5, feet or hands; 6, vertebrae; 7, clavicles; 8, sternum. The illustration is based on a field drawing made in 1976 upon reexcavation.

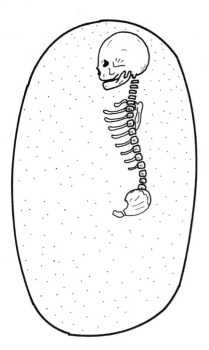

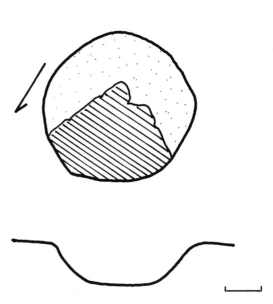

1976   B. 54   N 95.235−E 100.435
Fetus, ?   V. 3922   H. 20, in, under
L. 400/500

Comments: The burial had a covering of straw
and a straw pit lining. The grave was 8 to 10 cm.
deep, cutting into the pampa. It is probable
that the skeleton was flexed.

1973   B. 55   N 65.030−E 115.250
Less than 4 months, ?   V. —
Not near a known house   L. 300

Comments: This burial was reexcavated in
1976. The grave had been dug into the yellow
pampa. Only a few human bones were found,
mixed with tiny tufts of fiber, in the bottom
of the pit. These fibers may be the remains of
a fine twined textile. A large stone sloped
from the north edge of the pit to the center of
the grave. No signs of working or burning
could be seen on the stone, which was left
unexcavated. The drawing shows the stone in
the pit.

1973   B. 56   N 70.430—E 115.290
Fetus, ?   V. —   H. 16, in, under
L. 500

Comments: CIZA notes state that this burial
was slightly flexed with the head to the northwest and was wrapped in straw and covered
with the remains of a mat. 1976 excavations
discovered a pit 70 cm. in length, oriented east
to west; 35 cm. in width, oriented north to
south; and about 17 cm. deep. The pit was
steep-sided, filled with a great amount of ash,
and had a concentration of charcoal and burnt
rock on its floor.

1973   B. 57   N 50.510—E 115.260
Adult, ?   V. —   Between H. 22 and H. 23
L. 300

Comments: CIZA notes describe this burial as an adult with the head to the east. It was extended with the face on the ground. Reexcavation in 1976 supports the CIZA notes. The bones of the right hand were found in the central area of the pit. The fingers pointed westward and brown organic soil around them suggested that the hand had been in the stomach or pelvis area of the burial. Semi-articulated toe bones were found at the south-west end of the grave. The relatively small size of the burial pit (73 cm. × 33 cm.) suggests that the corpse may have been flexed to some degree. The upper edge of the pit was difficult to define due to a salitre layer, so the grave depth cannot be estimated. The burial pit contained traces of straw pit lining and fragments of a junco mat. A braided, three-ply fiber rope 18 mm. thick was found on what would have been the outside of the mat. The body was probably wrapped in the mat and then tied with the rope passing over the pelvic region.

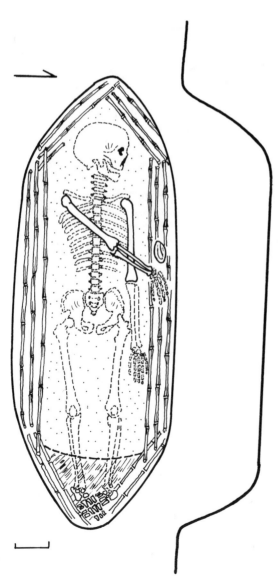

Pre-1976   B. 58   N 60.180−E. 115.420
3, ?   V. 4506   H. 34, in, on
L. 200

Artifacts: Somewhat disintegrated cane or sticks lined the burial pit. A *Mesodesma* shell was in the north wall of the grave near the approximate position of the right hand.
Comments: The right toe bones were found crossing over the left toe bones under a straw pit lining in the eastern end of the grave.

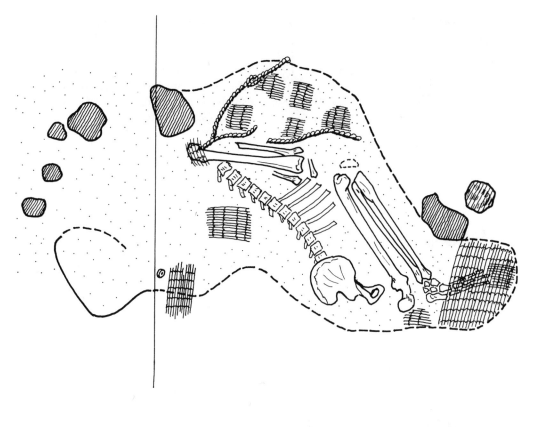

Pre-1976   B. 59   N 50.115—E 115.015
30, female?   V. 4505   H. 19, out, above
L. 300

Artifacts: A bone bead, near the southern edge of the pit next to a mat fragment. Two mats were apparently wrapped around the body, each in a different direction; probably one around the long axis and one around the width of the body. There was a junco rope, and a layer of straw was found over the mats.
Comments: The burial was close to the ground surface and in a poor state of preservation. The head and left leg of the skeleton appeared to be missing. The hatched areas indicate rocks. The other materials are ropes and mat fragments. Note the bead near the vertical line representing the edge of the excavation unit.

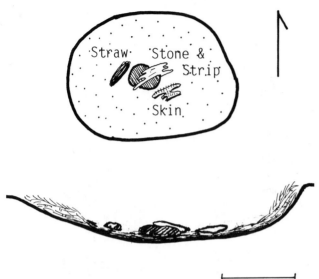

1976   B. 60   N 50.260–E 115.025
Fetus or neonate?   V. —   H. 22, out, over
L. 300 or later

Artifacts: A folded straw packagelike object,
8 × 4 × 1 cm., a strip of cut skin(?), and a
small piece of animal skin were found. Under
the cut skin strip was a small (1.5 cm. diameter) stone resting on top of the pit lining.
Comments: The grave appeared to have been
dug from near the modern ground surface. A
few small pieces of skull and some gray ash
were found near the small stone. The burial
had been covered with midden associated
with Level 200 and a small fire had been built
on it, as evidenced by burnt stones on top of
the grave.

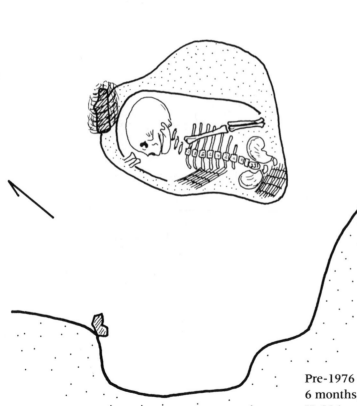

Pre-1976   B. 61   N 95.030–E 105.100
6 months, female?   V. 3989
H. 116, out, under   L. 400

Artifacts: A stone on the edge of the pit. A
straw wrapping, two junco mats, and a cloth
of very fine cordage were also found.

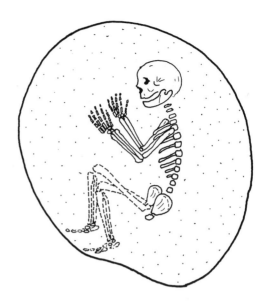

Pre-1976   B. 62   N 95.265–E 105.070
Fetus?, ?   V. —   H. 19, in, under
L. ?

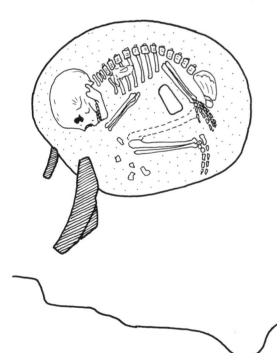

Pre-1976   B. 63   N 95.360–E 105.045
3, female?   V. 3987   H. 14, in, under
L. 400

Artifacts: No pit lining, but the body was
wrapped in very fine fiber.

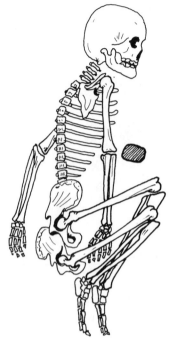

**Pre-1976   B. 64   N 75.380–E 115.450
7, male?   V. 3846   H. 14, in, under
L. 300**

Artifacts: Two mats, ropes, a straw pit lining, and a fine textile were found. A burnt rock is shown in the drawing, in front of the lower chest area. In 1976, the possible grave of this burial was located. It was a circular pit, 73 cm. in diameter and 23 cm. deep. Some straw lining, including the roots of the plant, was the only recovered material besides a few unidentifiable bone fragments.

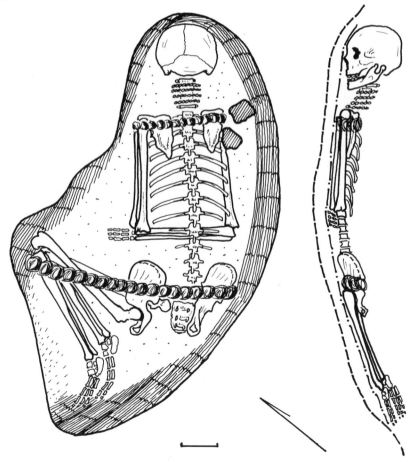

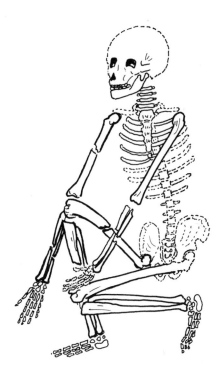

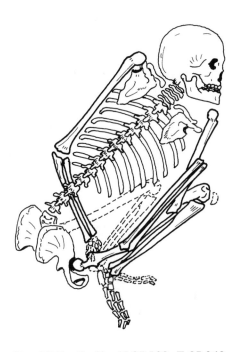

Pre-1976   B. 67   N 95.440–E 100.400
46, female   V. 3988   H. 20, out, above
L. 300

Artifacts (not shown in illustration): Traces of burnt junco, traces of three-strand braided rope near the left tibia and the proximal end of the right humerus. Red and yellow pigment on interior of junco covering the skull, and a straw pit lining. The pit appeared to have been lined with beach sand.

Pre-1976   B. 69   N 95.100–E 95.260
40, female   V. 3803   H. 117, in, under
L. 300

Artifacts: Fine cactus (?) textile around the thorax, a straw pit lining, and straw on the skeleton.

◀

Pre-1976   B. 65   N 50.420–E 115.200
32, female   V. 4341   N. 22, in, above
L. 300

Artifacts: Four ropes were found wrapped around the neck. A braided rope bound the shoulders and scapulae and another bound the pelvis and knees. There was a straw pit lining and two mats, one with possible irregular split twining. A fine textile was noted in

the head and shoulder region. Burnt rocks were on top of the mat near the right shoulder (as indicated in the drawing). A large three-strand braided rope, 2 cm. thick, was found underneath the lowest mat and running parallel to the vertebral column. It is likely that this rope had been tied, connecting the ropes in the shoulder and pelvis areas.

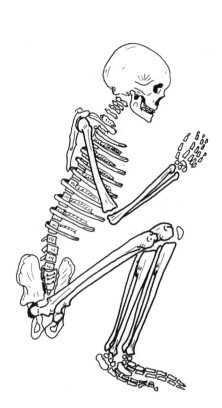

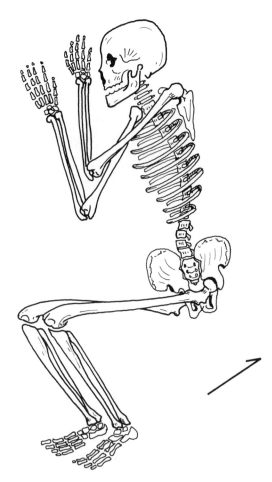

Pre-1976   B. 70   N 95.000−E 95.400
38, male   V. 3809   H. 117, in, under
L. 500

Artifacts: Two junco mats, one of which served
as a pit lining. Possibly, a fine fabric on the
skull.
Comments: A hearth may have been on top
of the grave. Field notes are not clear.

Pre-1976   B. 71   N 95−E 95
40, male   V. —   H. 21, in, under
L. 400

Artifacts: CIZA notes report a "needle," possibly a bone textile tool, and two junco mats.
Comments: The exact location is uncertain and
the remains were never recovered in 1976.

Pre-1976   B. 72   N 50.200−E 115.300
33, male   V. 4887   H. 22, in, on
L. 500

Artifacts: A textile tool and a shell in the
neck area. Two junco mats, one of which was
finely made, covered the skeleton; the other
may have been a cloth rather than a mat.

Pre-1976   B. 75   N 95.575—E 85.570
45, female   V. 5096   H. 26, out, ?
L. 300

Artifacts: The skull was covered with a tightly
looped cap; there were burnt rocks on the
skeleton; a three-strand braided rope was behind and below the left knee and a thicker
braided rope fragment was found on top of
the skeleton (not shown). The pit was lined
with straw. The dark circle represents a post;
the open circles are post holes.

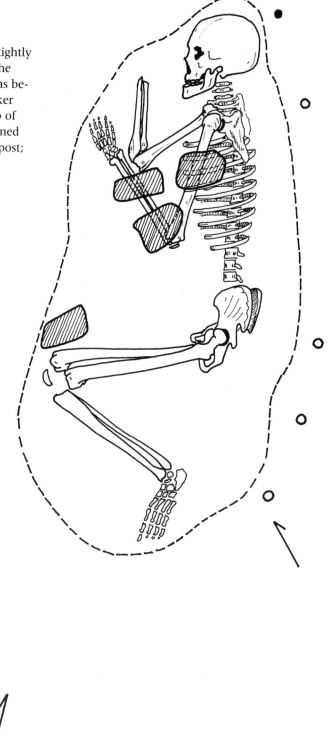

1973 B. 76 N 95.415–E 90.240
Infant, ? V. — H. 26, in, on
L. 400/500

Artifacts: In 1976, fish bones, gourd fragments, and small shell fragments were found in the grave.

1973 B. 77 N 95.390–E 90.215
Infant or fetus, ? V. — H. 26, in, on?
L. 400/500

Comments: No CIZA notes or skeletal materials are available for this burial. The extremely small size of the burial pit suggests that an infant or fetus had been in the grave.

1973 B. 78 N 95.515–E 90.315
Infant or fetus, ? V. — H. 26, in, on?
L. 400/500

Artifacts: In 1976, a few human bone fragments, fish bones, small rocks, and small shell fragments were found in this grave.

1973 B. 79 N 95.470–E 90.295
Infant or fetus, ? V. — H 26, in, on?
L. 400/500

Artifacts: In 1976, fragments of human bones, a piece of an unidentified bone tool, fish bones, and what appeared to be a squash seed were found in this grave.

1973 B. 80 N 95.575–E 90.220
Infant or fetus, ? V. — H. 26, in, on
L. 400/500?

1973 B. 81 N 95.375–E 90.250
Infant or fetus, ? V. — H. 26, in, on
L. 400/500?

1973 B. 82 N 95–E 80
?, ? V. — ?
L. ?

Comments: Except for its former existence and general location, no information is available concerning this burial.

1973 B. 83 N 94.100–E 130.155
35, male V. 5047 ?, in, under
L. 300

Artifacts: A stone projectile point was found in the burial fill and a junco mat and an animal skin (?) were found in the pelvis area of the burial.

Comments: Reexcavation in 1976 found a very poorly preserved skeleton. It appeared that the burial had been placed on the left side in a tight flexion. The grave dimensions were difficult to define, but were approximately 70 × 45 cm. Depth was indeterminate. Hearth stones were found on the edge of the grave and the burial pit was lined with straw.

Another poorly preserved burial, designated as Feature 345, was found on the same level as B. 83, south of it. The pit linings merged, but it was difficult to tell if the two individuals had been buried together or if this was a rare case of prehistoric grave disturbance by a somewhat later burial.

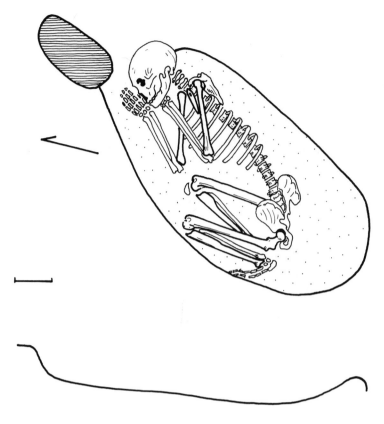

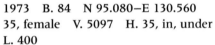

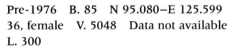

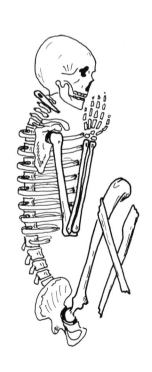

1973   B. 84   N 95.080–E 130.560
35, female   V. 5097   H. 35, in, under
L. 400

Artifacts: A grinding stone on the north edge of the grave, a bone textile tool in the thoracic area, and five limpet shells (not shown), probably once strung as a necklace, also found in the neck area. The pit was lined with straw and junco. In 1979, the condoyle of the left femur, the left patella, and a seismoid of the knee were recovered from this grave.

Pre-1976   B. 85   N 95.080–E 125.599
36, female   V. 5048   Data not available
L. 300

Artifacts: A bone textile tool was found in the throat area. A bead (not shown) was found in the grave fill near the skull. A large *Mytilus* sp. shell (not shown) was found in the bottom of the grave near the skull.

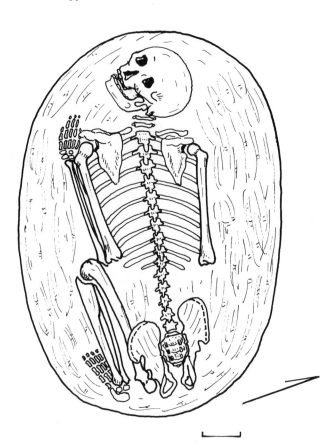

Pre-1976   B. 86   No data available
Adult, male   V. —   No data available
L. ?

Artifacts: A wrapping of straw.
Comments: The information above is from
CIZA notes, which also report that the skull
of the burial was deformed.

Pre-1976   B. 87   N 95.410−E 135.599
16, female   V. 5049   ?, ?, ?
L. 300

Artifacts: Straw pit lining.

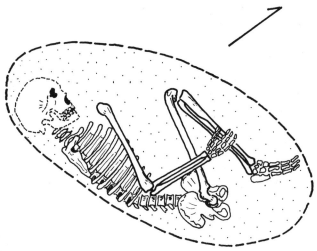

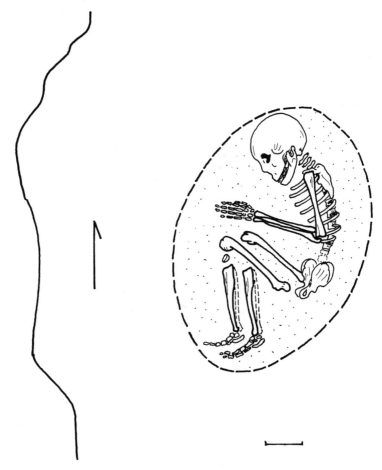

Pre-1976   B. 89   N 75.270–E 90.480
8, male   V. 5105   H. 42, in, under
L. ?

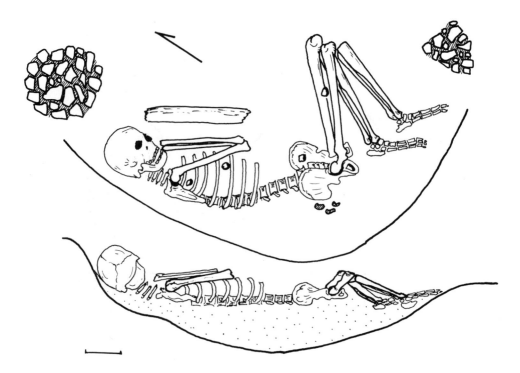

1976   B. 100   N 100–E 60
25, male   V. 3845   H. 100, in, under
L. 200 or later

Artifacts: Gourd fragments (not shown) on
the skull, upper chest, pelvis, and mid-femur.
Fine cordage or fabric (possibly a bag?) found
on the arms, especially the lower left arm,
and red (pigment?) stone in front of the chest
(not shown). Netting or cordage in the lower
pelvic area. Coprolites behind the pelvis. The
burial was wrapped in a junco mat.
Comments: The burial was located inside
House 100 and outside House 101; perhaps
this was a storage area. In addition to the two
hearths depicted in the illustration, a third
concentration of burnt rocks was found on
top of the grave. The three hearths and the
ashy soil surrounding them may have comprised one large fire with rock concentrations
in it.

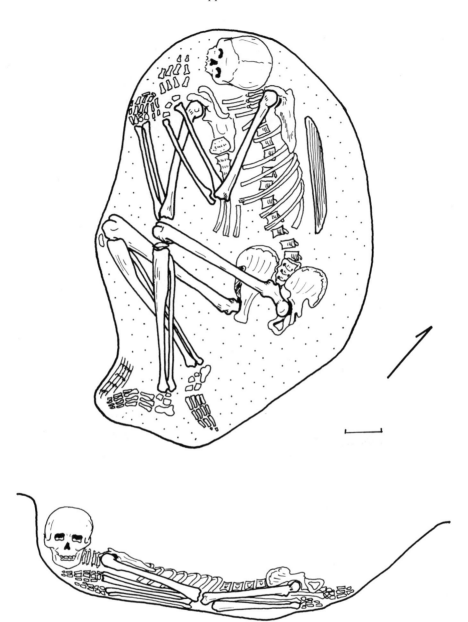

1976   B. 101   N 105–E 60
29, male   V. 4342   H. 101, in, under
L. 200

Artifacts: A junco mat, a basket, cane house poles, a junco roof mat, straw, and midden covered the burial.

Comments: This burial may have been the last to be placed in House 101. The top of the skull was above the level of the house floor, and the rest of the burial was covered with a junco mat and burnt house debris. Around the edge of the grave was a border of sand. Profile runs vertically from head through upper femur to pit edge.

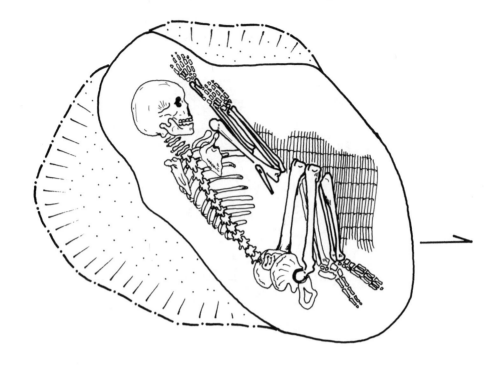

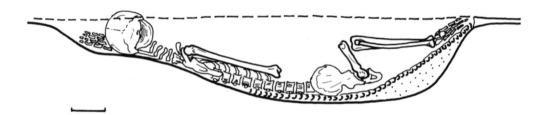

1976   B. 102   N 105.470–E 65.095
39, female   V. 3957
Not near a known house   L. 200

Artifacts: A textile tool was found near the distal end of the right humerus, and a small bead was found on the right mandible; it may have been in the grave fill. There was a straw pit lining.

Comments: The typical junco mat appeared to be absent from this burial. A thin, fine textile may have covered the skeleton. Traces of such material were found on the bones, especially in the area of the feet and the stomach. A shallow depression, different from the grave, was found on the west and south sides of the burial. The stippled area indicates the shallow depression.

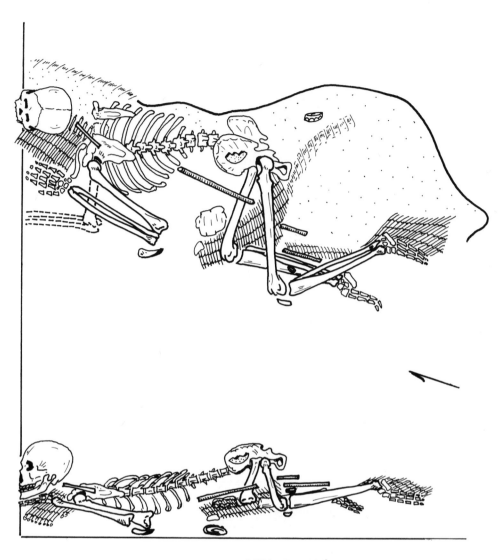

1976   B. 103A & B   N 95–E 70
35, male   V. 3959
In the remains of a destroyed house   L. 200
Artifacts: A mussel shell offering near the left
elbow. A gourd fragment on the pelvis. Chipped
stone southeast of the pelvis, near crushed
matting. A sea mammal bone near the left
knee. Bead on the right tibia. Crushed straw,
probably part of the house, near the legs. Burnt
matting, probably part of the house, near the
face. Burial 103B, an infant or child skull near
the right knee. House poles passing between
the legs. The vertical line represents the edge
of the excavation unit. The horizontal line
under the side view represents the house floor.

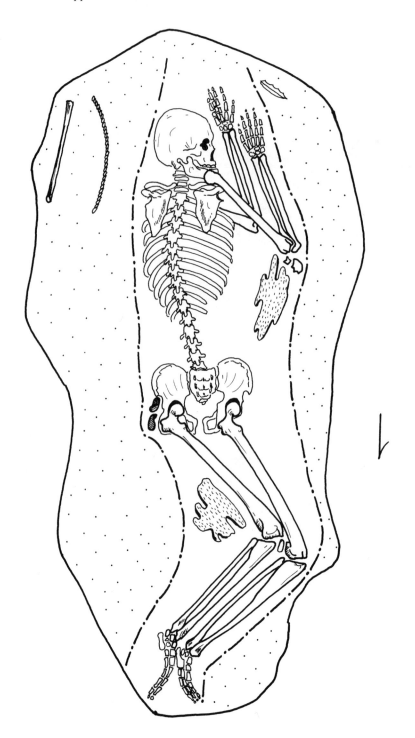

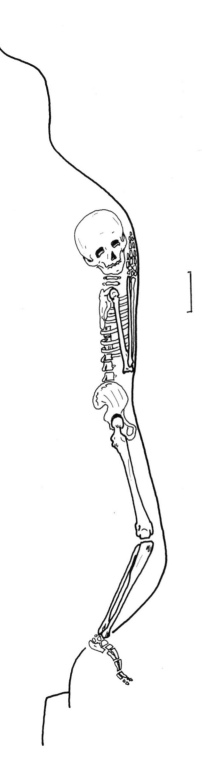

1976   B. 104   N 95–E 70
48, male   V. 3977   In destroyed house
L. 200

Artifacts: A wooden stick near the southeast
edge of the grave. A rope next to the stick;
the outline of a twined junco mat is shown as
a broken line. A chipped stone projectile
point near the hands. Gourd fragments and
animal fur or hair near the elbow and left hip.
Animal hair or fur also near the knee joints.

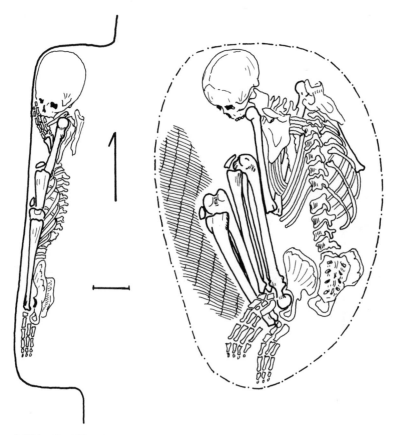

1976   B. 109   N 105–E 60
42, male   V. ?   H. 101, in, under
L. 200

Artifacts: A bone textile tool was in the neck
area. There was a rope on the neck and there
were fragments of a junco mat in the grave.
Comments: The burial was below the floor of
the house and in its center. Layers of junco
matting, straw, and earth were found above
the burial. The grave was underneath the
house floor, upon which rested a floor mat
with a large grinding stone on top.

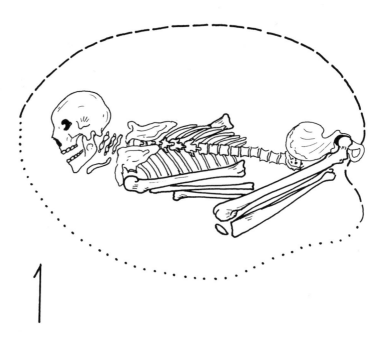

1976   B. 110   N 85.500—E 65.150
20, female   V. 4873
In the hearth/trash dump   L. 300?

Artifacts (not shown in illustration): A small piece of cordage (two-strand, Z-twist) was over the left orbit and neck area. Underneath the pelvis was a piece of braided cordage close to the skeleton. Underneath this cord were strands of junco and a wad (5 × 10 cm.) of the same material was near the inside of the right thigh. Gourd fragments were at the base of the left scapula; one fragment was perfo-rated and had a smooth edge. A small caplike piece of fine junco textile was on the back of the skull, probably held in place by a small string.

Comments: The grave was not lined. The neck appeared to be broken at the base of the cervical vertebrae. The left arm was bent with the hand in front of the chest and the fingers were in a gripping position. The right arm was straight with the hand passing under the pelvis, posterior to the hip (not visible in illustration).

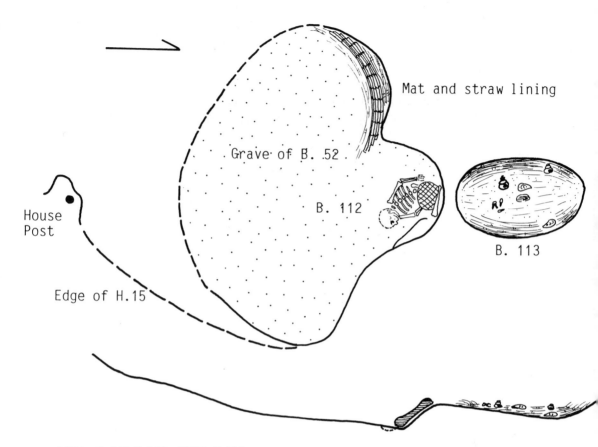

Mat and straw lining

Grave of B. 52

B. 112

B. 113

House Post

Edge of H.15

1976   B. 112 & 113   N 70–E 115
2 months, female   V. ?   H. 15, in, under
L. 500?

Artifacts and Comments: B. 112 was found in the northern edge of the grave of B. 52. It could not be determined whether the grave of B. 112 had been cut into that of B. 52 or whether it was an extension of the same pit. B. 112 was accompanied by a cut shell disk, red pigment, and animal hair or fur. It is uncertain whether B. 113 is a grave or some sort of offering pit, possibly associated with B. 52 or B. 112. B. 113 consisted of an oval straw-lined pit coated with a thin layer of ash. Three cut shell disks and a small *Tegula* sp. shell were found lying on the ash. In addition, there were also an uncertain number of poorly preserved teeth which have been identified as those of a 2-year-old child.

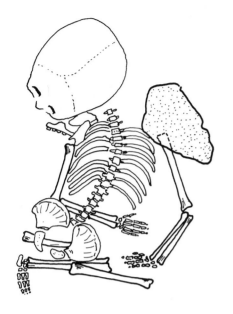

1976   B. 114   N 105—E 60
9 months, ?   V. —   H. 101, in, ?
L. 300

Artifacts: The body was in a mat with the edges folded from the bottom up around it. It may originally have totally enveloped the burial. A stone, possibly worked, was found on the right humerus and was covered by the mat.

Comments: Although first found in 1976, this burial was not removed from its grave until 1979. Both arms and legs were flexed. The body was prone, with the head directed to the southeast. The head was resting on the right side of the face, looking downward and to the east. The left arm crossed underneath the body with the hand palm up. The upper right arm paralleled the body, flexed back up toward it with the palm up. The right leg was in a skewed position.

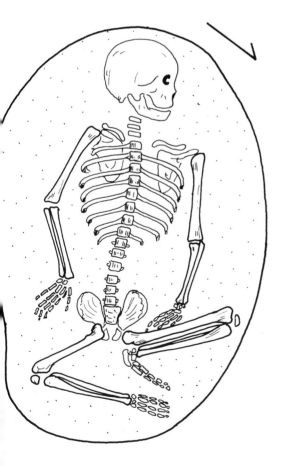

1976   B. 115   N 115—E 75
2 months, female?   V. 4871
H. 14, in, under   L. 400/500

Artifacts (not shown in illustration): Feathers and wool(?) on skull. A thin (5 mm.) string bound the skeleton and the burial was in a twined cradle or carrying strap. The pit was lined with a thin layer of junco.

Comments: There was a large amount of roofing material and straw found above the burial, suggesting that the house it was in had been destroyed, perhaps deliberately, as in House 100/101.

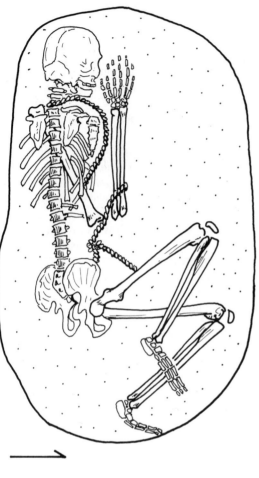

1976   B. 117   N 85−E 65
23, male   V. 4878   H. 103, in, under
L. 300

Artifacts: A three-strand braided rope. The body was completely covered in a poorly preserved junco mat formed into a neat rectangular package. Another mat may have been wrapped around the head and covered with straw. Straw was found elsewhere on top of the larger mat. There was white material on the skull which may have been decomposed animal skin. There were burnt rocks on top of the skull, and a gourd fragment was found on the edge of the pit (not shown). The pit was lined with straw.

Comments: Cracks in the skull suggest that the burnt rocks had been thrown into the grave. Feature 155 is a small pit directly above the skull. Liquid had apparently been poured into the skull area of B. 117, forming a hard salitre.

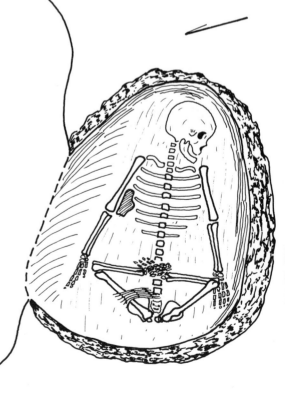

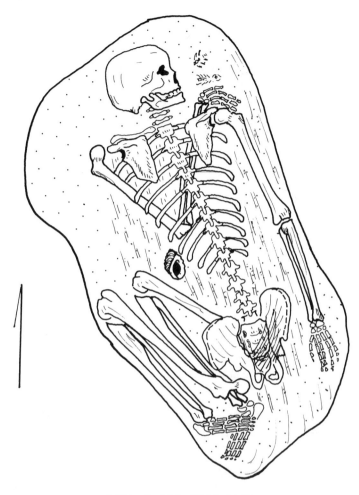

1976   B. 119   N 90–E 60
45, female   V. 4872   No data available
L. 200

Artifacts: Cordage around the sacrum; burnt shell in the stomach area; anchovy bones in front of the face; straw lining the pit and on the pelvis.

Comments: A pillar of salitre was above the skull, suggesting that it was poured into the grave in the same manner as observed in B. 117.

◄

1976   B. 118   N 105–E 60
1 month, male?   V. 4869
H. 101, in, under (Floor 3)   L. 200

Artifacts: Junco fiber under the skeleton; small sticks in the grave; junco matting fragments over the femurs and pelvis, some of which showed signs of burning; a rock under the right rib cage; straw pit lining; a ring of charred sticks and charcoal around the grave. The skeleton also showed signs of burning.

1973   B. 120A & B   N 80–E 115
Old adult, female   V. —   H. 13, in, under
L. 300

Artifacts: Fragments of a junco textile; 1 cm.
thick cordage; 2.5 cm. thick cordage; animal
skin found adhering to the textile; a lomas
shell (probably a snail?), a smooth pebble, a
fragment of a bone textile, all reported by
CIZA.
Comments: Only toe bones, found in the eastern end of the burial pit, were recovered in
1976. They suggested the individual was an
adult. Burial 120B is listed as a 4-month-old
of unknown sex; no additional information is
available concerning it. These burials may
have been given different numbers during the
CIZA excavations.

1973   B. 121A, B, & C
N 80.445–E 115.160   See Comments
V. —   H. 13, in, under   L. 300

Comments: Three sets of skeletal remains have
been found and designated as B. 121. They
consist of a fetus, a 32-year-old, and a child.
Sex designations have not been made. A grave
believed to be associated with B. 121 was located at the site. Its long axis was oriented
north to south, and its dimensions were 60 ×
38 cm. and 20 cm. deep. Gray ash and straw
pit lining were found in the grave. There appeared to have been a high concentration of
shell in the grave fill. One of these burials may
have been CIZA's B. 48.

1973   B. 123   N 85–E 115
1 month, female?   V. 4875
H. 13, in, under   L. 500

Comments: This burial was probably CIZA's
B. 30. The bones may have been disturbed
and possibly even removed from the grave
and then returned to it. The disturbance is
probably not prehistoric. In 1976, the skeleton appeared to have been flexed and placed
on the side with the head to the northeast.
There was a very small amount of straw pit
lining in the grave.

1973   B. 124   N 90–E 115
Fetus, male   V. 4876   H. 28, in, under
L. 400/500

Comments: This burial was probably CIZA's
B. 26. The burial pit appeared to have been
dug from the floor of H. 28 into the underly-
ing pampa. The long axis of the pit ran north
to south and the pit dimensions were 42 ×
36 cm. and 24 cm. deep.

1973   B. 125A & B   N 90–E 115
See Comments   V. 4874   H 28, in, under
L. 400/500

Comments: Only one set of skeletal remains
could be located in the CIZA laboratory. It is
uncertain whether this skeleton is that of
125A or 125B. One of these burials may have
been CIZA's B. 25. Reexcavation in 1976 determined that the pit size was 53 × 25 cm.
and 3 cm. deep. The shallowness of the pit is
probably due to disturbance from the 1973
excavation. CIZA field notes state that there
were two infants in the burial, one on top of
the other. B. 125A was on top of 125B. B.
125A was on the stomach, flexed, with the
right hand near the throat. B. 125B was flexed
on the left side, the head to the west, the
hands possibly near the face. One of the burials had a limpet shell under the skull and the
legs are reported to have been covered with a
fine junco textile. The bones of 125B showed
signs of burning, while those of 125A did not.
A narrow beltlike textile, folded to a width of
4 cm., was also reported to have come from
this grave. A thin layer of straw lined the
burial pit.

1973   B. 126   N 90–E 115
2 months, ?   V. 4896   H. 28, in, under?
L. 500

Comments: This burial was probably CIZA's
B. 28. The burial pit was circular, 40 cm. in
diameter and 15 cm. deep. The bones may
have been disturbed in 1973; they appeared
randomly scattered in the pit upon reexcavation in 1976. The grave contained a large
amount of small fish bones and shell.

1973   B. 127   N 90–E 115
1 month, male?   V. 4897   H. 28, in, under
L. 500

Comments: In 1976, this burial was a shallow pit in the floor of H. 28. The bones had been disturbed, probably in 1973, when it probably was labeled B. 29. Straw pit lining was found during reexcavation. In the southern end of the pit, animal wool was found in the straw pit lining. The pit was oriented north to south. The dimensions were 57 × 27 cm.; original depth unknown.

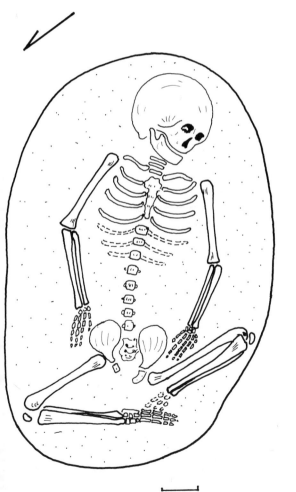

1976   B. 128   N 90–E 115
1, female   V. 4868   H. 28, in, ?
L. 500

Artifacts: Straw pit lining.

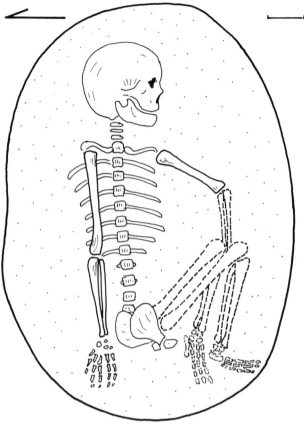

1976   B. 137   N 80–E 115
1 month, male?   V. 5051   H. 13, in, under
L. 300?

Artifacts: A mussel shell offering containing
junco was found near the skull (not shown).
A junco mat, possible fine cloth, red coloring,
a gourd fragment, and a lomas snail shell
were the grave goods (not shown). Many
small mussel shells were found in the burial
fill.

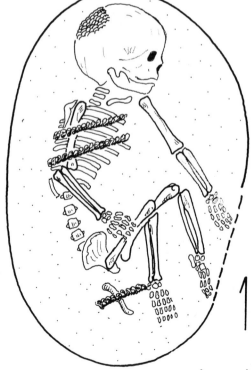

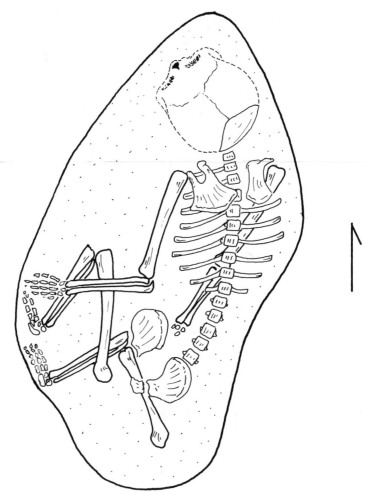

1976   B. 139   N 95–E 120
6 months, ?   V. 5147   H. 115, in, under
L. 300

Artifacts: A *Mytilus* sp. shell offering, fine textile under the feet, a rock in the grave (not shown); no pit lining.

◀

1976   B. 138   N 95–E 120
2, female?   V. 5098   H. 115, in, over
L. 500

Artifacts: Fine looped material on the skull; braided cordage around the shoulders-ribs and below the pelvis; three stone pendants, barnacle beads, and crab claws in the neck area appear to have been part of a necklace (not shown). There may have been an animal skin on the skeleton with fine textile wrapping it. There was straw and junco pit lining.

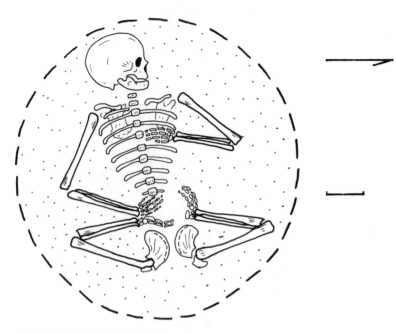

1976   B. 140   N 80–E 115
3 months, female?   V. 5052
H. 13, in, under
L. 400?

Artifacts: A *Mytilus* shell offering containing a
red pigment stone; red coloring on the skeleton; the pit was lined with alternating layers
of straw and animal skin; a calcite cube and
limpet shell beads were found on an animal
skin layer (not shown).

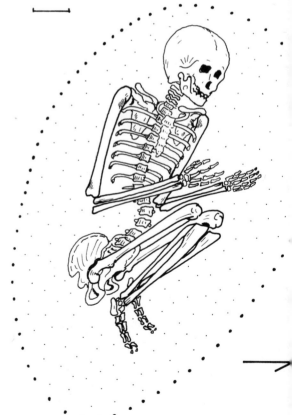

1976   B. 141   N 95–E 135
32, female   V. 5053   H. 35, in, under
L. 400

Artifacts: Junco mat fragments around the pelvis; a straw pit lining.

A   B

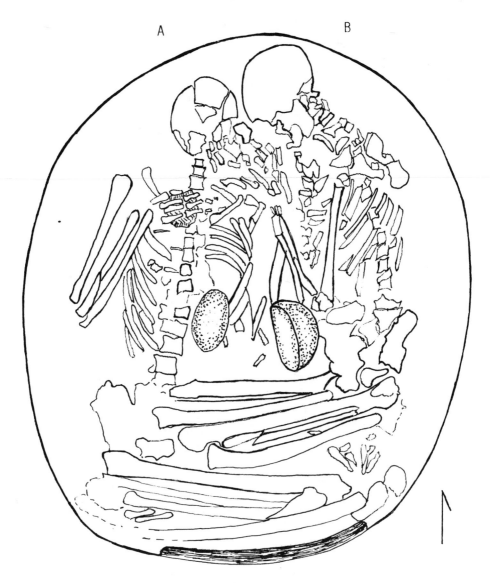

1976   B. 142A & B   N 95–E 135
A 21, male   V. 5099 & 5595
No house associated   B 47, male   L. 300
Artifacts: A hardwood stick was found in the southern end of the grave. A split mano or two manos were found on top of the central part of the burials. 142A had both twisted and braided rope associated and held a flat but sharp-edged rock, probably from nearby hills, in the right hand on the chest. 142B was found with fragments of two twined textiles and some twisted rope with knots. What appeared to be wool was on the top of the skull of B. 142B. A calcite crystal (not shown) was found near the feet of 142A in matting and cactus fruits were on top of the mat near this burial's right shoulder.

Comments: A small, circular, basin-shaped pit, Feature 344, was found on the southeast side of the burial. It was filled with straw and midden, and was about 20 cm. in diameter and 30 cm. deep.

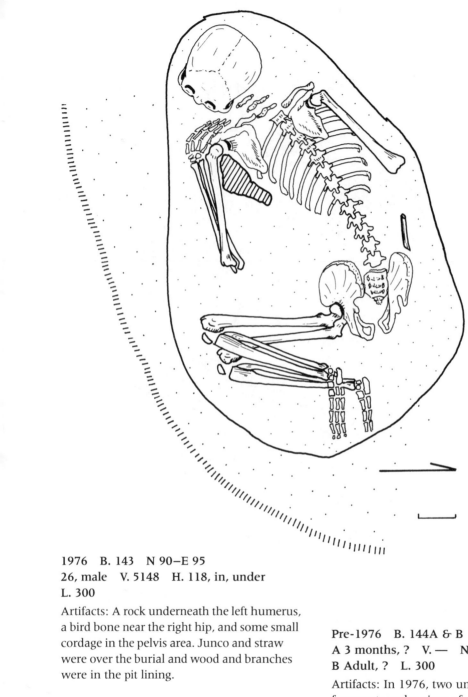

1976   B. 143   N 90–E 95
26, male   V. 5148   H. 118, in, under
L. 300

Artifacts: A rock underneath the left humerus, a bird bone near the right hip, and some small cordage in the pelvis area. Junco and straw were over the burial and wood and branches were in the pit lining.

Pre-1976   B. 144A & B   N 80–E 115
A 3 months, ?   V. —   No data available
B Adult, ?   L. 300

Artifacts: In 1976, two unidentifiable bone fragments and a piece of rope as well as a few fragments of straw pit lining were found in a pit with its long axis north to south, measuring 68 × 59 cm. and 18 cm. deep. The pit had a flat bottom. The original burial number is unknown.

Pre-1976   B. 145A & B   N 80–E 115
A Less than 1   V. —   No data available
B Adult   L. 300

Comments: One small finger bone, a fragment of human long bone, and small amounts of straw pit lining were found in 1976. The pit was oriented with its long axis northwest to southeast and measured 40 × 30 cm. The depth of the pit was 18 cm., and it had a flat bottom. Both burials 144 and 145 may have been labeled as B. 37 in 1973.

Pre-1976   B. 147–B. 150D   See Comments
See Comments   See Comments
See Comments   No known levels

Comments: These burials were found in the backdirt near the south end of the cross trench. Details on sexes and ages may be found in the supplementary tables. Animal fur, string, gourd fragments, straw, a fine mat, and rope were found, possibly associated.

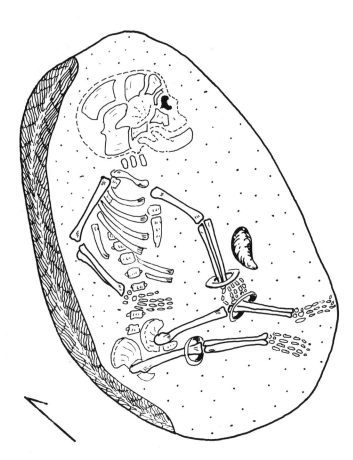

1976   B. 152   N 80–E 115
2 months, female   V. —   H. 13, in, under
L. 400

Artifacts: A mussel shell offering near the lower left arm. A bracelet on the left wrist and two knee bands of cordage. A 4 cm. wide rim of folded junco matting was on the edge of

the grave. The skeleton appeared to rest on a cradlelike object consisting of a mat and wool. There was blue powder on the skull.

Comments: A CIZA workman commented that he had seen similar bracelets and knee bands on infant burials at similar sites.

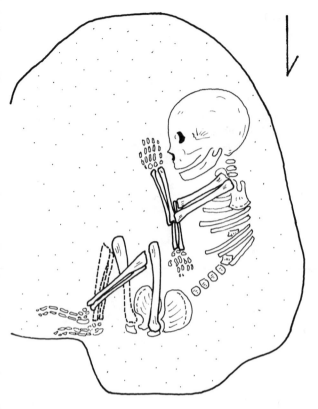

1976   B. 153A & B   N 75—N 90
2 months, male?   V. 5107
H. 42, in, in fill or under floor   L. 300?

Artifacts: Animal skin and a fine fabric were found in the grave of B. 153A. Fine twined textile and a bone bead were found in the grave of B. 153B.

Comments: Skeletal remains only available for 153B. B. 153A was probably also an infant.

1976   B. 158   N 90—E 95
2, male?   V. 5151   H. 117/118, in, under
L. 500?

Artifacts (not shown in illustration): Straw in the center of the grave; a mat folded at the edge below the straw; fine textile covering the skeleton and wrapped on the left humerus. A small *Tegula* sp. shell near the skull; wool below the matting.

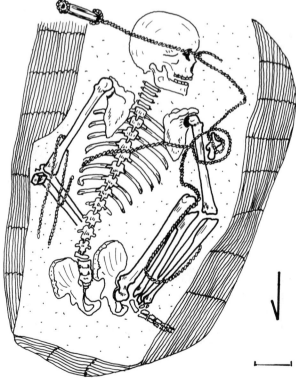

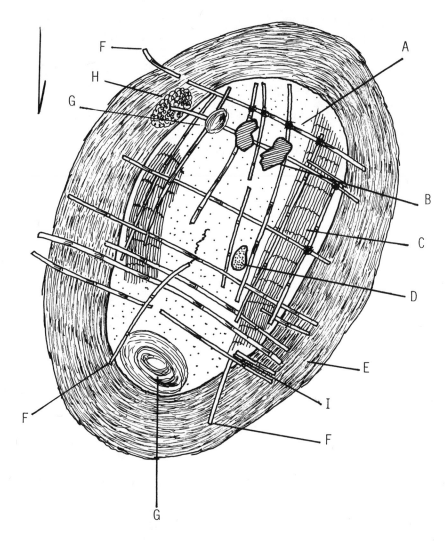

1976   B. 159   N 120–E 65
17, male   V. —   No house associated
L. 300

Artifacts in burial structure: An elaborate cane structure covered the grave. The gridlike framework was tied with unprocessed junco cord. A, cord knots; B, rocks on cane poles; C, coarse junco mat; D, mano; E, straw grave border; F, cane poles with ends implanted in ground; G, bunch of straw; H, camelid(?) wool; I, mussel shell offering with wool and a roll of junco (underneath the mat). Gourd bowl found in the upper fill (not illustrated). Comments on burial structure: The straw border averaged 35 cm. in thickness. The illustration shows the border peeled back from the edge of the pit. Large feathers, hair, and a bead strung on a quill were found in the northwest side of the pit. The skull of the skeleton was just south of B and the pelvis of the skeleton was south of G.

Artifacts with the burial: A sea mammal bone was entangled in rope on top of the upper right arm of the burial. A wedge-shaped rock was underneath the left elbow. One of the ropes had a decorative tassel near the left side of the head of the burial. A junco mat encased these artifacts and the burial itself.

Comments: The entire left leg was missing. There were cut marks on the pelvis. This individual apparently was the victim of a shark attack.

1979 B. 201 N 105–E 60
6, ? V. — H 101, in, under
L. 300

Artifacts: The grave walls were lined with junco but not the floor. Three mussel shells were found, one of which was in the shoulder area and upside down. A shell bead was located near the mandible and two *Pan pan* shells lay along the eastern wall of the grave.
Comments: The burial was flexed, resting on its left side. Both arms were extended down the body. The feet lay on the rim of the burial pit. The head was pointing to the south, facing west. Brock (1979) notes possible prehistoric disturbance in the cranium and feet areas of the human remains.

1979 B. 202 N 100–E 60
6 months, male V. — H. 101, in, under
L. 300

Artifacts: Grass-lined pit and matting apparently were only under the bones, suggesting they had served as an additional form of grave lining. A textile was also found around the skull and may have wrapped it. A gourd and a wooden stick were found in the grave, suggesting to Brock (1979) that they may be the remains of a rattle.
Comments: The burial was tightly flexed, lying on its right side. The head pointed north, facing west. The hands were in the chest area. Red pigment was found along the back of the skeleton and rimmed the mandible.

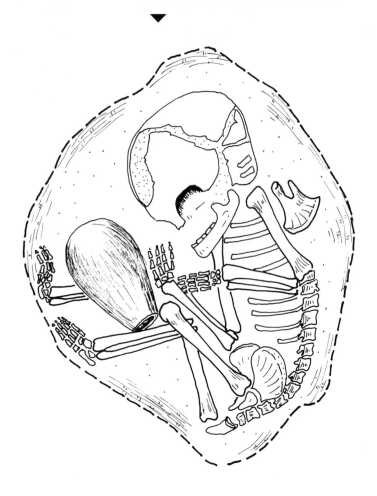

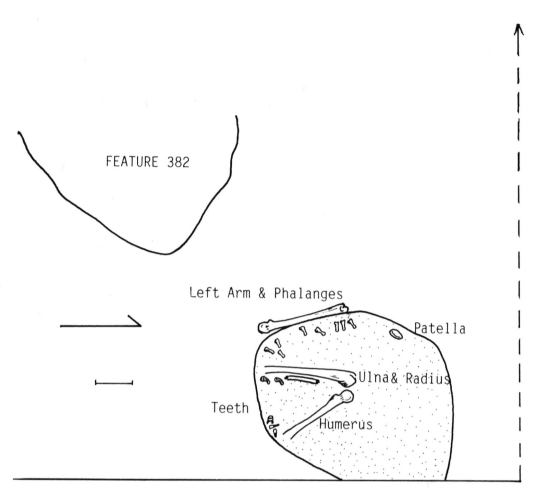

FEATURE 382

Left Arm & Phalanges

Patella

Teeth

Ulna & Radius

Humerus

1979   B. 203   N 95−E 65
Adult, female   V. —   H. 102, out, under
L. 220

Artifacts and Comments: A junco-lined pit held the body, which had been covered by a mat. String occurred near a humerus. Only fragments of this burial were found, but the orientation could be estimated as lying on the left side with the head to the south, facing west. The left leg and arm were probably flexed.

1979   B. 204   N 105–E 65
Adult, male?   V. —   H. 129, ?, ?
L. 230

Comments: This was a single cranium encased in caliche. It was facing north, leaning
slightly to the left. There was no clear evidence of a pit for the skull. Ojeda suggested to
Brock (1979) that the caliche was the result
of a thick layer of ash surrounding the skull.

1979   B. 205   N 95–E 80
Adult and child   V. —   H. 27, ?, ?
L. 400

Comments: It was assumed that this burial
had been disturbed by previous excavations.
Fragments of the foot and long bone of an
adult and scraps of materials from a child
were found amidst charcoal, fish remains, and
rock concentrations, although the human remains were not burnt.

1979   B. 206   N 115–E 65
20–23, male   V. —   Shell concentration
L. 230/300

Artifacts: Matting was found underneath a
foot of the burial and over it. A fine twined
textile was seen in the skull area. The pit was
lined with junco.
Comments: The skeleton was arranged face
down, in the manner of supplication. The
skull pointed north. The left arm was arranged
so that it was slightly flexed under the body
with the hand at the right knee. The right
hand was placed between the legs, over and
beside the left femur.

1979   B. 207   N 105–E 65
Adult, ?   V. —   H. 129, ?, ?
L. 220

Artifacts and Comments: Human remains
consisting of rib fragments and phalanges were
found in gray ashy soil flecked with charcoal.
A large hearth was east of this area, so the
burial may have been disturbed in prehistory.
A rib was burnt. String, netting, and scraps of
matting were found with the bones.

1979   B. 208   N 95–E 80
Adult, ?   V. —   H. 27, ?, ?
L. 400

Comments: A burial probably disturbed during earlier excavations. The pit had been grass-
lined. All human bone was broken and disturbed. The left foot was in the eastern end of
the pit, suggesting that the burial's head was
to the west.

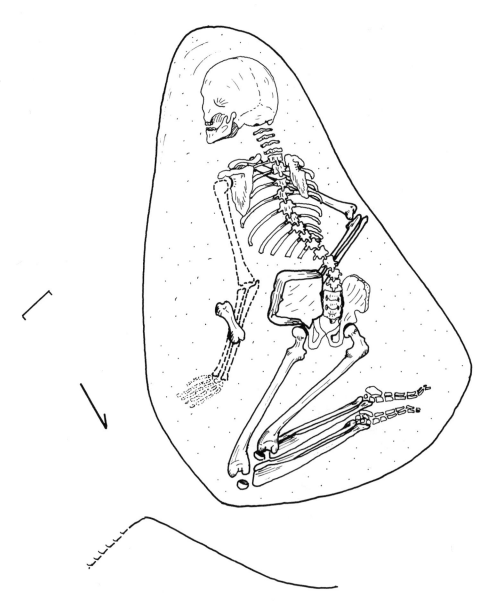

1979   B. 209   N 80–E 125
31–33, female   V. —   H. 135, out?, under
L. 220

Artifacts (not shown in illustration): The pit
was lined with grass and junco covered a mat
which was tied with thin cordage in the lower
leg, upper thigh, and leg areas. A smooth,
round rock was near the pelvis and below the
flexed right arm. Three small unidentified
shell valves were placed around the rock. In
the right hand of the burial was a piece of
worked wood resembling an awl.

Comments: Tightly flexed legs with the arms
flexed at the elbow. The right hand was in the
stomach area and the left hand was placed
flat on the ground as if pushing against it.
Brock (1979) suggests that numerous breaks
in the bones may indicate that the burial was
forced into the grave.

1979   B. 210   N 95−E 130
Old adult, male   V. —   Shell concentration
L. 230?

Comments: There was no clear indication of a
grave, although the general area around the
mat-encased skeleton was lined with junco.
The burial was on the right side with the skull
pointing east, face down. The burial was
flexed with the right arm slightly flexed and
the left arm straight alongside the body. Both
hands were between the flexed legs.

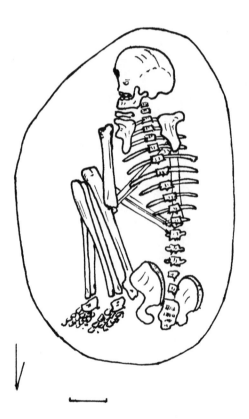

1979   B. 211   N 85−E 120
35−40, female   V. —   H 136, ?, ?
L. 220

Artifacts and Comments: The burial was encased in junco, lying on a mat in an oval
grass-lined pit. The body was on the right
side, the skull to the south. The legs were
tightly flexed. Both arms were also tightly
flexed, with the left hand on the rib cage and
the right on the right knee.

1979   B. 212   N 80−E 125
Adult, male   V. —   H. 135, ?, ?
L. 300

Artifacts and Comments: The grave of B. 209
was superimposed on the eastern wall of this
grave. The body rested on one mat, which
may have encased it. Alternatively, another
mat may have been on top of the body. A fine
net cap was on the skull and junco was over
the body. The individual was flexed on the
left side with the left leg crossed over the right.
The left arm was extended along the body,
while the right was flexed at the elbow, crossing the body with the right hand near the left
shoulder.

1979   B. 213   N 80−E 120
25−30, male   V. —   H. 137 (Ossuary)
L. 220

Artifacts (not shown in illustration) and Comments: Under the body was junco or matting.
Over it were two mats, each of a different
type, as well as a third mat (burnt). A three-
strand braided rope was round the middle of
the skeleton. The bones were partially burnt.
A bone pendant was in the upper chest area of
the skeleton.

1979   B. 214   N 80−E 120
13, male   V. —   H. 137 (Ossuary)
L. 220

Artifacts and Comments: The burial was on
an unburnt mat with a burnt mat on top of it.
Junco was on top of the uppermost mat. The
foot bones were in disarray and were almost
certainly disturbed in prehistory. A burnt
nonhuman vertebral fragment was found in
the pelvic basin.

1979   B. 215   N 80−E 120
35−40, female   V. —   H. 137 (Ossuary)
L. 220

Artifacts and Comments: Disturbance was
noted in this burial, including the feet and
hand bones, some of the phalanges of which
were missing.

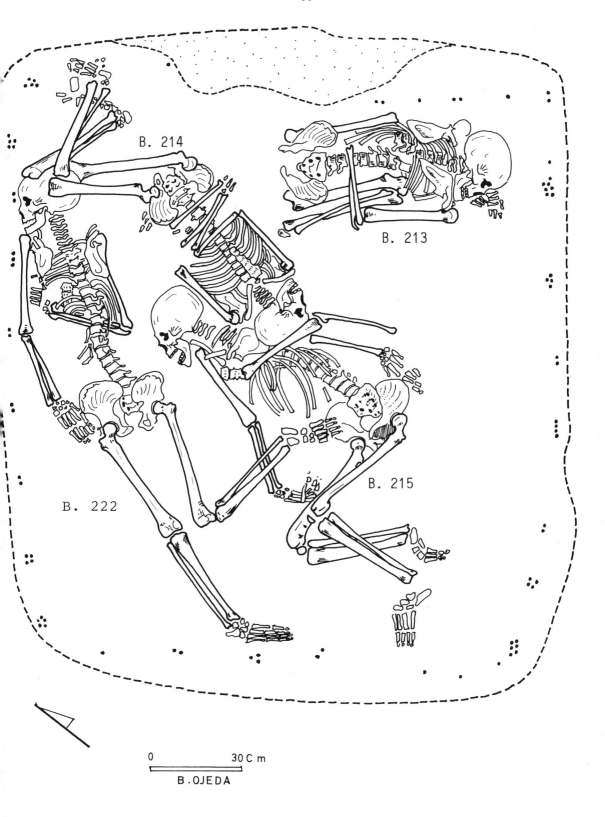

B. 214

B. 213

B. 222

B. 215

0   30 C m

B.OJEDA

1979   B. 216   N 110–E 65
2–3, female   V. —   H. 131, ?, ?
L. 300

Artifacts and Comments: Burial in a deep, mat-lined pit. The map wrapping was tied at mid-body with three strands of cordage. The burial was on the back with the upper body twisted to the right. The skull was pointed to the west. The legs were flexed, resting on the left side. The left leg crossed the right knee. The right arm extended along the body, the left was bent.

1979   B. 217   N 110–E 65
6–12 months, ?   V. —   H. 131, ?, ?
L. 300

Artifacts and Comments: A mat was found on top of the grave. The body was in a camelid hide with the pit packed with junco. The burial was loosely flexed, on its left side, with the head to the southeast. The right foot and left leg protruded from the grave. The left arm was loosely bent at the elbow. The right arm was tightly flexed, with the hand next to the ribs.

1979   B. 218   N 100–E 60
30–35, female   V. —   H. 100, in, under?
L. 230

Artifacts: Five *Pan pan* shells were along the spinal column. A red rock was in the fill above the legs. A large purple mussel valve was placed, concave side down, near the shoulder. There was little pit lining and no burial wrapping.
Comments: The burial was tightly flexed on the left side with the head pointed to the north. The burial was looking directly in the face of the newborn, B. 219. Both arms were flexed, with the right hand next to the right cheek. The left arm was also flexed, with the hand in the upper body area.

1979   B. 219   N 100–E 60
Newborn, ?   V. —   H. 100, in, under?
L. 230

Comments: The burial had been placed on a mat laid near the right wrist of B. 218. Either another mat was over the body or the mat on which it was laid had been wrapped around or over it. It seems likely that the body had been sitting up with the legs flexed underneath and to the left. The arms also appear to have been flexed. The skeleton was looking over the right shoulder at B. 218.

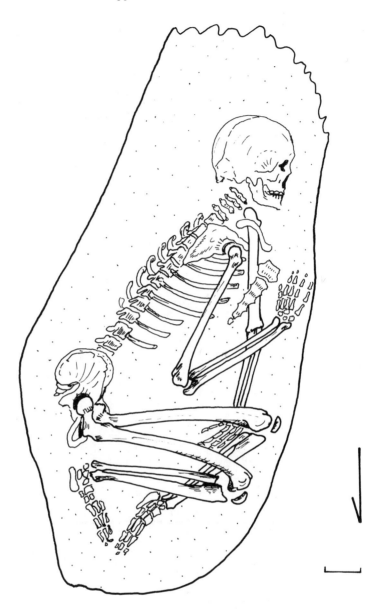

1979   B. 220   N 90–E 95
30–35, male   V. —   H. 120, ?, ?
L. 400

Artifacts: The grave was lined with a fine mat and another was over the burial, over which were mussel shells, stones, and a stick. Artifacts with the skeleton (not shown) included a fine twined cap on the head covered with junco. Nine mussel shells were placed around the body. Gourd fragments were near the pelvis and skull. Two sticks were placed as if radiating from the skull and there were small *pique* shells on the upper mat and in the grave fill.

Comments: The burial was flexed, lying on the left side. The left arm was alongside the body and the right arm was flexed. The face looked west, with the skull oriented to the south-southwest.

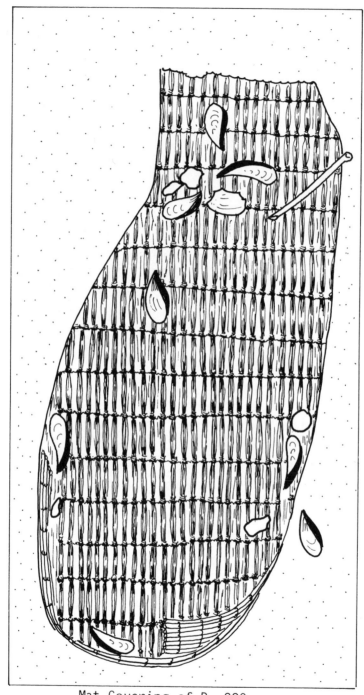

Mat Covering of B. 220

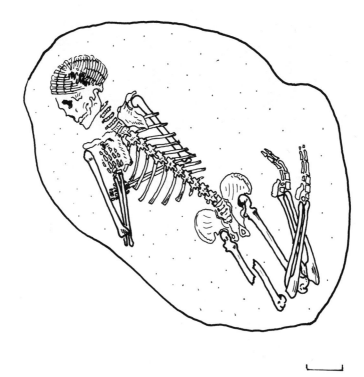

1979   B. 221   N 85–E 105
12–13, ?   V. —   H. 141, in, ?
L. 300

Artifacts and Comments: Burial was in a junco-lined pit with the material also packed around the body. The remains were lying on the stomach, leaning to the right, flexed at the arms and knees. The arms were crossed in front of the chest, with the right hand holding the left forearm. A piece of worked bone was found near the eastern wall of the grave. Junco was stuck to the head.

1979   B. 222   N 80–E 120
30–31, female   V. —   H. 137 (Ossuary)
L. 220

Artifacts: The remains lay on an unburnt mat and were covered by a burnt mat extending from the northern wall of the house-ossuary. Over the pelvis were three fire-cracked rocks which had crushed that part of the skeleton. A worked bone awl was held in the right hand of the burial.

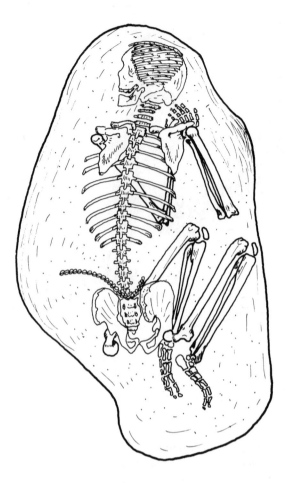

1979   B. 223   N 85–E 115
33, female   V. —   H. 136, ?, ?
L. 230

Artifacts: The body was wrapped in a hide and then placed on a mat in the grave. Another mat was on top of the grave and the entire burial was encased in junco. Two braided ropes were part of the mat and overlay the burial, one across the lower back and the other near the hips. A *Pan pan* shell was near the left scapula and a fragment of possible worked bone was in the northeastern pit wall (not shown).

Comments: The burial was flexed, on the stomach, facing left. The skull was on the right side with the head pointing south. Both the legs and arms were tightly flexed. Both hands rested against the right shoulder.

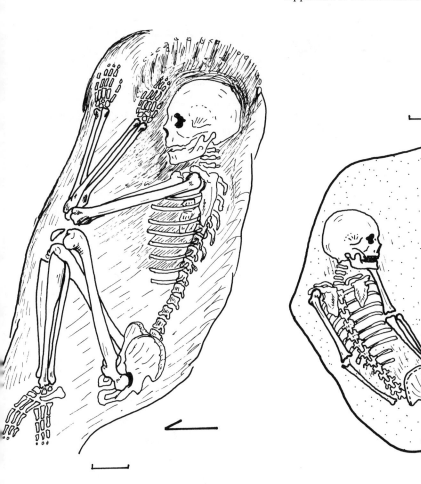

1979   B. 224   N 50−E 120
32−38, female   V. —
No known association   Pampa

Artifacts: The body had been wrapped in a mat secured with rope and packed with junco in the grave. A gourd covered the skull area and a fragment of a passive grinding stone lay on the abdomen (not shown). Two unworked stones were on top of the burial mat. A bone pendant was found in the rib cage.

Comments: The grave was in an area below a shell concentration. The lower legs extended beyond the grave wall. The burial was flexed, on the right side with the head directed to the southeast. Both hands were near the face.

1979   B. 225   N 110−E 65
0−6 months, female   V. —   H. 131, ?, ?
L. 300

Artifacts and Comments: An animal hide had been placed in the grave, covered with a fine mat on which the body rested, then a mat was laid over the burial. The infant had been tightly flexed at the hip and knees, leaning toward the left with the arms behind the body. The head was up, facing east.

1979   B. 226   N 50−E 120
2−4 months, ?   V. —
No known association   Pampa

Artifacts and Comments: The burial was not fully excavated. The infant was in a grass-lined pit.

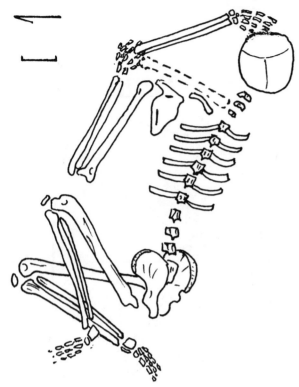

1979   B. 227   N 80–E 120
25–30, female   V. —   ?, in, on
L. 300

Artifacts and Comments: The burial was in a shell concentration above the floor of an unspecified house. An area had been made by placing junco and a mat on top of it in the midden. The grave was covered with shell and rock. The burial was flexed, on the right side with the head to the south, facing east. Both arms were flexed, with the left hand holding the right forearm and the right hand in a loose fist against the face.

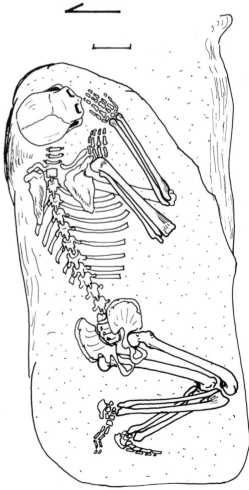

1979   B. 228   N 85–E 120
41, male   V. —   H. 136, in, under
L. 230

Artifacts and Comments: The man had been placed in a junco-lined pit. The burial was flexed on the ventral-left side of the body. The head pointed east-northeast with the face toward the south-southeast. The knees were together with the right leg crossing the left. The arms were flexed underneath the body with the right hand against the right shoulder and the left hand near the mouth. This hand may have held a rock. In the fill above the grave a round stone, a large flat rock (possibly, a *batan*), and a bone needlelike object were found.

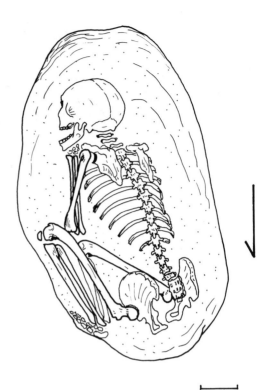

1979   B. 229   N 80−E 100
40−45, female   V. —   H. 142, out, under
L. 300

Artifacts and Comments: The burial was in an irregularly shaped ovoid pit lined with junco. A mat covered the entire body and matting was also found below the burial. It was uncertain whether this represented one or two mats. The burial was tightly flexed on the right side. The feet were on the upper margin of the pit. Both arms were flexed, with the left across the body, fingers close to the face. The right was bent upward with the fingers near the chest. The skull pointed south, facing east. A single broken stone was found in the southern end of the pit near the occipital (not shown).

1979   B. 230   N 90−E 95
0−6 months, ?   V. —   H. 139, ?, ?
L. 500 ?

Comments: The burial was not completely excavated; details on mortuary practices are not available.

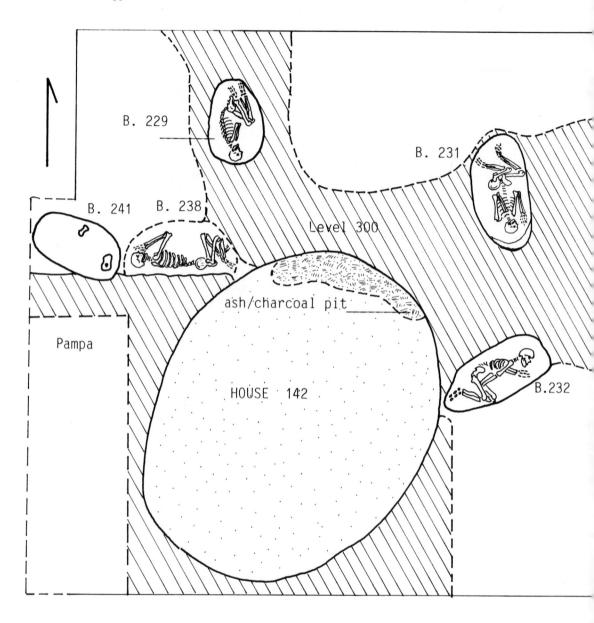

B. 229

B. 231

B. 241

B. 238

Level 300

ash/charcoal pit

Pampa

HOUSE 142

B. 232

1 meter

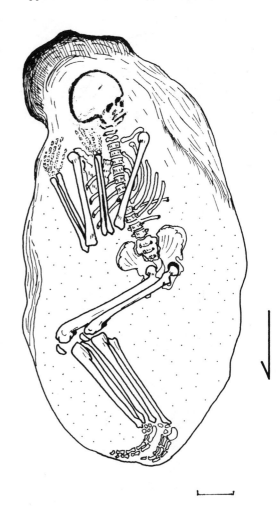

1979   B. 231   N 80−E 100
29, female   V. —   H. 142, out, ?
L. 300

Artifacts: The burial was in a deep junco-lined pit and a junco-packed mat covered the remains, also covering the body itself. A mat which may have been a skull cap was also found on the cranium. A small round stone was on top of the uppermost mat but it is uncertain whether this was part of the fill or a deliberate inclusion with the burial. A stone point fragment and an awl were also found in the grave fill.

Comments: The burial was reclined with the back against the southern wall of the pit with the pelvis on the floor. The body leaned to the right side and both arms and legs were flexed. The feet overlapped and both hands were at the upper body. The right was on the right cheek and the left was against the chest. The skull leaned to the right side with the top of the skull pointing south, facing north-northwest.

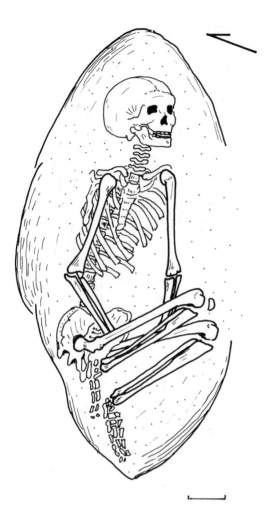

1979   B. 232   N 80–E 100
40–45, male   V. —   No known association
L. 300

Artifacts and Comments: A mat may have
wrapped the body. Junco was found above
the mat and around the body. The human remains were tightly flexed below the waist,
with the body resting on the back to the left
side. The arms extended down the body, with
the hands between the legs.

1979   B. 233   N 90–E 110
2–6 months, ?   V. —   H. 28, in, under
400/500?

Artifacts and Comments: This burial was not
examined in detail. It appeared that a grass-
lined pit held only the skull and mandible of
the infant, but a thorough examination was
not made.

1979   B. 234   N 50–E 125
7, female?   V. —   No known association
L. 230

Artifacts and Comments: This was a shallow
grave with matting around its southern edge
and on the skull of the burial. Junco encased
the skeleton, which was not removed from
the grave. The remains were flexed, lying
on the right side. The hands may have been
around the knees. The skull pointed south,
facing east. Red pigment was noted in the
upper body on the mandible, chest, and arms.

1979   B. 235   N 90–E 110
0–6 months, ?   V. —
No known association   L. 500?

Artifacts and Comments: The burial was not
completely excavated. The remains were in a
junco-lined pit, with an animal hide detected
at least above the body.

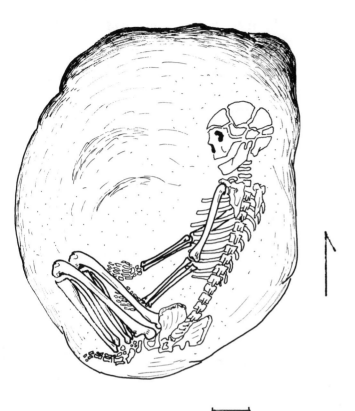

1979   B. 236   N 85–E 125
28–32, female   V. —
No known association   L. 300

Comments: The burial was exposed but not removed from the grave. It was in a junco-lined pit. No textiles were seen. The burial was tightly flexed at the knees on the right side with arms extended. The head pointed north, facing west-southwest. The left hand was near the legs. Burning was evident on the right forearm and ribs.

1979   B. 237   N 75–E 120
35, female   V. —   H. 144, ?, ?
L. 300?

Artifacts: Parts of the body may have been covered with either a mat or loose junco. A "boiling" stone, a large clam shell, and a small "conch shaped" shell (a whelk?) were found among the bones.

Comments: This burial was exposed but not excavated. The burial was flexed and lying on the left side. Arms were flexed, with the right hand at the face and the left hand near the forehead. Part of the left leg and all of the right were missing, presumably due to pre-historic grave disturbance.

1979   B. 239   N 105–E 65
8–12, ?   V. —   H. 129, ?, ?
L. 400

Comments: The burial was not fully excavated; details on position and artifacts are not available.

1979   B. 240   N 100–E 65
Child, ?   V. —   No known association
Pampa

Artifacts and Comments: The burial had been disturbed in prehistory, probably by activities involving features surrounding it. The pit was shallow, with a mat lining and grass over the remains. Body orientation and other information could not be determined.

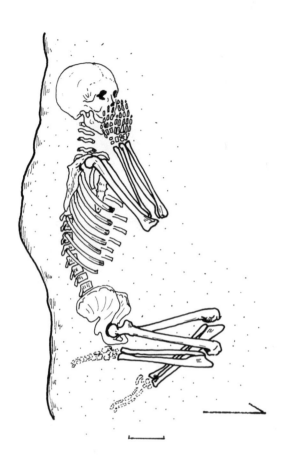

1979   B. 238   N 80–E 100
25, male   V. —   H. 142, out, under
L. 300

Artifacts and Comments: The burial had been placed in a dug-out area rather than a well-defined pit. A mat was over the skull and an obsidian flake was below the ribs. The burial was flexed at the knees and elbows, lying on the left side. Both hands were at the face.

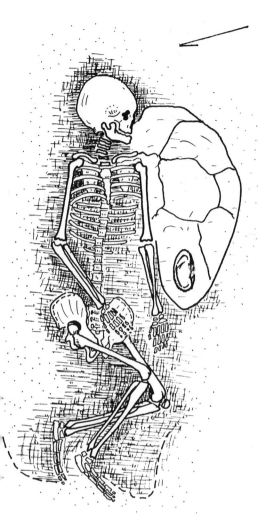

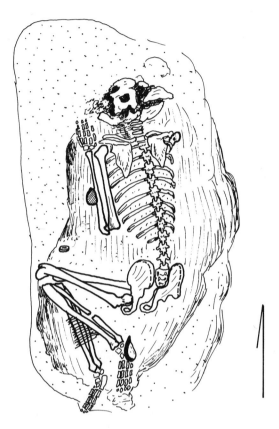

1979   B. 241   N 80–E 100
12, male   V. —   H. 142, out, under
L. 300

Artifacts: A very fine twined textile, possibly of cactus fiber, was below the skull and around the neck. A large gourd with a clam shell on top of it was found near the left forearm.
Comments: The burial was loosely flexed on the left dorsal side. The left arm was extended along the body and the right arm was loosely flexed at the elbow, crossing the body with the hand near the left femur. The head was to the southeast, facing southwest.

1979   B. 242   N 90–E 105
20, female   V. —   H. 141, ?, ?
L. 300

Artifacts and Comments: A smooth round stone was found adjacent to the midsection of the lower left arm. A bead was located above the knees. A mussel shell was placed on the left foot. The right tibia was covered in junco.

1979   B. 243   N 90–E 105
Adult, female   V. —   H. 141, near wall
L. 300

Artifacts and Comments: The burial was not fully excavated. The skull was found covered in junco, but the rest of the skeleton was not exposed.

1979   B. 244   N 80−E 125
2−2.5, ?   V. —   H. 135, ?, ?
Pampa

Artifacts and Comments: The burial was only
partly exposed. Junco grass overlay the grave
and the burial was on a mat. The skull was
wrapped in material made of braids and fine
filaments. The upper torso rested on the stomach with the head on the left side, pointed
to the east, and facing down. The legs were
loosely flexed at the hip and knees, resting on
the right side. The left arm was flexed at the
elbow, with the forearm lying below the body
on the chest, and the right arm was very
slightly flexed and resting between the legs.

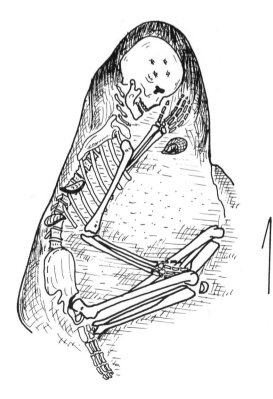

1979   B. 245   N 80−E 120
45+, male   V. —   H. 135, in wall
Pampa

Artifacts and Comments: The grave was dug
into the house wall and lined with junco,
with some over the burial. The burial was not
completely excavated. The burial was on the
left side. The left hand was at the face and the
right hand was near the right knee. The toes
overflowed the pit. The skull was on the left
side with the head pointing north, facing
southeast. Numerous unspecified shell artifacts were found with the burial.

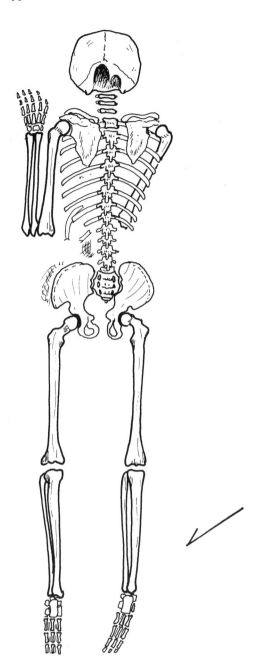

1979   B. 246   N 90−E 105
31−33, male   V. —   H. 141, in, under?
L. 300

Artifacts (not shown in illustration) and Comments: The burial had been placed in the center of the floor of the house in a canoe-shaped pit lined with a mat. Rope was around the body at the scapula, pelvis, knees, and ankles. Stones were concentrated over the legs, and there was a hearth on the grave which had burnt some of the fill. The burial was prone and extended, with the head pointed southeast and the face down and to the south. Both arms were flexed, with the left hand near the neck and the right arm crossing the chest.

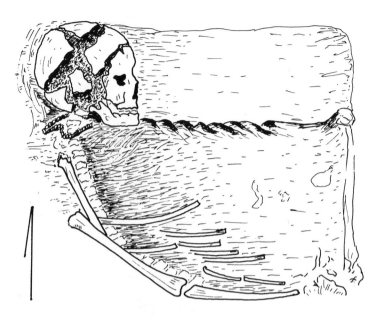

1979   B. 247   N 75−E 120
8, male?   V. —   H. 144, ?, ?
L. 300

Artifacts and Comments: This burial was not completely excavated. It lay in a basin of caliche rather than a fully excavated grave. The feet of this burial protruded into the grave of B. 237; this disturbance may have resulted in the missing materials in that grave. The burial was covered with a mat and bound in several places by rope. It appeared that the burial was tightly flexed at the hip. It was on the left side with the right arm extending along the body. The left arm may also have been extended. The head rested on the left side directed west-northwest and facing north-northeast.

1979   B. 248   N 105−E 110
Adult, male   V. —   H. 140, in, ?
L. 300

Comments: This burial was discovered during excavation of a small test pit in the house. No details concerning mortuary practices could be ascertained.

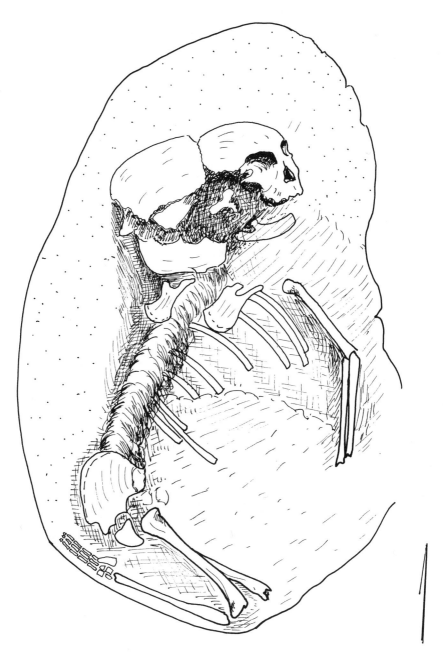

1979   B. 249   N 75−E 120
1.5−2, ?   V. —   H. 144, in, under
L. 300

Artifacts (not shown in illustration) and Comments: The burial was not completely excavated. Only one mat covered or slightly wrapped the body. There were no other fiber materials in the pit. The burial was tightly flexed on the left (?) side. The skull was to the north, facing east. The right arm was away from the body and roughly parallel to it. The left arm was flexed at the elbows, below the body, with the hand just above the right hip. An animal bone was found with the burial and a "boiling" stone was in the grave fill.

1979   B. 250   N 85–E 115
0–6 months, ?   V. —   H. 136, in, under
L. 300

Artifacts and Comments: The burial was not
excavated in detail. The grave was lined with
junco, which was also packed around the
body. The burial was near B. 223, an adult
female.

1979   B. 251   N 85–E 115
Less than 1, ?   V. —   H. 136, in, under
L. 300

Artifacts and Comments: Similar to B. 250.
Not fully excavated. Junco-lined grave and
packed body. It was also near B. 223. A feature was contiguous to B. 251, consisting of a
junco-lined pit containing articulated fish and
crab remains.

Appendix 2. Supplementary Tables

The following conventions are used to standardize the data in the supplementary tables. For detailed information on each burial, consult burial illustrations and data (appendix 1).

Burial Number. Decimal places were substituted for letter designations for burials with the same number. Thus, Burial 27a is listed as 27.1, Burial 27b as 27.2, etc.

Level. Burials for which more than one level designation is listed in the master table, due to uncertainty, are presented with the highest number (lowest level). Burials associated with the Pampa level are listed as 600.

Sex. 1 = males, 2 = females.

Age. .1 = fetuses and newborns.
    .5 = "less than one year of age" (when exact age is indeterminate).
  10.9 = "child" (when exact age is indeterminate).
  13.9 = "juvenile" (when exact age is indeterminate).
  30.9 = "adult" (when exact age is indeterminate).
  40.9 = "old adult" (when exact age is indeterminate).
  Children less than 1 year of age are listed as a decimal percentage: .5 = 6 months, .3 = 3 or 4 months, etc.

All missing data are designated by "0."
When ages have been given in a range (35–40) they have been averaged (e.g., 37) in these tables.
Use of zeros for integers and fractions varies per table on basis of clarity for reading.

TABLE 1. Burials by Burial Number

No.	Level	Sex	Age
1	400	1	31
3.1	500	2	28
3.2	500	2	55
7	500	2	34
8	500	1	24
9	500	2	31
10	500	2	34
11	500	2	50
12	300	2	40
13	300	1	42
14	400	2	27
15	500	1	31
16	500	0	30.9
17	500	2	42
18	400	2	39
19	500	1	25
20	500	2	32
21	200	2	40.9
22	200	1	30.9
25	0	1	05
27.1	500	1	00.3
27.2	500	2	00.6
31	300	1	43
32	300	1	40
33	500	0	10.9
34	300	2	00.4
35	0	0	07
36	300	1	30
37	300	0	11
38	300	0	30.9
39	300	2	47
42	300	2	50

TABLE 1. *continued*

No.	Level	Sex	Age	No.	Level	Sex	Age
44	300	1	11	112	500	2	00.2
47	500	1	23	114	300	0	00.8
50	300	2	30.9	115	500	2	00.2
51	500	1	25	117	300	1	23
52	500	2	24	118	200	1	00.1
53	500	2	01	119	200	2	45
54	500	0	00.1	120.1	300	2	40.9
55	300	0	00.3	120.2	300	0	00.3
56	500	0	00.1	121.1	300	0	00.1
57	300	0	30.9	121.2	300	0	32
58	200	0	03	121.3	300	0	10.9
59	300	2	30	123	500	2	00.1
60	300	0	00.1	124	500	1	00.1
61	400	2	00.5	125	400	2	00.3
63	400	2	03	126	500	0	00.1
64	300	1	07	127	500	1	00.1
65	300	2	32	128	300	2	01
66	400	0	30.9	129	300	0	10
67	300	2	46	130	300	0	01
69	300	2	40	132	300	2	01
70	500	1	38	133	300	0	00.3
71	500	1	33	135	300	1	07
73	300	1	28	136	0	0	30.9
75	300	2	45	137	0	1	00.1
76	500	0	00.5	138	500	2	02
77	500	0	00.5	139	300	0	00.5
78	500	0	00.5	140	0	2	00.3
79	500	0	00.5	141	400	2	32
80	500	0	00.5	142.1	300	1	21
81	500	0	00.5	142.2	300	1	47
82	500	0	00.5	143	300	1	26
83	300	1	35	144.1	300	0	00.3
84	400	2	35	144.2	300	0	30.9
85	300	2	36	145.1	300	0	00.5
86	0	1	30.9	145.2	300	0	30.9
87	300	2	16	147.1	0	0	05
89	0	1	08	147.2	0	0	07
100	200	1	25	147.3	0	0	00.3
101	200	1	29	150.1	0	2	50
102	200	2	39	150.2	0	0	00.8
103.1	200	1	35	150.3	0	0	02
103.2	200	0	10.9	150.4	0	1	48
104	0	1	48	151	0	2	05
108	200	2	00.1	152	400	2	00.1
109	200	1	42	153.1	0	0	00.1
110	0	2	20	153.2	0	1	00.2
				154	0	0	07

TABLE 1. *continued*

No.	Level	Sex	Age	No.	Level	Sex	Age
155	0	1	01	217	300	0	00.8
157	0	0	30.9	218	230	2	33
158	500	1	02	219	230	0	00.1
159	300	1	17	220	400	1	24
160.1	0	2	25	221	300	0	13
160.2	0	0	08	222	220	2	30
161	0	2	50	223	300	1	35
162.1	0	0	30.9	224	600	2	33
162.2	0	0	00.3	225	300	2	00.3
163	0	0	30.9	226	0	0	00.3
164	0	0	30.9	227	300	1	28
165	0	0	30.9	228	230	1	34
166	0	0	10.9	229	300	2	42
167	0	0	30.9	230	0	0	00.1
169.1	0	1	30.9	231	300	2	29
171	300	0	30.9	232	300	1	43
172	0	0	13.9	233	600	0	00.3
173	0	0	00.5	234	230	0	07
178.1	0	1	30.9	235	0	0	05
178.2	0	0	04	236	300	2	30
201	300	0	06	237	300	2	21
202	300	0	00.5	238	300	1	25
203	220	2	30.9	239	0	2	28
204	230	1	30.9	240	600	0	00.1
205	400	1	40.9	241	300	1	12
206	200	2	21	242	300	2	20
207	220	0	30.9	243	300	2	32
208	400	0	30.9	244	600	0	02
209	220	2	32	245	220	1	28
210	200	1	40.9	246	300	1	23
211	220	2	37	247	300	0	05
212	300	2	25	248	300	1	40
213	220	1	27	249	300	0	02
214	220	1	13	250	300	0	00.1
215	220	2	37	251	300	0	01
216	300	0	02.5	252	0	2	24

TABLE 2. Burials by Level

No.	Level	Sex	Age	No.	Level	Sex	Age
086	0	1	30.9	109	200	1	42
089	0	1	08	118	200	1	00.1
160.1	0	2	25	119	200	2	45
161	0	2	50	103.1	200	1	35
160.2	0	0	08	103.2	200	0	10.9
155	0	1	01	108	200	2	00.1
154	0	0	07	210	200	1	40.9
157	0	0	30.9	206	200	2	21
165	0	0	30.9	058	200	0	03
164	0	0	30.9	214	220	1	13
235	0	0	05	213	220	1	27
166	0	0	10.9	203	220	2	30.9
162.2	0	0	00.3	222	220	2	30
162.1	0	0	30.9	211	220	2	37
230	0	0	00.1	215	220	2	37
163	0	0	30.9	245	220	1	28
226	0	0	00.3	207	220	0	30.9
147.2	0	0	07	209	220	2	32
150.1	0	2	50	204	230	1	30.9
147.3	0	0	00.3	218	230	2	33
137	0	1	00.1	228	230	1	34
136	0	0	30.9	234	230	0	07
147.1	0	0	05	219	230	0	00.1
140	0	2	00.3	159	300	1	17
150.3	0	0	02	142.2	300	1	47
150.2	0	0	00.8	143	300	1	26
151	0	2	05	142.1	300	1	21
150.4	0	1	48	139	300	0	00.5
104	0	1	48	135	300	1	07
110	0	2	20	144.1	300	0	00.3
150.1	0	2	40.9	201	300	0	06
167	0	0	30.9	216	300	0	02.5
035	0	0	07	212	300	2	25
025	0	1	05	202	300	0	00.5
239	0	2	28	171	300	0	30.9
252	0	2	24	145.1	300	0	00.5
169.1	0	1	30.9	144.2	300	0	30.9
172	0	0	13.9	217	300	0	00.8
178.2	0	0	04	145.2	300	0	30.9
178.1	0	1	30.9	133	300	0	00.3
173	0	0	00.5	044	300	1	11
021	200	2	40.9	236	300	2	30
022	200	1	30.9	050	300	2	30.9
100	200	1	25	042	300	2	50
101	200	1	29	037	300	0	11
102	200	2	39	038	300	0	30.9
				039	300	2	47

TABLE 2. *continued*

No.	Level	Sex	Age	No.	Level	Sex	Age
059	300	2	30.9	013	300	1	42
064	300	1	07	063	400	2	03
065	300	2	32	061	400	2	00.5
057	300	0	30.9	018	400	2	39
232	300	1	43	208	400	0	30.9
231	300	2	29	220	400	1	24
055	300	0	00.3	066	400	0	30.9
036	300	1	30	001	400	1	31
247	300	0	05	071	400	1	40
246	300	1	23	205	400	1	40.9
243	300	2	32	152	400	2	00.1
248	300	1	40	084	400	2	35
251	300	0	01	014	400	2	27
250	300	0	00.1	141	400	2	32
249	300	0	02	125	400	2	00.3
060	300	0	00.1	019	500	1	25
031	300	1	43	017	500	2	42
032	300	1	40	016	500	0	30.9
034	300	2	00.4	020	500	2	32
237	300	2	21	047	500	1	23
242	300	2	20	027.2	500	2	00.6
241	300	1	12	027.1	500	1	00.3
238	300	1	25	015	500	1	31
121.1	300	0	00.1	007	500	2	34
121.2	300	0	32	003.2	500	2	55
121.3	300	0	10.9	003.1	500	2	28
120.2	300	0	00.3	008	500	1	24
114	300	0	00.8	011	500	2	50
117	300	1	23	010	500	2	34
120.1	300	2	40.9	009	500	2	31
129	300	0	10	051	500	1	25
130	300	0	01	112	500	2	00.2
132	300	2	01	126	500	0	00.1
128	300	2	01	072	500	1	33
225	300	2	00.3	124	500	1	00.1
223	300	1	35	123	500	2	00.1
221	300	0	13	115	500	2	00.2
227	300	1	28	070	500	1	38
229	300	2	42	053	500	2	01
073	300	1	28	138	500	2	02
067	300	2	46	158	500	1	02
069	300	2	40	052	500	2	24
075	300	2	45	056	500	0	00.1
087	300	2	16	127	500	1	00.1
085	300	2	36	054	500	0	00.1
083	300	1	35	033	500	0	10.9
012	300	2	40	076	500	0	00.5

TABLE 2. *continued*

No.	Level	Sex	Age	No.	Level	Sex	Age
077	500	0	00.5	082	500	0	00.5
078	500	0	00.5	240	600	0	00.1
079	500	0	00.5	233	600	0	00.3
080	500	0	00.5	224	600	2	33
081	500	0	00.5	244	600	0	02

TABLE 3. Burials by Sex

No.	Level	Sex	Age	No.	Level	Sex	Age
076	500	0	0.5	164	0	0	30.9
077	500	0	0.5	171	300	0	30.9
078	500	0	0.5	201	300	0	06
079	500	0	0.5	202	300	0	00.5
080	500	0	0.5	178.2	0	0	04
081	500	0	0.5	172	0	0	13.9
082	500	0	0.5	173	0	0	00.5
060	300	0	0.1	162.2	0	0	00.3
153.1	0	0	0.1	147.3	0	0	00.3
130	300	0	01	150.2	0	0	00.8
216	300	0	02.5	147.2	0	0	07
129	300	0	10	145.2	300	0	30.9
126	500	0	00.1	147.1	0	0	05
217	300	0	00.8	150.3	0	0	02
133	300	0	00.3	160.2	0	0	08
144.2	300	0	30.9	162.1	0	0	30.9
145.1	300	0	00.5	207	220	0	30.9
144.1	300	0	00.3	154	0	0	07
136	0	0	30.9	157	0	0	30.9
139	300	0	00.5	058	200	0	03
219	230	0	00.1	247	300	0	05
226	0	0	00.3	235	0	0	05
103.2	200	0	10.9	250	300	0	00.1
230	0	0	00.1	035	0	0	07
233	600	0	00.3	251	300	0	01
208	400	0	30.9	240	600	0	00.1
066	400	0	30.9	056	500	0	00.1
114	300	0	00.8	054	500	0	00.1
121.2	300	0	32	055	300	0	00.3
121.3	300	0	10.9	057	300	0	30.9
121.1	300	0	00.1	244	600	0	02
221	300	0	13	038	300	0	30.9
120.2	300	0	00.3	249	300	0	02
166	0	0	10.9	016	500	0	30.9
167	0	0	30.9	234	230	0	07
165	0	0	30.9	037	300	0	11
163	0	0	30.9	033	500	0	10.9

TABLE 3. *continued*

No.	Level	Sex	Age	No.	Level	Sex	Age
086	0	1	30.9	044	300	1	11
089	0	1	08	135	300	1	07
032	300	1	40	238	300	1	25
142.1	300	1	21	008	500	1	24
143	300	1	26	051	500	1	25
142.2	300	1	47	117	300	1	23
153.2	0	1	00.2	223	300	1	35
213	220	1	27	109	200	1	42
036	300	1	30	178.1	0	1	30.9
214	220	1	13	220	400	1	24
169.1	0	1	30.9	118	200	1	00.1
155	0	1	01	061	400	2	00.5
019	500	1	25	050	300	2	30.9
013	300	1	42	059	300	2	30.9
245	220	1	28	252	0	2	24
015	500	1	31	236	300	2	30
158	500	1	002	222	220	2	30
159	300	1	17	237	300	2	21
246	300	1	23	218	230	2	33
025	0	1	05	229	300	2	42
248	300	1	40	231	300	2	29
031	300	1	43	224	600	2	33
027.1	500	1	00.3	225	300	2	00.3
150.4	0	1	48	242	300	2	20
210	200	1	40.9	209	220	2	32
022	200	1	30.9	206	200	2	21
241	300	1	12	243	300	2	32
137	0	1	00.1	239	0	2	28
227	300	1	28	215	220	2	37
228	230	1	34	211	220	2	37
205	400	1	40.9	212	300	2	25
100	200	1	25	042	300	2	50
104	0	1	48	052	500	2	24
103.1	200	1	35	039	300	2	47
101	200	1	29	27.2	500	2	00.6
083	300	1	35	034	300	2	00.4
204	230	1	30.9	053	500	2	01
232	300	1	43	069	300	2	40
064	300	1	07	075	300	2	45
070	500	1	38	067	300	2	46
073	300	1	28	063	400	2	03
072	500	1	33	065	300	2	32
071	400	1	40	021	400	2	40.9
001	400	1	31	009	500	2	31
047	500	1	23	010	500	2	34
127	500	1	00.1	007	500	2	34
124	500	1	00.1	003.1	500	2	28
				003.2	500	2	55

TABLE 3. *continued*

No.	Level	Sex	Age	No.	Level	Sex	Age
011	500	2	50	160.1	0	2	25
018	400	2	39	151	0	2	05
020	500	2	32	152	400	2	00.1
017	500	2	42	128	300	2	01
012	300	2	40	108	200	2	00.1
014	400	2	27	110	0	2	20
084	400	2	35	102	200	2	39
141	400	2	32	085	300	2	36
150.1	0	2	50	087	300	2	16
140	0	2	00.3	112	500	2	00.2
132	300	2	01	123	500	2	00.1
138	500	2	02	125	400	2	00.3
150.1	0	2	40.9	120.1	300	2	40.9
161	0	2	50	115	500	2	00.2
203	220	2	30.9	119	200	2	45

TABLE 4. Burials by Age

No.	Level	Sex	Age	No.	Level	Sex	Age
060	300	0	0.1	027.1	500	1	0.3
056	500	0	0.1	226	0	0	0.3
054	500	0	0.1	162.2	0	0	0.3
123	500	2	0.1	225	300	2	0.3
124	500	1	0.1	147.3	0	0	0.3
153.1	0	1	0.1	034	300	2	0.4
127	500	1	0.1	076	500	0	0.5
137	0	1	0.1	077	500	0	0.5
152	400	2	0.1	078	500	0	0.5
126	500	0	0.1	079	500	0	0.5
219	230	0	0.1	080	500	0	0.5
240	600	0	0.1	081	500	0	0.5
118	200	1	0.1	082	500	0	0.5
108	200	2	0.1	061	400	2	0.5
250	300	0	0.1	202	300	0	0.5
230	0	0	0.1	145.1	300	0	0.5
121.1	300	0	0.1	173	0	0	0.5
112	500	2	0.2	139	300	0	0.5
115	500	2	0.2	27.2	500	2	0.6
153.2	0	1	0.2	217	300	0	0.8
055	300	0	0.3	114	300	0	0.8
140	0	2	0.3	150.2	0	0	0.8
144.1	300	0	0.3	251	300	0	1
125	400	2	0.3	128	300	2	1
120.2	300	0	0.3	130	300	0	1
133	300	0	0.3	132	300	2	1
233	600	0	0.3	155	0	1	1

TABLE 4. *continued*

No.	Level	Sex	Age	No.	Level	Sex	Age
053	500	2	1	008	500	1	24
249	300	0	2	019	500	1	25
138	500	2	2	212	300	2	25
158	500	1	2	051	500	1	25
150.3	0	0	2	100	200	1	25
244	600	0	2	238	300	1	25
216	300	0	2.5	160.1	0	2	25
058	200	0	3	143	300	1	26
063	400	2	3	213	220	1	27
178.2	0	0	4	014	400	2	27
025	0	1	5	239	0	2	28
147.1	0	0	5	245	220	1	28
151	0	2	5	03.1	500	2	28
235	0	0	5	227	300	1	28
247	300	0	5	073	300	1	28
201	300	0	6	231	300	2	29
154	0	0	7	101	200	1	29
147.2	0	0	7	222	220	2	30
064	300	1	7	036	300	1	30
234	230	0	7	236	300	2	30
035	0	0	7	086	0	1	30.9
135	300	1	7	167	0	0	30.9
160.2	0	0	8	162.1	0	0	30.9
089	0	1	8	165	0	0	30.9
129	300	0	10	163	0	0	30.9
121.3	300	0	10.9	164	0	0	30.9
103.2	200	0	10.9	178.1	0	1	30.9
166	0	0	10.9	208	400	0	30.9
033	500	0	10.9	207	220	0	30.9
044	300	1	11	204	230	1	30.9
037	300	0	11	169.1	0	1	30.9
241	300	1	12	171	300	0	30.9
221	300	0	13	016	500	0	30.9
214	220	1	13	022	200	1	30.9
172	0	0	13.9	050	300	2	30.9
087	300	2	16	145.2	300	0	30.9
159	300	1	17	038	300	0	30.9
242	300	2	20	136	0	0	30.9
110	0	2	20	066	400	0	30.9
142.1	300	1	21	157	0	0	30.9
206	200	2	21	057	300	0	30.9
237	300	2	21	144.2	300	0	30.9
047	500	1	23	059	300	2	30.9
117	300	1	23	203	220	2	30.9
246	300	1	23	015	500	1	31
220	400	1	24	001	400	1	31
252	0	2	24	009	500	2	31
052	500	2	24				

TABLE 4. *continued*

No.	Level	Sex	Age	No.	Level	Sex	Age
065	300	2	32	032	300	1	40
020	500	2	32	069	300	2	40
209	220	2	32	120.1	300	2	40.9
243	300	2	32	021	400	2	40.9
121.2	300	0	32	150.1	0	2	40.9
141	400	2	32	205	400	1	40.9
218	230	2	33	210	200	1	40.9
224	600	2	33	109	200	1	42
072	500	1	33	017	500	2	42
010	500	2	34	229	300	2	42
007	500	2	34	013	300	1	42
228	230	1	34	031	300	1	43
103.1	200	1	35	232	300	1	43
223	300	1	35	119	200	2	45
083	300	1	35	075	300	2	45
084	400	2	35	067	300	2	46
085	300	2	36	142.2	300	1	47
211	220	2	37	039	300	2	47
215	220	2	37	104	0	1	48
070	500	1	38	150.4	0	1	48
102	200	2	39	150.1	0	2	50
018	400	2	39	042	300	2	50
071	400	1	40	161	0	2	50
248	300	1	40	011	500	2	50
012	300	2	40	003.2	500	2	55

References Cited

Allison, M. J.
  1985 Chile's Ancient Mummies. *Natural History* 94:74–81.
Allison, M. J., and E. Gerszten
  1982 *Paleopathology in South American Mummies: Application of Modern Techniques.* Richmond: Medical College of Virginia.
Alva, Walter
  1986 *Las Salinas de Chao: Frühe Siedlung in Nord-Peru.* Materialen zur Allgemeinen und Vergleichenden Archäologie, Band 34. Munich: Verlag C. H. Beck.
Barjenbruch, Margaret W.
  1977 Preliminary Summary of Gross Pathologies Found at Paloma. Manuscript on file, Department of Anthropology, University of Missouri-Columbia.
Barr, A. J., J. H. Goodnight, J. P. Sall, and J. I. Helwig
  1976 *A User's Guide to SAS '76.* Raleigh, N.C.: SAS Institute.
Bateson, Gregory
  1967 *Naven.* Stanford, Cal.: Stanford University Press.
Bauer, Brian, and M. Munsters
  1985 The Manufacture, Use, and Storage of Stone Tools in Present Day Andean Communities. Paper presented at the thirteenth Annual Midwestern Conference on Andean and Amazonian Archaeology and Ethnohistory, Field Museum of Natural History, Chicago.
Bender, Barbara
  1985 Prehistoric Developments in the American Midcontinent and in Brittany, Northwest France. In T. D. Price and J. A. Brown (eds.), *Prehistoric Hunter-Gatherers,* pp. 21–57. Orlando, Fla.: Academic Press.
Benfer, Robert A.
  1977 Post Pleistocene Biological/Cultural Evolution in Coastal Peru. Paper presented at the Seventy-sixth Annual meeting of the American Anthropological Association, Houston.
  1981 (comp.) Adaptations to Sedentism and Food Production: The Paloma Project, Part 1. *Paleopathology Newsletter* 36:11–13.
  1982a Adaptations to Sedentism and Food Production: The Paloma Project, Part 2. *Paleopathology Newsletter* 37:6–9.
  1982b El Proyecto Paloma de las Universidades de Missouri y El Centro de Investigaciones de Zonas Aridas. *Zonas Aridas* 2:33–51.
  1984 The Challenges and Rewards of Sedentism: The Preceramic Village of Paloma, Peru. In M. N. Cohen (ed.), *Paleopathology at the Origins of Agriculture,* pp. 531–558. Orlando, Fla.: Academic Press.
  1986a Holocene Coastal Adaptations: Changing Demography and Health at the Fog Oasis of Paloma, Peru 5,000–7,800 B.P. In R. Matos M., S. A. Turpin, H. H. Eling, Jr. (eds.), *Andean Archaeology, Papers in Memory of Clifford Evans,* pp. 45–64. Monograph 27, Institute of Archaeology. Los Angeles: University of California.
  1986b The Site of Paloma, Chilca Valley, Peru. Unpublished manuscript.
  1986c Adaptation in the Preceramic Periods of

Central Coastal Peru. Revised version of a paper presented at the symposium Maritime Foundations: Preceramic Subsistence and Society on the Andean Coast, Society for American Archaeology, Fifty-first Annual Meeting, New Orleans.

Benfer, Robert A., and Jeremy Edward
1988 Paloma Burials Were Toasted, Then Salted. Paper presented to the Midwest Conference on Andean and Amazonian Archaeology and Ethnohistory, Ann Arbor.

Benfer, Robert A., B. Ojeda, and G. H. Weir
1987 Early Water Management Strategies on the Coast of Peru. In D. L. Browman (ed.), *Risk Management and Arid Land Use Strategies in the Andes,* pp. 195–206. Boulder, Colo.: Westview Press.

Binford, Lewis R.
1968 Post-Pleistocene Adaptations. In S. R. Binford and L. R. Binford (eds.), *New Perspectives in Archeology,* pp. 313–341. Chicago and New York: Aldine.
1971 Mortuary Practices: Their Study and Their Potential. In James A. Brown (ed.), *Approaches to the Social Dimensions of Mortuary Practices.* Memoirs of the Society for American Archaeology 35:6–29.
1978 *Nunamuit Ethnoarchaeology.* New York: Academic Press.
1983 *Working at Archaeology.* New York: Academic Press.

Binford, Lewis R., and W. J. Chasko
1978 Nunamuit Demographic History: A Provocative Case. In Ezra B. W. Zubrow (ed.), *Demographic Anthropology: Quantitative Approaches,* pp. 63–143. Albuquerque: University of New Mexico Press.

Bird, Junius B.
1943 Excavations in Northern Chile. *Anthropological Papers of the American Museum of Natural History,* vol. 38, part 4: 179–318.
1948 Preceramic Cultures in Chicama and Virú. In W. C. Bennett (ed.), *A Reappraisal of Peruvian Archaeology.* Memoirs of the Society for American Archaeology 4:21–28.
1969 A Comparison of South Chilean and Ecuadorian "Fishtail" Projectile Points. *Kroeber Anthropological Society Papers*

40:52–71. Berkeley: Department of Anthropology, University of California.
1985 *The Preceramic Excavations at the Huaca Prieta, Chicama Valley, Peru,* John Hyslop (ed.). Anthropological Papers of the American Museum of Natural History, vol. 62, part 1.

Bonavia, Duccio, and A. Grobman
1979 Sistema de depósitos y almacenamiento durante el período precerámico en la costa del perú. *Journal de la Société des Américanistes* 66:21–45.

Brock, Sharon
1981 Report on the La Paloma Burials. Department of Anthropology, University of Missouri, 1979 excavations on file.

Bryan, Alan L.
1973 Paleoenvironments and Cultural Diversity in Late Pleistocene South America. *Quaternary Research* 3:237–256.
1978 (ed.) Early Man in America from a Circum-Pacific Perspective. Occasional Papers, 1, Department of Anthropology. Edmonton: University of Alberta, Archaeological Researches International.

Burger, Richard L., and Frank Asaro
1977 Obsidian Distribution and Provenience in the Central Highlands and Coast of Peru during the Preceramic Period. *Contributions of the University of California Archaeological Research Facility* 36:51–83.

Burger, Richard L., and Lucy Salazar Burger
1979 Resultados preliminares de excavaciones en los distritos de Chavín de Huanta y San Marcos, Perú. In Ramiro Matos M. (ed.), *Arqueología peruana: Investigaciones arqueológicas en el Perú, 1976,* pp. 133–155. Lima: Centro de Proyección Cristiana.
1986 Early Organizational Diversity in the Peruvian Highlands: Huaricoto and Kotosh. In R. Matos M., S. A. Turpin, H. H. Eling, Jr. (eds.), *Andean Archaeology, Papers in Memory of Clifford Evans,* pp. 45–64. Monograph 27, Institute of Archaeology. Los Angeles: University of California.

Cardenes M., Mercedes
1978 Obtención de una cronología del uso de los recursos marinos en el antiguo Perú. Arqueología PUC, *Boletín del Seminario de Arqueología* 19–20 (1977–

1978). Publicación 107 del Instituto Riva Aguero, Lima.

Cardich, Augusto
1964 Lauricocha: Fundamentos para una prehistoría de los Andes centrales. *Studia Praehistorica* 3.
1985 The Fluctuating Upper Limits of Cultivation in the Central Andes and Their Impact on Peruvian Prehistory. *Advances in World Archaeology* 4:293–333. New York: Academic Press.

Chapman, Robert, I. Kinnes, and K. Randsborg
1981 *The Archaeology of Death.* Cambridge and New York: Cambridge University Press.

Chauchat, C.
1976 The Paiján Complex, Pampa de Cupisnique, Peru. *Nawpa Pacha* 13 (1975):85–96.
1979 Additional Observations on the Paiján Complex. *Nawpa Pacha* 16 (1978): 51–64.

Childe, Vere Gordon
1952 *New Light on the Most Ancient Near East.* 4th ed. London: Routledge and Kegan Paul.

Cieza de León, Pedro de
1947 Primera parte de la crónica del Perú. *Biblioteca de Autores Españoles* 26: 349–458.
1959 *The Incas of Pedro de Cieza de León.* Translated by Harriet de Onis; edited by Victor Wolfgang von Hagen. Norman: University of Oklahoma Press.

Cook, Sherbour F.
1972 *Prehistoric Demography.* Palo Alto: Addison-Wesley Modules in Anthropology I.

Deza, Jaime
1988 Entierros de cenizas funerarias, Chao, 4500 A.P. Paper presented at the I Convención Peruana de Arqueología Andina, Lima.

Dillehay, Tom D.
1986 Monte Verde: An Early Man Site in South Central Chile. In R. Matos M., S. A. Turpin, H. H. Eling, Jr. (eds.), *Andean Archaeology, Papers in Memory of Clifford Evans,* pp. 1–17. Monograph 27, Institute of Archaeology. Los Angeles: University of California.

Donnan, Christopher B.
1964 An Early House from Chilca, Peru. *American Antiquity* 30(2):137–144.

1985 (ed.) *Early Ceremonial Architecture in the Andes.* Washington, D.C.: Dumbarton Oaks.

Donnan, Christopher B., and Carol Mackey
1978 *Ancient Burial Patterns of the Moche Valley, Peru.* Austin: University of Texas Press.

Draper, Patricia
1975 !Kung Women: Contrasts in Sexual Egalitarianism in Foraging and Sedentary Contexts. In R. R. Reiter (ed.), *Toward an Anthropology of Women,* pp. 77–109. New York and London: Monthly Review Press.

Edward, Jeremy B.
1987 Studies of Human Bone from the Preceramic Amerindian Site at Paloma, Peru, by Neutron Activation Analysis. Ph.D. dissertation, University of Missouri-Columbia.

Edwards, Daniel Stewart
1984 Dental Attrition and Subsistence at the Preceramic Site of Paloma, Peru. Master's thesis, University of Missouri-Columbia.

Engel, Frederic A.
1957a Early Sites on the Peruvian Coast. *Southwestern Journal of Anthropology* 13:54–68.
1957b Sites et établissements sans céramiques de la côte péruvienne. *Journal de la Société des Américanistes* 44:67–155.
1960 Un groupe humain de 5000 ans à Paracas, Pérou. *Journal de la Société des Américanistes* 49:7–35.
1963 A Preceramic Settlement on the Central Coast of Peru: Asia, Unit 1. *Transactions of the American Philosophical Society* 53(3) (entire volume).
1966a Le complexe précéramique d'El Paraíso (Pérou). *Journal de la Société des Américanistes* 55:43–96.
1966b *Paracas, Cien siglos de la cultura peruana.* Lima: Editorial Juan Mejia Baca.
1970 Exploration of the Chilca Canyon, Peru. *Current Anthropology* 11(1):55–58.
1976 *An Ancient World Preserved.* New York: Crown Publishers.
1980 *Paloma.* Prehistoric Andean Ecology Series, 1. New York: Humanities Press.
1981 *Prehistoric Andean Ecology, Man, Settlement, and Environment in the Andes, The Deep South.* New York: Humanities Press.

1984   *Chilca.* Prehistoric Andean Ecology Series, 4. New York: Humanities Press.

1987   *De las begonias al maíz, Vida y producción en el Perú antiguo.* Lima: Universidad Nacional Agraria.

1988   *Ecología prehistorica andina, Chilca, Pueblo 1, Implementos de hueso.* Lima: Universidad Nacional Agraria.

Fairservis, Walter A., Jr.

1975   *The Threshold of Civilization.* New York: Scribner's.

Feinman, Gary, and J. Neitzel

1984   Too Many Types: An Overview of Sedentary Prestate Societies in the Americas. In M. B. Schiffer (ed.), *Advances in Archaeological Method and Theory,* pp. 39–102. Orlando, Fla.: Academic Press.

Feldman, Robert

1980   Aspero, Peru: Architecture, Subsistence Economy, and Other Artifacts of a Preceramic Maritime Chiefdom. Ph.D. dissertation, Department of Anthropology, Harvard University, Cambridge, Mass.

Flannery, Kent V.

1972   The Cultural Evolution of Civilizations. *Annual Review of Ecology and Systematics* 3:399–426.

1976   *The Early Mesoamerican Village.* New York: Academic Press.

Fung Pineda, Rosa

1988   The Late Preceramic and Initial Period. In R. W. Keatinge (ed.), *Peruvian Prehistory,* pp. 67–96. Cambridge and New York: Cambridge University Press.

Fung Pineda, Rosa, C. F. Cenzano L., and A. Zavaleta

1972   El taller lítico de Chivateros, valle de Chillón. *Revista del Museo Nacional* 38:61–72.

Gehlert, Sarah G.

1979   Dental Asymmetry in Two Peruvian Populations. Master's paper, University of Missouri-Columbia.

Greenberg, Joseph H., C. G. Turner, and S. L. Zegura

1986   The Settlement of the Americas: A Comparison of the Linguistic, Dental and Genetic Evidence. *Current Anthropology* 27(5):477–497.

Greer, John

1977   The 1976 Field Season at Paloma: Intra-Site Structure and Patterning— Investigative Procedures, Observations, Initial Impressions, and Recommendations. Paper on file, Department of Anthropology, University of Missouri-Columbia.

Grieder, Terence, and A. Bueno Mendoza

1981   La Galgada: Peru before Pottery. *Archaeology* 34(2):44–51.

Harner, Michael J.

1972   *The Jívaro, People of the Sacred Waterfall.* Garden City, N.Y.: Natural History Press.

Hartweg, Raoul

1958   Les squelettes des sites sans céramiques de la côte du Pérou. *Journal de la Société des Américanistes* 47:179–198.

Heusser, C. J.

1983   Quaternary Pollen Record from Laguna de Tagua Tagua, Chile. *Science* 219:1429–1432.

Hodder, Ian

1987   *Reading the Past.* Cambridge and New York: Cambridge University Press.

Holmberg, Allan R.

1969   *Nomads of the Long Bow, The Sirionó of Eastern Bolivia.* American Museum Science Books. Garden City, N.Y.: Natural History Press.

Howell, Nancy

1979   *Demography of the Dobe !Kung.* New York: Academic Press.

Howells, William W.

1965   Estimating Population Numbers through Archaeological and Skeletal Remains. In Robert F. Heizer and Sherburne F. Cooks (eds.), *The Application of Quantitative Methods in Archaeology,* pp. 158–185. Viking Fund Publication in Anthropology 28. Chicago: Quandrangle Books.

Jackson, Barbara E.

1981   Histomorphometric Analysis of Twenty-two Human Rib Segments from the Preceramic Site of Paloma, Peru. Master's paper, University of Missouri-Columbia.

Jackson, Barbara, and T. Stocker

1982   Peru's Preceramic Menu. *Field Museum of Natural History Bulletin* 53(7):12–23.

Kennedy, G. E.

1986   The Relationship between Auditory Extoses and Cold Water: A Latitudinal Analysis. *American Journal of Physical Anthropology* 71:401–415.

Kirchoff, Paul
1948 The Tribes North of the Orinoco River. In Julian H. Steward (ed.), *Handbook of South American Indians*, vol. 4, *The Circum-Caribbean Tribes*, pp. 481–493. Bureau of American Ethnology, Bulletin 143. Washington, D.C.: Smithsonian Institution.

Kosok, Paul
1965 *Life, Land, and Water in Ancient Peru.* New York: Long Island University Press.

Krieger, Alex D.
1964 Early Man in the New World. In J. D. Jennings and E. Norbeck (eds.), *Prehistoric Man in the New World*, pp. 23–85. Chicago: University of Chicago Press.

Krieger, Herbert W.
1943 Island Peoples of the Western Pacific, Micronesia and Melanesia. Smithsonian Institution War Background Studies 16. Washington, D.C.: U.S. Government Printing Office.

Kroeber, Alfred
1927 Disposal of the Dead. *American Anthropologist* 29 : 308–315.

Lanning, Edward P.
1963 A Preagricultural Occupation on the Central Coast of Peru. *American Antiquity* 28 : 360–371.
1967 *Peru before the Incas.* Englewood Cliffs, N.J.: Prentice-Hall.

Lathrap, Donald W.
1975 Ancient Ecuador: Culture, Clay, and Creativity 3000–300 B.C. Chicago: Field Museum of Natural History.
1977 Our Father the Cayman, Our Mother the Gourd: Spinden Revisited, or a Unitary Model for the Emergence of Agriculture in the New World. In Charles A. Reed (ed.), *Origins of Agriculture*, pp. 713–751. The Hague: Mouton.

Lathrap, D. W., J. G. Marcos, and J. A. Zeidler
1977 Real Alto: An Ancient Ceremonial Center. *Archaeology* 30(1) : 2–13.

Lester, C. W.
1966 Notes on the Skeletons from Huaca Prieta. Unpublished manuscript on file, Department of Anthropology, American Museum of Natural History.

Lippi, Ronald D.
n.d. Proyecto Pichincha Occidental—Cuarto informe provisional: Excavaciones en Nambillo (Agosto 1985–Enero 1986). Report on file at Museo del Banco Central, Quito, Ecuador.

Lothrop, S. K.
1946 Indians of the Paraña Delta and La Plata Littoral. In J. H. Steward (ed.), *Handbook of South American Indians*, vol. 1, *The Marginal Tribes*, pp. 177–190. Smithsonian Institution, Bureau of American Ethnology Bulletin 143. Washington, D.C.: United States Government Printing Office.

Lumbreras, Luis G.
1974 *The Peoples and Cultures of Ancient Peru.* Translated by Betty J. Meggers. Washington, D.C.: Smithsonian Institution Press.

Lynch, Thomas F.
1971 Preceramic Transhumance in the Callejón de Huaylas, Peru. *American Antiquity* 36 : 139–148.
1974 Current Research: Andean South America. *American Antiquity* 39(2): 383–386.
1978 The South American Paleo-Indians. In J. D. Jennings (ed.), *Ancient Native Americans*, pp. 455–589. San Francisco: W. H. Freeman and Company.
1980 *Guitarrero Cave, Early Man in the Andes.* New York: Academic Press.
1983 The Paleo-Indians. In J. D. Jennings (ed.), *Ancient South Americans*, pp. 87–137. San Francisco: W. H. Freeman and Company.
1986 Climate Change and Human Settlement around the Late-Glacial Laguna de Punta Negra, Northern Chile: The Preliminary Results. *Geoarchaeology* 1(2): 145–162.

MacNeish, Richard S., A. G. Cook, L. G. Lumbreras, R. K. Vierra, and A. Nelken-Turner
1981 *Prehistory of the Ayacucho Basin, Peru*, vol. 2, *Excavations and Chronology.* Ann Arbor: University of Michigan Press.

Malpass, Michael A.
1983 The Preceramic Occupation of the Casma Valley, Peru. In D. H. Sandweiss (ed.), *Investigations of the Andean Past*, pp. 1–20. Ithaca: Cornell Latin American Studies Program.

Mandeville, Marnie M.
1979 Report on Textiles from Paloma

(1979). Report on file at the Department of Anthropology, University of Missouri-Columbia.

Martin, M. Kay, and B. Voorhies
1975 *Female of the Species.* New York: Columbia University Press.

Matos M., Ramiro
1975 Prehistoria y ecología en las punas de Junín. *Revista del Museo Nacional* (Lima) 41:37–80.

Mayer-Oakes, W.
1982 El Inga Broad Stemmed Projectile Points—A New Horizon Marker for Early Man in South America? Paper presented at the Tenth Midwest Conference on Andean and Amazonian Archaeology and Ethnohistory, Ann Arbor.

McAnulty, Sarah D.
1977 Preliminary Report on the Textiles from Paloma. Unpublished manuscript.

McGimsey, Charles R.
1958 Further Data and a Date from Cerro Mangote, Panama. *American Antiquity* 23:434–435.

Menzel, Dorothy
1976 *Pottery, Style, and Society in Ancient Peru.* Los Angeles: University of California Press.
1977 *The Archaeology of Ancient Peru and the Work of Max Uhle.* Berkeley: Robert H. Lowie Museum of Anthropology.

Mercer, J. H.
1983 Cenozoic Glaciation in the Southern Hemisphere. *Annual Review of Earth and Planetary Science* 11:99–132.

Metraux, Alfred
1947 Mourning Rites and Burial Forms of the South American Indians. *American Indígena* 7(1):7–44.

Moseley, Michael E.
1968 Changing Subsistence Patterns: Late Preceramic Archaeology of the Central Peruvian Coast. Ph.D. dissertation, Department of Anthropology, Harvard University.
1972 Demography and Subsistence: An Example of Interaction from Prehistoric Peru. *Southwestern Journal of Anthropology* 28(1):25–49.
1975 *The Maritime Foundations of Andean Civilization.* Menlo Park, Cal.: Cummings Press.

1978 *Pre-agricultural Coastal Civilizations in Peru.* Carolina Biology Readers 90. Burlington, N.C.: Carolina Biological Supply Company.

Moseley, M. E., and E. E. Deeds
1982 The Land in Front of Chan Chan: Agrarian Expansion, Reform, and Collapse in the Moche Valley. In M. E. Moseley and K. E. Day (eds.), *Chan Chan: Andean Desert City,* pp. 25–54. Albuquerque: University of New Mexico Press.

Moseley, Michael E., and G. R. Willey
1973 Aspero, Peru: A Reexamination of the Site and Its Implications. *American Antiquity* 38(4):452–468.

Muelle, Jorge C., and R. Ravines
1973 Los estratos precerámicos de Ancón. *Revista del Museo Nacional* (Peru) 39:49–70.

Murra, John V.
1972 El control vertical de un máximo de pisos ecológicos en la economía de las sociedades andinas. In Iñigo Ortiz de Zuñiga (ed.), *Vista de la provincia de León de Húanuco en 1562,* vol. 2, pp. 427–476. Huánuco, Peru: Universidad Nacional Hermilio Valdizan.

Naroll, R.
1962 Floor Area and Settlement Population. *American Antiquity* 27:587–589.

Osborn, Allan J.
1977 Strandloopers, Mermaids, and Other Fairy Tales. Ecological Determinants of Marine Resource Utilization—The Peruvian Case. In Lewis R. Binford (ed.), *For Theory Building in Archaeology,* pp. 157–243. New York: Academic Press.

O'Shea, John
1981 Social Configurations and the Archaeological Study of Mortuary Practices: A Case Study. In T. Chapman, I. Kinnes, and K. Randsborg (eds.), *The Archaeology of Death,* pp. 39–52. Cambridge and New York: Cambridge University Press.

Page, J. W.
1974 Human Evolution in Peru: 9000–1000 B.P. Ph.D. dissertation, University of Missouri-Columbia.

Parsons, Jeffrey R., and Norbert P. Psuty
1975 Sunken Fields and Prehispanic Subsis-

tence on the Peruvian Coast. *American Antiquity* 40(3):259–282.

Parsons, Mary H.
1970 Preceramic Subsistence on the Peruvian Coast. *American Antiquity* 35:292–304.

Patterson, Thomas C.
1971a Central Peru: Its Economy and Population. *Archaeology* 24(4):316–321.
1971b The Emergence of Food Production in Central Peru. In Stuart Struever (ed.), *Prehistoric Agriculture,* pp. 181–208. Garden City, N.Y.: Natural History Press.
1973 *America's Past: A New World Archaeology.* Glenview, Ill.: Scott, Foresman, and Company.
1983 The Historical Development of a Coastal Andean Social Formation in Central Peru, 6000 to 500 B.C. In D. H. Sandweiss (ed.), *Investigations of the Andean Past,* pp. 21–37. Ithaca, N.Y.: Cornell Latin American Studies Program.

Patterson, Thomas C., and M. E. Moseley
1968 Late Preceramic and Early Ceramic Cultures of the Central Coast of Peru. *Nawpa Pacha* 6:115–134.

Paulsen, A.
1974 The Thorny Oyster and the Voice of God: *Spondylus* and *Strombus* in Andean Prehistory. *American Antiquity* 39(4):597–607.

Petersen, Georg
1970 *Minería y metalurgia en el antiguo Perú.* Arqueológicas 12. Lima: Museo Nacional de Antropología y Arqueología.

Pittock, A. B.
1980 Patterns of Climatic Variation in Argentina and Chile, 1931–1960. *Monthly Weather Review* 108:1347–1362.

Pozorski, Shelia, and T. Pozorski
1979 Alto Salaverry: A Peruvian Coastal Preceramic Site. *Annals of the Carnegie Museum of Natural History* 49:337–375.
1987 *Early Settlement and Subsistence in the Casma Valley, Peru.* Iowa City: University of Iowa Press.

Pulgar Vidal, Javier
1987 *Geografía del Perú: Las ocho regiones naturales del Perú.* Lima: Editorial Universo S.A.

Quilter, Jeffrey
1980 Paloma: Mortuary Practices and Social Organization of a Preceramic Peruvian Village. Ph.D. dissertation, Department of Anthropology, University of California, Santa Barbara.
1985 Architecture and Chronology at El Paraíso, Peru. *Journal of Field Archaeology* 12:279–297.
n.d. To Fish in the Afternoon: Beyond Subsistence Economies in the Study of Early Andean Civilization. Unpublished manuscript.

Quilter J. and T. Stocker
1983 Subsistence Economies and the Origins of Andean Complex Societies. *American Anthropologist* 85(3):545–562.

Ramos de Cox, J.
1972 Marcadores y niveles de ocupación en Tablada de Lurín, Lima. *Arqueología PUC* 13:7–30.

Ranere, Anthony J.
1980 Preceramic Shelters in the Talamancan Range. In O. F. Linares and A. J. Ranere (eds.), *Adaptive Radiations in Preceramic Panama,* pp. 16–43. Peabody Monographs 5. Cambridge, Mass.: Harvard University.

Raymond, J. Scott
1981 The Maritime Foundations of Andean Civilization: A Reconsideration of the Evidence. *American Antiquity* 46(4):806–821.

Reitz, Elizabeth J.
1986 Maritime Resource Use at Paloma, Peru. Paper presented at the Fifty-first Annual Meeting of the Society for · American Archaeology, New Orleans.
1988 Faunal Remains from Paloma, An Archaic Site in Peru. *American Anthropologist* 90(2):310–322.

Renfrew, Colin
1975 Trade as Action at a Distance. In J. A. Sabloff and C. C. Lamberg-Karlovsky (eds.), *Ancient Civilization and Trade,* pp. 3–59. Albuquerque: University of New Mexico Press.

Richardson, James B., III
1978 Early Man on the Peruvian North Coast: Early Maritime Exploitation and the Pleistocene and Holocene Environment. In A. Bryan (ed.), *Early Man in America from a Circum-Pacific Perspective,* pp. 247–259. Edmonton: University of Alberta Press.

1981   Maritime Adaptations on the Peruvian Coast: A Critique and Future Directions. Paper Presented at the Forty-Seventh Annual Meeting of the Society for American Archaeology, San Diego.

1986   Maritime before Maritime: 8,500 B.C. Evidence for Maritime Economies in Southern Peru. Paper presented at the Fifty-first Meeting of the Society for American Archaeology, New Orleans.

Rick, John
1980   *Prehistoric Hunters of the High Andes.* New York: Academic Press.

1987   Dates as Data: An Examination of the Peruvian Preceramic Radiocarbon Record. *American Antiquity* 52(1):55–73.

Rindos, David
1984   *The Origins of Agriculture: An Evolutionary Perspective.* New York: Academic Press.

Roosevelt, Anna C.
1980   Parmana, Prehistoric Maize and Manioc Subsistence along the Amazon and Orinoco. New York: Academic Press.

Rostworowski de Diez Canseco, María
1981   Recursos renovables y pesca, siglos XVI y XVII. Lima: Instituto de Estudios Peruanos.

Rowe, John H.
1962   Worsaae's Law and the Use of Grave Lots for Archaeological Dating. *American Antiquity* 28(2):129–137.

1969   The Sunken Gardens of the Peruvian Coast. American Antiquity 34:320–325.

Sandweiss, D., and J. Quilter
n.d.   Malacoarchaeology of El Paraíso, Peru. Unpublished manuscript.

Sandweiss, Daniel, H. Rollins, and J. Richardson III
1983   Landscape Alteration and Prehistoric Human Occupation on the North Coast of Peru. *Annals of the Carnegie Museum* 52(12):277–298.

Saxe, Arthur A.
1970   Social Dimensions of Mortuary Practices. Ph.D. dissertation, University of Michigan.

Schiappacasse F., Virgilio, and Hans Niemeyer F.
1984   *Descripción y análisis interpretativa de un sitio archaico temprano en la Quebrada de Camarones.* Publicación ocasional 41, Museo Nacional de Historia Nacional. Tarapaca, Chile: Universidad de Tarapaca.

Sharon, Douglas
1978   *Wizard of the Four Winds.* New York: Free Press (Macmillan).

Sheets, Payson D.
1971   An Ancient Natural Disaster. *Expedition* 14(1):24–31.

Silverblatt, Irene
1987   *Moon, Sun, and Witches.* Princeton, N.J.: Princeton University Press.

Spinden, H. J.
1917   The Origin and Distribution of Agriculture in America. Proceedings of the Nineteenth International Congress of Americanists, Washington, D.C. (1915).

Stevenson, M. R., and H. R. Wicks
1975   Bibliography of El Niño and Associated Publications. Interamerican Tropical Tuna Commission. *Bulletin* 16:451–501.

Steward, Julian H.
1936   The Economic and Social Basis of Primitive Bands. In R. H. Lowie (ed.), *Essays in Anthropology Presented to A. L. Kroeber,* pp. 331–350. Berkeley: University of California Press.

Stothert, Karen E.
1985   The Preceramic Las Vegas Culture of Coastal Ecuador. *American Antiquity* 50(3):613–637.

Tainter, Joseph
1971   Ethnographic Documentation for a Theory of Mortuary Practices. Unpublished manuscript.

1975   The Archaeological Study of Social Change: Woodland Systems in West Central Illinois. Ph.D. dissertation, Northwestern University.

1978   Mortuary practices and the Study of Prehistoric Social Systems. In M. G. Schiffer (ed.), *Advances in Archaeological Method and Theory,* no. 1, pp. 105–146. New York: Academic Press.

Tattersall, Ian.
1985   The Human Skeletons from Huaca Prieta, with a Note on Exostoses of the External Auditory Meatus. In Junius B. Bird, *The Preceramic Excavations at the Huaca Prieta, Chicama Valley, Peru,* ed. John Hyslop, pp. 60–64. Anthropological Papers, 62, part 1. New York: American Museum of Natural History.

Topic, John R.
  1987 A Pre-cotton Preceramic "Fortified"
        Site of the Santa Valley, Peru. Paper
        presented at the Twentieth Annual
        Chacmool Conference. University of
        Calgary, Alberta.
Torres G., Juan, and C. López Ocaña
  1982 Estudio bioecológico de la loma Pa-
        loma. *Zonas Aridas* 2:61–66.
Tosdal, Richard M., A. H. Clark, and E. Farran
  1984 Cenozoic Polyphase Landscape and
        Tectonic Evolution of the Cordillera
        Occidental, Southern-most Peru. *Geo-
        logical Society of America Bulletin* 95:
        1318–1332.
Troll, Karl
  1931 Die geografische Grundlagen der an-
        dinen Kulturen und des Inca Reiches.
        Ibero-amerikanisches Archiv 5 (entire
        volume).
  1958 Las culturas superiores andinas y el
        medio geográfico. *Revista del Instituto
        Geográfico* (Lima) 5:3–55.
Tylor, Edward B.
  1891 *Primitive Culture: Researches into the De-
        velopment of Mythology, Philosophy, Re-
        ligion, Language, Art and Customs.*
        London: J. Murray.
Uhle, Max
  1919 La arqueología de Aríca y Tacna.
        *Boletín de la Sociedad Ecuatoriana de Es-
        tudios Históricos Americanos* (Quito)
        3(7–8):1–48.
Vallejos A., Miriam
  1982 El hombre preagrícola de las Cuevas
        Tres Ventanas de Chilca, Perú: Tex-
        tilería. *Zonas Aridas* 2:21–32.
Vehik, Susan
  1977 Climate, Population, Subsistence and

the Central Peruvian Lomas between
        8000 and 2500 B.C. Unpublished
        manuscript.
Weir, Glendon H., R. A. Benfer, and J. G. Jones
  1985 Preceramic to Early Formative Subsis-
        tence on the Central Coast of Peru.
        Paper presented at the Fiftieth Annual
        Meeting of the Society for American
        Archaeology, Denver.
Weir, Glendon H., and J. Phillip Dering
  1986 The Lomas of Paloma: Human En-
        vironmental Relations in a Central
        Peruvian Fog Oasis: Archaeobotany
        and Palynology. In R. Matos M.,
        S. A. Turpin, H. H. Eling, Jr. (eds.), *An-
        dean Archaeology, Papers in Memory of
        Clifford Evans*, pp. 18–44. Monograph
        27, Institute of Archaeology. Los An-
        geles: University of California.
Wendt, W. E.
  1964 Die präkeramische Siedlung am Río
        Seco, Perú. *Baessler Archiv* 11(2):
        225–275.
West, Frederick H.
  1987 Migrationism and New World Origins.
        Quarterly Review of Archaeology
        8(1):11–14.
Wilson, David
  1981 Of Maize and Men: A Critique of the
        Maritime Hypothesis of State Origins
        on the Coast of Peru. *American Anthro-
        pologist* 38(1):93–120.
Yacovleff, Eugenio, and Jorge C. Muelle
  1934 Notas al trabajo "Colorantes de Para-
        cas." *Revista del Museo Nacional* (Peru)
        3(1–2):157–163.
Yellen, John
  1977 *Archaeological Approaches to the Present.*
        New York: Academic Press.

Index

Boldface indicates pages with illustrations

Abraders, 34
Alto Salaverry Site, 80
Amazon, 82; comparisons of Paloma with, 56–57. *See also* Jívaro
Anchovies, xi
Ancón, burials at, xv, 74
Asia Site, 32, 38, 76, 82, 84
Aspero Site, 78, 82, 84
Avic Site, 22

Bandurria Site, 78
Beads, 29, 32, **38**, 53, 58, 64, 65, 85; at Aspero, 79; barnacle, 29; at Chilca I, **12**, 74; Chilean, 79; at Paracas 514, 71; stone, 37
Benfer, Robert, xvi, 19, 20, 47, 64, 88
Binford, Lewis, 24, 44
Bird, Junius, 7
Birds, in diet, 8; in lomas, 3; parrots, 3; seabirds, 24
Boats (watercraft), 8
Bone, artifacts, 32–34, **33–35**, 58

Cabezas Largas Site, 71, 84
Cacti, 24
Camelids, in lomas, 3
Cane, 14–15, 34
Chilca I Site, 17, 26, 56, 74, 83, 101
Chilca Valley, 10
Chile, 82, 84; burials in northern, xv, 69
Chimú, culture, 8
Chinchorro burials, 66
Cieza de León, Pedro de, 4
Cluster analysis, 46–49, 53
Colinas Site, Ancón, 74
Coprolites, in graves, 26, 76; pollen in, 23

Cotton, preceramic period, xii; site near Paloma, 19; textiles, 32, 41
Culture change, environmental causes of, 9

Deer, in lomas, 3
Dering, Phil, 23
Desert, Peruvian coastal, 1
Diseases, of Palomans, 20–21
Disks and crescents (shell), 29–32, **31**, 58
Disturbance, of burials, 26
Donnan, Christopher, 74, 101

Ecuador, xv, 76, 82. *See also* Vegas Site
El Niño, 8–9
El Paraíso Site, 32, 80
Engel, Frédéric-André, 7, 11, 17, 19, 34, 36, 38, 39, 71
Environment, regions of, 1; vertical nature of, 1
Excavation, stages, **15**; strategy, 11, 14,
Exostoses, 21

Features, **18**, **35**; hearths, 18; pits, 18
Feldman, Robert, 78, 82
Fetuses, numbers of, 20
Fire rituals, 27, 46, 54, 66, 83
Fish, 5, 8–9; anchovies, 5; paste, 22
Fishhooks, **33**, 34
Fung Pineda, Rosa, 78

Gourds, 23, 27, **28**, 46, 51, 59, 62; at Aspero, 78; at Huaca Prieta, 76, **77**; at Vegas Site, 69
Greer, John, 19
Guitarrero Cave Site, 42

Harris Lines, at Paloma, 20
Horticulture, regions suitable for, 1; shift to, xii, 64; sunken gardens, 20

Houses, **17**, **55**, **56**; abandonment/destruction, xii, 54, 56–57, 66, 82; burials in, 54; characteristics of, 14–18; number of, 19; size of, 18
Huaca Prieta, 7, 65, 75, **77**, 80, 84, 85; baskets at, 42; bodkins at, 32; exostoses at, 21

Ice Age, 5–6
Ideology, in mortuary studies, 43
Inbreeding, xii
Inca, mummies of, xv, 83, 85
Infanticide, 20, 66–67
Infants, **33**, 66; burial, 58, 112; burial facility (House 28), 62–63, **63**; grave goods, 29; mortality of, 20
Initial Period, 7
Irrigation, preceramic, 4

Jívaro, comparisons with Paloma, xii

Kennedy, G. E., 21
Kroeber, Alfred, 44

La Galgada Site, 80, 84
Lanning, Edward, 7, 8, 30, 36
Las Haldas Site, 75
Lathrap, Donald, 82
Level 200, culture changes in, xi
Lomas, **4**, 7, 57, 64; degradation, 3, 23, 65; plants, 23–24; richness, 3; trees, 3

Maize, in late Paloma midden, 20; at Vegas Site, 69–70
Marcos, Jorge, 31
Maritime Hypothesis, 8
Martin, M. Kay, 65
Mats, 23, **39**, 71, 74, 75, 76; raw materials, **41**
Melanesia, 69
Mollusks, 5, 21
Monkey, bone, 24
Moseley, Michael, 30, 76
Murra, John, 1
Musculature, of burials, xi, 64

Obsidian, 24, 36–37, 65
O'Shea, John, 44
Ossuary, 59, **60**, 61; at Chilca I, 74; at Vegas, 70
Ostra Camp Site, 85

Paloma project, goals of, xi, xvii; history of, xi, xv
Paracas sites, 71
Patrilineality-Patrilocality, xii, 65
Patterson, Thomas, 7, 65
Peru Current, 3, 5

Piedras Negras Site, 75
Pigments, 38, 51, 58, 66, 71, 82, 83; at Asia, 76; at Aspero, 78; at Tres Ventanas, 71; at Vegas Site, 70
Pollen, 23
Population, replacement at Paloma, 19, 53; sizes of at Paloma, 20
Pozorski, Shelia and Thomas, 80
Preceramic Stage, development of concept of, xv; early, 5–6; middle, xvii; late, 6–7; pre-projectile point stage of, 6
Preservation at Paloma, xi
Projectile points, as culture indicators, xi; early preceramic, 6
Pulgar Vidal, Javier, 1

Radiocarbon dates, of Cotton Preceramic site near Paloma, 19; of earliest Americans, 5; of late Paloma maize, 20; of Paloma, 11
Ranere, Anthony, 82
Reiss and Stubel, work at Ancón, xv
Reitz, Elizabeth, 21
Rick, John, 5, 7
Río Seco Site, 79–80, 85
Rostworowski de Diez Canseco, María, 4

Saxe, Arthur, 44
Seafood, role of, 8–9, 21–23
Sea levels, rise in preceramic, 5
Sea lions, 22
Seasons, 3
Sexes, distinctions in burial practices of, xii, 47, 50–52; exostoses of, 21
Shell, as site indicator, 10, **14**; disks and crescents, 27, 29, 66; grave inclusions, 28–29; offerings, **29–30**; worked, 29–31, **31–32**
Silverblatt, Irene, 67
Social organization, in mortuary studies, 43
Spinden, H. J., 82
Spondylus, 24, 29, 65
Stone tools, 46, **52**, 54, 56, 58; axe at Vegas site, 70; chipped, xi, 36–37; ground/grinding, 19, 34, 36, 59, 66; miscellaneous, 37, 59; Table 9, 52
Stothert, Karen, 69
Stratigraphy, at Paloma, xi–xii, 11, 47
Sunken gardens, 5

Tainter, Joseph, 44
Teeth, of burials, xi
Territories, political, xii; Paloman range, 24–25
Textiles, 39–**41**, 46, 51, 53, 64, 65, 82; at Alto Salaverry, 80; at Aspero, 78; at Cabezas Largas,

71; at Huaca Prieta, 80; manufacture of, 32–33; at Las Haldas, 74; at Paracas, 71; at Piedras Negras, 75; at Tres Ventanas, 71
Transhumance, 7
Trees, 3, 23
Troll, Karl, 1

Uhle, Max, 68

Vegas Site, Ecuador, 69, **72–73**, 82, 83, 84
Village, organization of Paloma, 19

Villareal, Gloria, 36
Violence, at Asia, 78; at Ostra, 85; lack of, xii, 65, 85
Voorhies, B., 65

Water, availability of, 4–5; sources, 10
Weir, Glendon, 23
Wilson, David, 9
Women, marriage patterns of, xii; status decrease of, xii, 65
Worsaae, J. J. A., 43